THE PROFESSIONAL APPROACH TO MODEL RAILWAYS

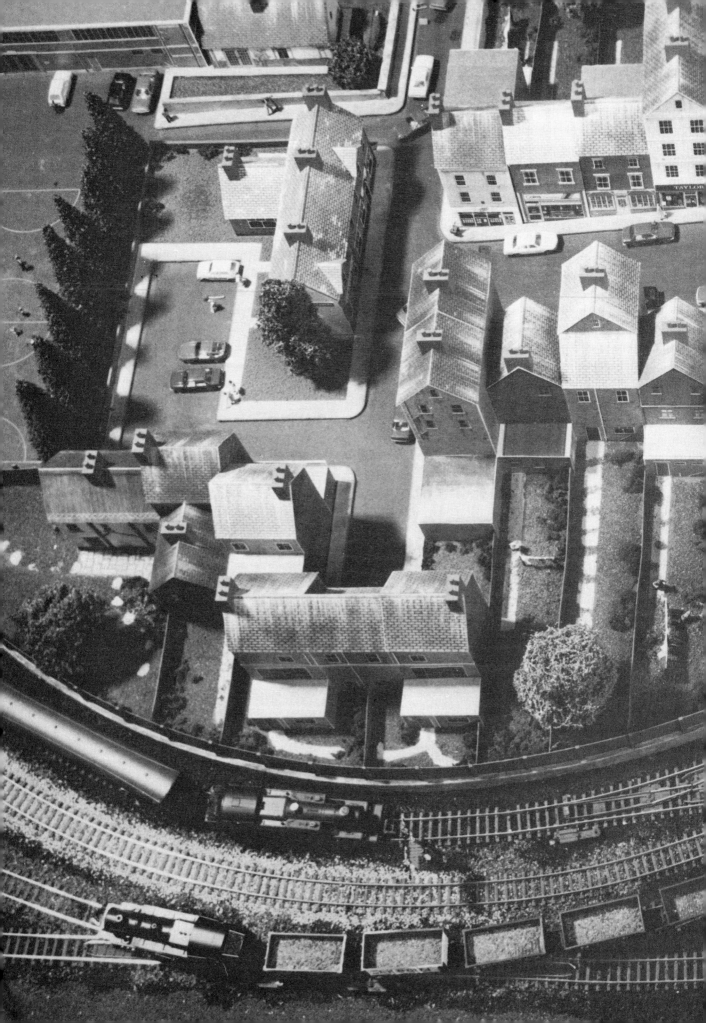

THE PROFESSIONAL APPROACH TO MODEL RAILWAYS

John Wylie

Patrick Stephens
Wellingborough, Northamptonshire

First published 1987

British Library Cataloguing in Publication Data

Wylie, John
    The professional approach to model
    railways.
    1. Railroads—Models
    I. Title
    625.1'9   TF197

    ISBN 0-85059-833-8

Patrick Stephens is part of the
Thorsons Publishing Group

Printed and bound in Great Britain

10 9 8 7 6 5 4 3 2 1

CONTENTS

Front end paper
Bases 01 and 02 joined together to form a realistic townscape at various levels.

Half title page
Bases 01, 02 and 03 joined together to form a 7 ft by 4 ft layout.

Title page
An aerial view of the oval base which is self-contained and measures 4 ft by 3 ft.

Left
A typical country scene with roads and bridges. The construction methods used will be found on base 6.

PREFACE

In welcoming you as a reader to this book perhaps I ought to tell you a little about myself. For over a quarter of a century I have worked as a professional model maker. My work has also involved photography and lecturing to various students in colleges. This book is based upon this experience and is designed to help you progress from beginner through to expert status in easy-to-follow stages.

Each chapter contains progressive step-by-step procedures, starting with the easier models to allow the beginner to the hobby to learn the very basic techniques of model making, using the book as a reference for gathering information.

While the basic knowledge will be learnt very quickly, the development of craft skills takes longer, so as the modeller improves his skills he will be able to undertake far more difficult and complex types of model making. To illustrate this, compare two photographs. The first on page 24, is constructed on a flat baseboard with track, and is ready for some houses and trees—ideal for the beginner to make or purchase. The second layout, shown below, has a contoured base and the houses are in a scenic

setting. Such a layout could be easily constructed by the average modeller, but would be too complex a project for the inexperienced to start with.

My advice to the newcomer to the hobby is always to start with a simple layout and find out the problems involved. The layout can always be rebuilt at a later date, when skills and knowledge have been developed.

With this in mind, the book shows how to construct an interesting layout for use with one or two controllers which is initially built on a flat base, but can be contoured afterwards. The design of the layout is based on a simple oval with passing loops and a siding allowing up to three locomotives to be run, one at a time using a single controller, two with the double controller system, or all three independently controlled irrespective of track position by using the 'Zero One' system of control (see Chapter 7).

Instructions are given for wiring the layout, including signals that change automatically as the turnouts (points) are set, and for sectioning the layout for several operators to use at once.

Below The oval layout's basic construction using plywood battens and contiboard edging. Expanded polystyrene foam forms the foundation for the embankments. The step by step construction methods, shown below, for this layout and others are shown within the book.

This progressive method of construction is favoured by many modellers, as it allows improvements to be carried out whilst still being able to operate the layout. The layout gradually progresses as the skills of the modeller improve.

The expert modeller, having developed his skills, still never ceases to learn. In fact quite often the newcomer, having fresh ideas, can cause the expert to rethink his own methods of model making. We can all learn from each other.

The newcomer should remember that we all have our 'disaster box' which we don't like to talk about, so don't be disappointed if your first model is not as good as you would have hoped.

John Wylie, FSAI, ABIPP, ARPS
Erith, Kent, June 1986

Below The finished oval layout as constructed from the plans shown in this book. The ground levels change above and below the track's level, to make it visually more interesting. The size of this layout built at N scale is only 3 ft by 4 ft. By using selective compression and building at OO scale a similar layout would measure 4 ft 6 in by 6 ft, and plans of this are shown on page 34.

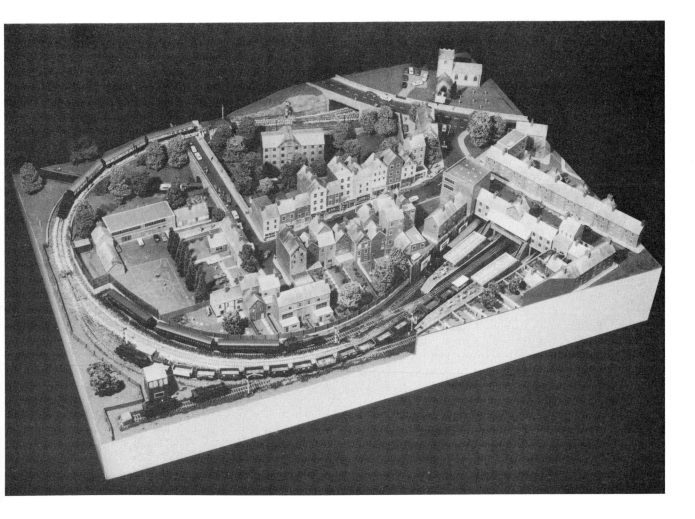

INTRODUCTION

Above The hand over the OO scale *Flying Scotsman* locomotive clearly shows its size. OO and HO scale rolling stock use the same track gauge but are of different scales.

Modelling railways is a hobby that is followed by millions in all walks of life throughout the world. For many people the fascination is in modelling replicas of magnificent engineering feats which in full size are enormously powerful, capable of pulling many times their own weight, and in model form produce their very own engineering problems.

It is a challenging and relaxing pastime to model the peaceful scenic settings and the modeller will gain considerable knowledge and a number of skills; for example, a person who builds baseboards can also put up shelves, as wives will be quick to point out! As a hobby it is expensive in terms of the amount of money one invests in it, but note that I say invest, for model railways are always resaleable items.

A railway layout will provide hours of enjoyment irrespective of age. How many new dads I wonder have, at the excuse of a first baby, rushed off and started a model railway? Or perhaps when the youngster grows up, having reached the age of six or seven, they might say: 'Dad can you make me a model railway?' These are typical beginnings to a hobby that for many remains into old age.

In the early stages the beginner, or indeed the old hand returning to the hobby, is often overwhelmed by the choice of rolling stock available and the wide variety of scales. Coming across a term such as HO/OO can be very confusing, for although the

track gauge remains the same size the modelling scale is very different. The smallest commercially-produced scale is Z gauge from Marklin. This ultra-tiny scale has a track gauge of 6 mm (0.24 in) and uses mainly German rolling stock. Its size is so small that a complete layout can be built on a coffee table and a locomotive fits comfortably into a matchbox.

At the other end of the scale are 5.5 in gauge live steam locomotives that will allow passengers to be carried. These live steam models are in many respects not so much 'models' as simply small locomotives, especially those which are a freelance

Right Graham Farish's N scale locomotive shown on a box of matches to display its size. The same track gauge is also used for other scales.

design rather than based on a full-size prototype. Miniature steam locomotives are subject to the same boiler pressure checks, maintenance problems and so on that one would find on the largest counterpart. For practical reasons, therefore, this book does not attempt to cover this type of modelling.

SCALES AVAILABLE

Gauge 1 (10 mm to 1 ft, previously 3/8 in to 1 ft) This gauge is normally accepted as the start of model as opposed to miniature railways, although they are usually found laid out in a garden. This is also a popular scale for model town layouts that visitors flock to see, as due to its size it is very impressive. It is a specialist scale usually involving the use of live steam, through coal, oil, methylated spirit or gas firing, although model village layouts are generally electrically driven.

O Gauge (7 mm to 1 ft) This is the largest scale suitable for an indoor model railway layout, but is also sometimes used for tracks running round the garden, perhaps starting from inside a garden shed. It is the smallest practical size for live steam running, although in recent years smaller scales have been built and successfully run by an expert. The O gauge live steam locomotive is often these days controlled by radio, as the advent of small transmitters, reliable receivers and servos has made this possible. This method of control is also useful for electric outdoor layouts, overcoming the problems of the weather short-circuiting the track and the restrictions of being only able to run a very limited amount of rolling stock on a single track. Electrically-powered rolling stock carry their own rechargeable battery sources of power, controlled through radio using proportionally-controlled power outputs. This allows not only forward and reverse operation in a completely scale-like manner, but most important of all multi-use of a single line, as the transmitters and receivers have up to 24 frequencies, allowing far more than 24 locomotives to be operated at the same time along a single length of track, all independently controlled.

S Gauge (3/16 of one inch to 1 foot) This is half the size of gauge 1 and being so close to 00 scale has not really caught on, there being little or no trade support for it apart from in North America.

OO Gauge (4mm to 1 ft) The most popular gauge in Britain, although not a true scale track gauge-wise, is OO. It is extremely well catered for commercially. The history of the gauge is derived from HO (3.5 mm to 1 ft) which is popular with European and American manufacturers. The large electric motors, which were all that were available at the time, could be fitted into model American and European locomotives but unfortunately not into British locomotives which are considerably smaller in average size. So the British manufacturers decided to increase the scale from 3.5 mm to 1 ft to 4 mm to 1 ft and rename it OO for British outline rolling stock, but to retain the

Above A live steam 5.5 in gauge locomotive, capable of pulling both driver and passengers. When such a locomotive is constructed to the builder's own design it ceases to be a model, and becomes a small real locomotive.

Left The diminutive Marklin Z scale locomotive, displayed next to a pen to show its size. The track gauge is the same as that for N scale narrow gauge rolling stock.

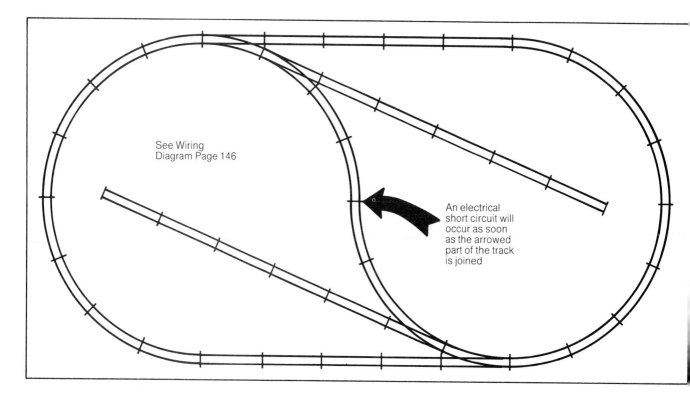

See Wiring
Diagram Page 146

An electrical
short circuit will
occur as soon
as the arrowed
part of the track
is joined

Above A classic
beginner's mistake is
joining a layout together
without insulators,
sections or switches.
The layout does not
work due to the built-in
electrical short circuit.
See the chapter on
wiring for a complete
explanation.

same track gauge to allow a running compatibility. Unfortunately mixing HO and OO does not work because an HO scale locomotive run alongside a OO scale model looks very wrong, as the HO locomotive is smaller than the OO locomotive at model size whilst in real life it is the reverse. Buildings also become extremely noticeable as HO scale buildings are dwarf-like compared with OO scale buildings, so again they should not be mixed.

EM Gauge Modellers who were disillusioned with OO gauge, as the track gauge is really much too narrow for its corect scale, began to remake the axles and wheels, moving the wheels outwards to give the maximum track width possible (18 mm gauge). Then came the introduction of specialized components in 18.25 mm track gauge. This dimension remains to the present, but as always the true scale modeller was not really satisfied with this which led to the development of the next gauge listed.

Scale four or Protofour This is the final development to date of the 4 mm to 1 ft scale. It is a virtually accurate 18.83 mm track gauge and is building up a following in Britain, although as yet it is still very much a specialist's and expert's scale as the vast majority of components have to be hand-built.

HO Scale (3.5 mm to 1 ft) The most popular scale of all in Europe and America is HO, standing for half O gauge, which dates from about 1920. It was established by manufacturers producing models in the early years of railway modelling and is very accurate. This scale provides the modeller with the widest choice of additional components of any scale; buildings, cars, people and other accessories, all with appropriate national characteristics to the countries of origin.

TT Gauge (3 mm to 1 ft) Unfortunately TT, or table top, gauge has now ceased to be commercially produced in quantity in Britain although it flourishes in America. It was the first of the smaller scales to be developed, but like HO/OO two variations arise. The scale ratio 120:1 was adopted by American and European manufacturers, while British manufacturers worked to a scale of 100:1. As with HO/OO, this means that the British models are not strictly to scale and true scale specialist modellers change wheels and track gauge in order to create the correct gauge for the British rolling stock modelled at 3 mm to 1 ft.

N Gauge N gauge or nine gauge refers to the track gauge of 9 mm. This is unquestionably the smallest of the standard gauges but as with HO/OO and TT the scales vary—160:1 for North American and European prototypes and 148:1 (2 mm to 1 ft) for British outline rolling stock. Once again it was the fitting of the working components into the models of British rolling stock which presented problems—it is quite surprising just how small our locomotives are compared with those of other countries. British specialist scale modellers therefore started hand-building to the wider 9.5 mm track gauge so as to keep to the true track gauge for 2 mm to 1 ft scale. This is the N gauge equivalent of EM gauge and protofour/scale four. Poor old Britain always seems to be left struggling with a non-standard international scale size.

Z Gauge The tiniest of all the model sizes are the micro-miniature locomotives using a 6 mm (0.24 in) track gauge established by Marklin once again using mainly German rolling stock. If this scale catches on I foresee all the problems of scale difference recurring as the manufacturers will want to standardize on a track gauge, as in previous cases, with the

Left Many clubs cater for a wide range of different scales and the members help newcomers to the hobby. Exhibitions advertised in the hobby magazines are a good place to make a contact with a club.

supposed advantage of running rolling stock on a standard gauge track.

LAYOUTS

Obviously the larger the modelling scale chosen, the larger the layout will be. O gauge layouts require an enormous amount of room which is why they are generally built in gardens, whilst a Z gauge layout requires the area of a coffee table. The middle of the range, and the most popular scale, is HO or OO. To build a reasonable oval layout at this scale will require a 2 m × 1.5 m (6 ft 6 in × 4 ft 10 in)

baseboard area. An equivalent N gauge layout will require a baseboard 2 m × 0.75 m (6 ft 6 in × 2 ft 5 in)—the size of a standard door panel—as this scale is half the HO/OO scale.

An oval layout is a good compromise in that it allows continuous running and has provision for sidings, landscaping and buildings, all built on a single baseboard which allows access from all sides. It is ideal for the younger modeller.

The alternative is to build an end-to-end layout fixed to a wall. By utilizing further walls the layout

Below A gauge 1 locomotive being run at 'Tucktonia' open air seaside attraction at Christchurch.

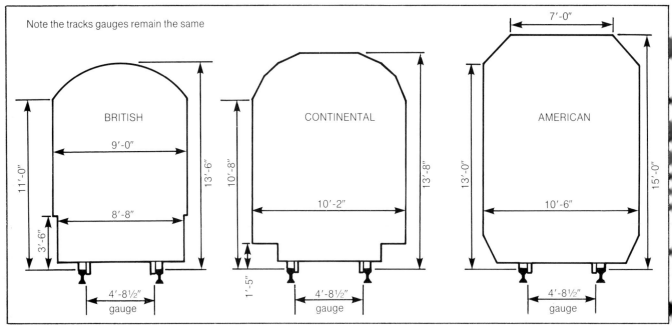

Note the tracks gauges remain the same

BRITISH

9'-0"

11'-0"

13'-6"

10'-8"

8'-8"

3'-6"

4'-8½"
gauge

CONTINENTAL

13'-8"

10'-2"

1'-5"

4'-8½"
gauge

AMERICAN

7'-0"

13'-0"

15'-0"

10'-6"

4'-8½"
gauge

Above The overall size of different countries' rolling stock varies. This caused manufacturing problems in the early days, resulting in HO scale and OO scale running on the same track gauge.

Below Side-on photographs of (top) N scale and (bottom) Z scale locomotives for comparison.

can then be extended until it runs around all the walls of the room, leaving a clear space in the middle for the operator. This type of layout arrangement allows for greater scale-like curves of the track and considerable room for landscaping, buildings and backdrop. This all looks far more realistic, but unfortunately it also requires a large permanent room. If you have the opportunity, the loft is ideal for this purpose and has the added advantage that you can retract the ladder behind you when privacy is required!

SCALE SIZES

With all the different types of scales and ratios, it is very difficult at first to understand the relationship between scale and ratio, so let us see precisely what

is meant, for example, by 32:1. If we take a full size object 32 in long and divide this by 32 the answer would be 1 in. Thus, if we were to make a model of our object totaling 1 in long this would represent a full size to model ratio of 32 to 1 (32:1) as our real object is 32 times bigger. This forms a straight division scale by dividing up one inch by 32 equalling 1/32 of an inch, each 1/32 in on the model equalling 1 in full size. If the object was bigger, say 32 ft long, and the finished model is 1 ft long, the ratio remains the same (the 32 ft divided by 32 equals 1 ft). The 1 ft is multiplied by 12 to give inches, ie, 12 in, then the 12 in are divided by 32 to form scale feet. At model size 12 over 32 equals 12/32 of 1 in; expressed as a fraction 12/32 = 6/16 = 3/8, the smallest number. This 3/8 of 1 in now represents 1 in full size. Instead of our ratio of 32 to 1, we could have used inches, by saying each inch represents a foot, so our 32-ft full size object would become 32 in long; this is a one-twelfth scale model, 1:12, the foot being divided by 12.

It is the same with metric dimensions. One metre divided by 100 equals 1:100, but note the way the figures have changed over and are now reversed, one being 32:1 and the other 1:100. The main difficulty arises when scales of 4 mm to 1 ft occur and how the conversion to metric is accomplished (1 m equals 39.37 in). The nearest we can get conveniently is 39 in, as 1 mm now equals 3 in full size, therefore 13 mm equals 39 in full size (this is arrived at by dividing 39 by 3 equalling 13 so that at 4 mm to 1 ft scale 1 mm equals 3 in full size). Next we have 13 mm to 1 m giving a full size ratio of 76:1 (OO scale). This 13 mm is a close approximation which is convenient, but when it is multiplied over a considerable length the error becomes exaggerated due to the 0.37 in ignored. Fortunately in Britain one rarely mixes these dimensions either modelling in Imperial or metric measurements, but Continental modellers have a worse problem as the HO scale is

3.5 mm to 1 ft. Hence the ratio of 87:1 is used, the metric measurement of 1 m being divided up by 87 providing a close approximate equivalent dimension of 11.5 mm (model size) to 1 m full size. These dimensions for convenience are rounded up or down; for example, N gauge at 160:1 and OOO gauge 152:1, yet both are modelled at 2 mm to the foot.

GAUGES

When George Stephenson first invented the *Rocket* railway engine and decided upon a distance between the tracks of 4 ft 8½ in, he was just not thinking about the railway modeller! This awkward dimension was not, of course, adopted throughout the world or even by other British companies, and different gauges were introduced, both narrower and wider. The narrow gauge name has remained, its gauge (or distance between the tracks) being anything less than the 'Stephenson standard' width. A wider gauge introduced by Brunel became known as broad gauge. The terms narrow, standard and broad gauge are still used throughout the world today but, since different countries use various gauges, the modeller should ideally use the correct gauge and rolling stock of that country, all modelled to a common scale. In practice, and for commercial reasons, a series of standard model track gauges have appeared. HO and OO share the same track gauge as explained earlier, the scale of the model changing—an arrangement allowing for the interchangeability of rolling stock upon the layout. But, and it is a big 'but', this of course means either the rolling stock is out of scale to the buildings or visa versa. A layout designed at a given scale is either one or the other (OO or HO) never half-and-half, and is a point to remember.

Below A comparison of sizes, showing the popular scales used and their relationship to each other.

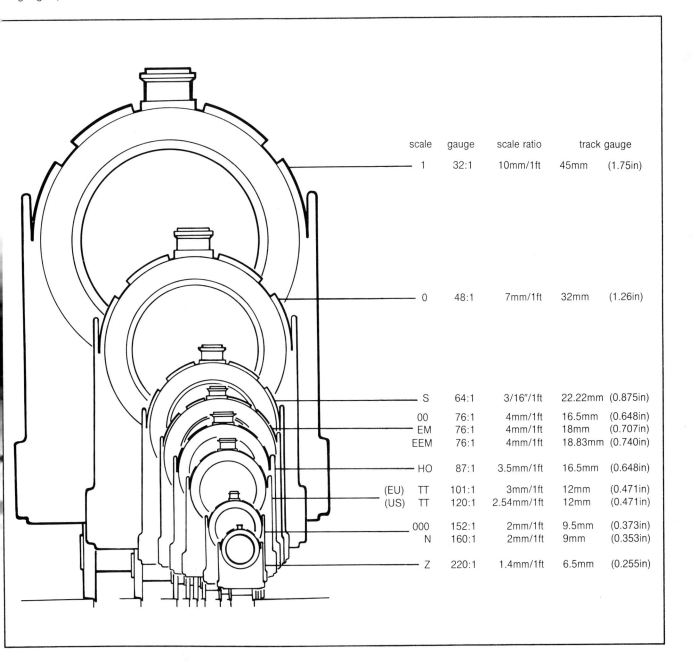

scale	gauge	scale ratio	track gauge	
1	32:1	10mm/1ft	45mm	(1.75in)
0	48:1	7mm/1ft	32mm	(1.26in)
S	64:1	3/16"/1ft	22.22mm	(0.875in)
00	76:1	4mm/1ft	16.5mm	(0.648in)
EM	76:1	4mm/1ft	18mm	(0.707in)
EEM	76:1	4mm/1ft	18.83mm	(0.740in)
HO	87:1	3.5mm/1ft	16.5mm	(0.648in)
(EU) TT	101:1	3mm/1ft	12mm	(0.471in)
(US) TT	120:1	2.54mm/1ft	12mm	(0.471in)
000	152:1	2mm/1ft	9.5mm	(0.373in)
N	160:1	2mm/1ft	9mm	(0.353in)
Z	220:1	1.4mm/1ft	6.5mm	(0.255in)

Right The *Flying Scotsman* OO scale Hornby locomotive and tender reproduced scale size. The scale rules show the comparison of sizes between OO and HO for the same length of locomotive.

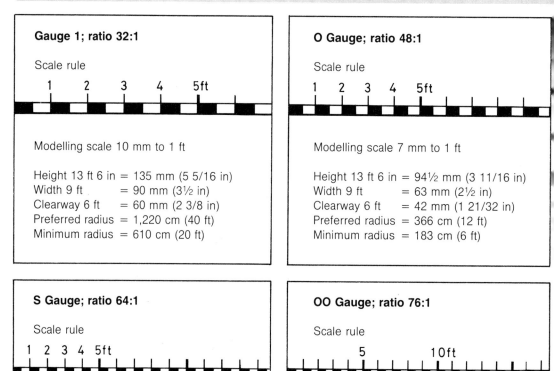

British loading gauge size This is a device used to size the load within its limitations. The maximum permitted height is 13 ft 6 in. The maximum width is 9 ft. The Continental and American loading sizes are larger.

Clearway This is the gap between the sets of tracks. The scale distance is much too small to provide sufficient clearance for model railway use so increase as necessary.

Gauge 1; ratio 32:1

Scale rule

Modelling scale 10 mm to 1 ft

Height 13 ft 6 in = 135 mm (5 5/16 in)
Width 9 ft   = 90 mm (3½ in)
Clearway 6 ft   = 60 mm (2 3/8 in)
Preferred radius = 1,220 cm (40 ft)
Minimum radius   = 610 cm (20 ft)

O Gauge; ratio 48:1

Scale rule

Modelling scale 7 mm to 1 ft

Height 13 ft 6 in = 94½ mm (3 11/16 in)
Width 9 ft   = 63 mm (2½ in)
Clearway 6 ft   = 42 mm (1 21/32 in)
Preferred radius = 366 cm (12 ft)
Minimum radius   = 183 cm (6 ft)

S Gauge; ratio 64:1

Scale rule

Modelling scale 3/16 in to 1 ft

Height 13 ft 6 in = 66 mm (2 19/32 in)
Width 9 ft   = 43 mm (1 11/16 in)
Clearway 6 ft   = 29 mm (1 1/8 in)
Preferred radius = 274 cm (9 ft)
Minimum radius   = 137 cm (4 ft 6 in)

OO Gauge; ratio 76:1

Scale rule

Modelling scale 4 mm to 1 ft

Height 13 ft 6 in = 54 mm (2 1/8 in)
Width 9 ft   = 36 mm (1 7/16 in)
Clearway 6 ft   = 24 mm (15/16 in)
Preferred radius = 182 cm (6 ft)
Minimum radius   = 61 cm (2 ft)

HO Gauge; ratio 87:1

Scale rule

5   10   15ft

Modelling scale 3.5 mm to 1 ft

Height 13 ft 6 in = 47¼ mm (1 7/8 in)
Width 9 ft   = 31½ mm (1¼ in)
Clearway 6 ft   = 21 mm (53/64 in)
Preferred radius = 182 cm (6 ft)
Minimum radius   = 61 cm (2 ft)

TT Gauge (EU); ratio 101:1

Scale rule

5   10   15ft

Modelling scale 3 mm to 1 ft

Height 13 ft 6 in = 40½ mm (1 19/32 in)
Width 9 ft   = 27 mm (1 1/16 in)
Clearway 6 ft   = 18 mm (47/64 in)
Preferred radius = 152 cm (5 ft)
Minimum radius   = 45 cm (1 ft 6 in)

OOO Gauge; ratio 152:1

Scale rule

5   10   15   20ft

Modelling scale 2 mm to 1 ft

Height 13 ft 6 in = 27 mm (1 1/16 in)
Width 9 ft   = 18 mm (47/64 in)
Clearway 6 ft   = 12 mm (15/32 in)
Preferred radius = 91 cm (3 ft)
Minimum radius   = 23 cm (9 in)

Z Gauge; ratio 220:1

Scale rule

10   20   30ft

Modelling scale 1.4 mm to 1 ft

Height 13 ft 6 in = 18.9 mm (¾ in)
Width 9 ft   = 12.6 mm (½ in)
Clearway 6 ft   = 8.4 mm (21/64 in)
Preferred radius = 69 cm (2 ft 3 in)
Minimum radius   = 14.5 cm (5 3/16 in)

Peco Ltd produce an excellent number of booklets on track information, which include layout plans and rolling stock for both standard and narrow gauge modelling. In addition to this the company also produces a wide range of modelling accessories and a monthly magazine.

Note. The minimum radius should always be checked against the rolling stock that is used for reversed shunting, as buffers can become locked on very tight bends.

1. UNDERSTANDING MAPS AND CONTOURS

Below A typical small-scale map showing a hilly countryside. Reading the map from left to right, the track is at ground level +50, then it runs through a cutting, which has a road bridge, confirmed by the raised contours; the ground then falls to meet the track level at the next road crossing on the 50 contour level. the ground continues to fall away and the track now becomes raised on an embankment with a road and stream passing underneath it. The ground then rises to meet the track level. At +50, this provides us with three track spot heights.

To successfully model a landscape with its hills, trees and rivers requires a basic knowledge of how the landscape is formed, by making a visual study of different areas. This can be accomplished through studying books, magazines and observing the countryside. This provides one with a natural instinct for knowing just what could happen at a particular point. For example, where the edge of a field adjoins a stream, one forms a mental picture of how the ground may have been eroded away, the possible colour of the soil and the plant life that grows upon its banks.

Basic information on how the ground heights are shaped (known as contours) can be obtained from maps. The 6 in to 1 mile maps produced in Britain by Ordnance Survey will show this, the rivers, roads and railways also being clearly marked. For modelling purposes the larger the scale of the map the better as the information is shown more clearly. A 1:1,250 scale map will contain detailed information on the house shapes and boundaries, shown in plan form, and since these maps have been reduced from larger scale maps, they are extremely accurate. Unfortunately some of the larger-scale maps do not show the contour lines and are marked out in spot

heights only. Spot heights are normally shown in the centre of the road but on occasions they will be located on a wall. These are called 'Bench marks' and since they are located on the wall, the height indicated can be a few feet above the actual ground level. Reading the map only, this 'Bench mark' level cannot be assessed so a site visit will be needed. Spot heights at ground level are shown as plus sign followed by a number representing height above sea level. A Bench mark above ground level is shown as the plus sign, number, then an arrow underneath to denote that it is above ground level.

Since the scale of any map obtainable is too small to make the model directly from it, the map will have to be enlarged in size. One of the easiest ways of doing this is to grid the map with squares then redraw it. Do not as yet redraw to the full size of the layout, but to a convenient sketch size, just showing the main features of roads and railways, rivers and buildings, to form an outline map so as to provide an idea of the landscape and the way the contours and other heights of the ground work, since these will probably need ultimately to be changed to fit the base board of the layout.

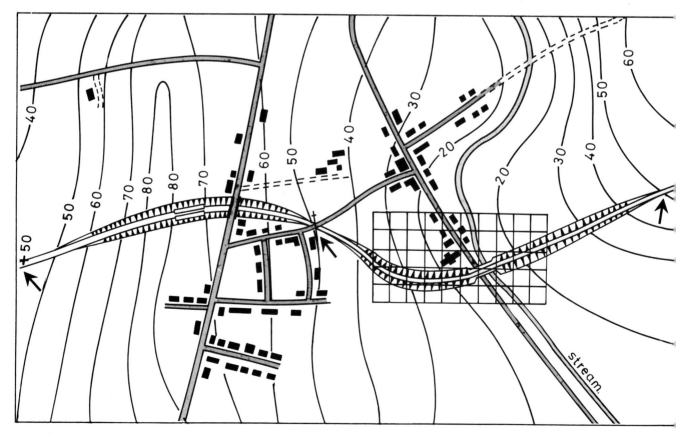

UNDERSTANDING MAPS AND CONTOURS

Modern maps are marked out in metric dimensions but older ones are in Imperial, so it is important first to establish the way the map has been measured out. Quite often both scales are used on one map, the heights of the contours being shown in metric, longitude distances in miles, with the gridding of the map in kilometres, just to confuse everything! This is due to the British change-over from Imperial to metric which will continue for a long time in the future. Thus how modern the map you use will affect the way in which the information is shown. This extends right down to the style of the graphics that represent trees, woodland, marshes etc, since these will also change as the maps become more international.

GRIDDING

I have found through practice that the best way of gridding up is to use the existing grid on the small-scale map and sub-divide this by ten. Then you regrid to a convenient sketch scale, by plotting the intersecting points on both the small and the larger grid by eye, estimating the intersecting point on each line. Start with the railway. Having plotted the intersections, the points can be joined up by freehand sketching in of the radii of the track's curves (see illustration). Then plot in the roads, followed by the rivers or streams, thus slowly building up the enlarged portion of the map. Having completed this I next mark in the spot heights shown on the roads and join up corresponding heights of the same level, or using the grid follow the contour lines marked out so as to establish how the ground

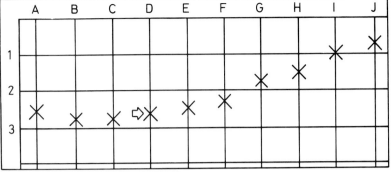

levels change. The railway line itself tends to run at an almost continuous level, very slowly changing height either running through a cutting or built up upon an embankment, whilst roads change height very quickly in comparison. In modelling though, do remember that there is a restriction upon the gradient of a hill, a 1 in 4 hill being extremely steep in Britain and only very occasionally encountered, and then for very short distances only. (One in four means one foot rise (25 percent) in four feet distance (100 percent), expressed as a percentage these days of 25 percent.) This should be the maximum gradient on roads that travel up or down hill when we change the map to suit the layout, so the roads will look more natural.

UNDERSTANDING CONTOURS

It is a matter of common observation that hillsides and valleys vary greatly in size and to indicate this on a map contour lines are used. These show the changes of level and are either marked out in feet or metres. So that all maps have a zero level or datum,

Above By estimating the position of intersecting lines, the small map can be enlarged. Mark a cross where lines intersect on the large grid.

Below Then join the crosses up, starting with the railway track, followed by the road and stream, then the contours. Below the +20 ft contour level no contours are shown, but the stream could well be at +11 ft, thus effectively obscuring the next lower contour line.

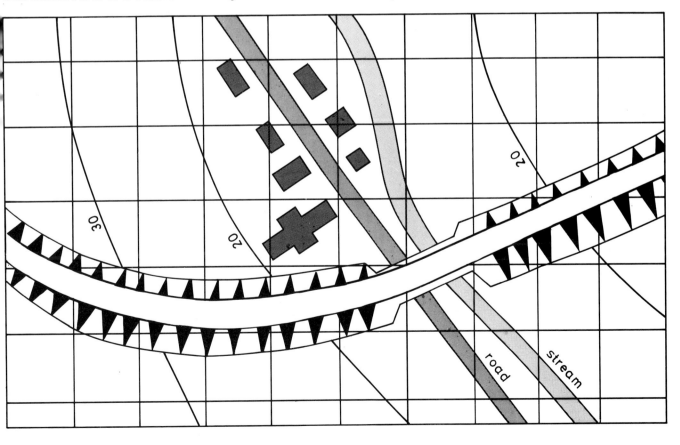

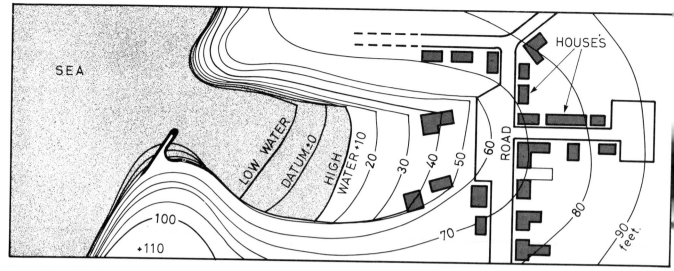

SEA

LOW WATER

DATUM ±0

HIGH WATER +10

20

30

40

50

60

ROAD

70

80

90 feet.

100

+110

HOUSES

Above A typical Cornish cove found among a hilly landscape. The gap between the cliff faces form a natural harbour. The beach is formed by sand and small stones being washed into the cove, and from the landscape deposited by the weather over thousands of years. The ground level rising from the water datum of zero (mean tide) to 90 ft, is shown in 10 ft contour intervals. The maximum height of the ground is 110 ft on top of the cliff. The road shown drops in its levels from both sides to its lowest at +60 ft, dwellings being built alongside it. Since these houses are built into the hillside they will have the ground changing all around their foundation levels.

a common level is necessary, and this generally is the sea's mean tide level, ie, the tide is neither in or out. Low and high water marks are also shown on maps to indicate the lowest and the highest levels at spring and neap tides, so there are three points that can be used as the datum zero level.

As one travels inland the ground level generally rises above the sea level, and to make it clear on the map that this happens, the heights that form the contour lines are marked with a plus sign, showing that this is above sea level. The ground itself varies in height due to the formation of the earth's crust, the ice age, wind and weather. Then the elements, with the passing of time, have eroded away the softer layers of soil, leaving the harder rock as high ground, the earth being washed down by the rain into the valleys producing good soil areas with plenty of growth whilst the rock faces remain barren. The rain that has fallen forms streams which join up to form rivers which eventually reach the sea. Since the ground varies in its levels the streams and rivers always follow the lowest ground level available. The steeper the slope the faster the water flows, causing considerable erosion of the stream's or river's banks. The flatter the ground the more likely the water is to form lakes, wide shallow streams or rivers, and where it has changed its course over the years, half moon shaped ponds will be left along its banks. Man has also contributed by building sea walls and reclaiming land which is below sea level. This is shown as a minus sign on the contour levels of the maps. Drainage ditches now become above ground level with a series of banks on each side, the water from the lower ditches being pumped up into each higher level of ditch.

To interpret the contour lines shown one simply looks at their height above or below the datum level. The slope of the ground determines how the contour lines will be spaced out. If the ground is very steep, ie, on a hillside, the contour lines will be close together. If the ground is very flat the contour lines will hardly exist and will be spaced extremely far apart. Where a very sharp fall occurs in the contour level, eg, a man-made embankment, the contour

lines are replaced with a series of signs like an arrow head, wide and heavily marked at the top becoming a point at the bottom of the slope, so as to denote which is the top and bottom of the embankment or fall in the ground's level.

To translate the heights from the map on to the model, first establish the scale it is going to be enlarged to and then draw the zero datum line; from this measure vertically either to the scale you are using on the model, OO/HO, etc, or to the scale being used on the working drawing. Mark the height of the first contour, then scale out the spacing of the next. Repeat this for each contour level required then finally join up these points in a series of radiuses so that the ground level looks natural. This forms a section through the landscape.

ROADS AND BRIDGES

Roads and bridges form a very important part of the layout, in the way they provide a scale to the model. The eye seeing this automatically sizes things to the reality it knows. If a model is made of an area of landscape in an unnatural way the eye simply will not accept what it sees as being realistic; for example, a model hump-back road bridge over a canal might have the angle of the road almost approaching 45 degrees to go up each side of the bridge and a small radius at the top. In practical terms the approach road either side would be too steep to allow the safe transportation of a vehicle up the slope of the bridge and due to the small radius at the top of the bridge, the passing vehicle would hit its underside on the crest of the bridge (see illustration) leaving its wheels airborne. Alongside this hump-back bridge might be a railway bridge, level with the river banks and having just a few inches clearance over the water, so if the modeller puts canal barges travelling up and down the canal either side of the railway bridge, the onlooker will know that the barges simply could not have passed underneath the bridge. If the railway bridge is fixed in position and not of the 'swing out of the way type' to the eye, this is an impractical situation that is not true to life so the mind does not accept what it is seeing as being realistic.

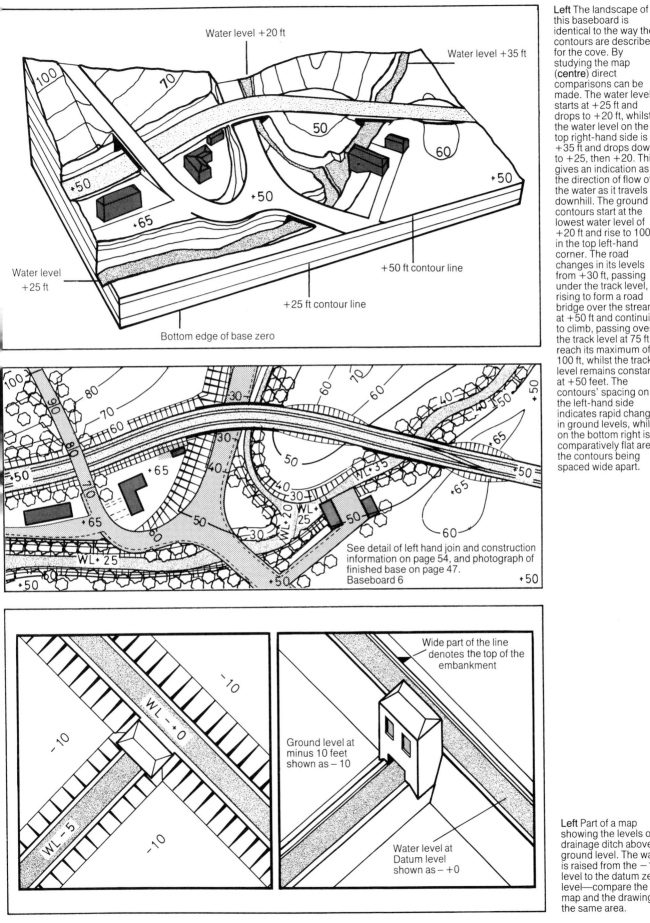

Water level +20 ft

Water level +35 ft

100

70

50

60

+50

+50

+65

+50

Water level +25 ft

+25 ft contour line

+50 ft contour line

Bottom edge of base zero

100

80

70

60

90

60

70

30

50

+65

+50

+65

60

50

40

40

30

50

30

30

WL + 20

WL + 25

WL + 25

WL + 35

40

60

70

60

40

50

65

+50

+65

60

+50

+50

+50

+50

See detail of left hand join and construction information on page 54, and photograph of finished base on page 47.
Baseboard 6

+50

−10

−10

WL − +0

WL − 5

−10

−10

Wide part of the line denotes the top of the embankment

Ground level at minus 10 feet shown as − 10

Water level at Datum level shown as − +0

Left The landscape of this baseboard is identical to the way the contours are described for the cove. By studying the map (**centre**) direct comparisons can be made. The water level starts at +25 ft and drops to +20 ft, whilst the water level on the top right-hand side is at +35 ft and drops down to +25, then +20. This gives an indication as to the direction of flow of the water as it travels downhill. The ground contours start at the lowest water level of +20 ft and rise to 100 ft in the top left-hand corner. The road changes in its levels from +30 ft, passing under the track level, rising to form a road bridge over the stream at +50 ft and continuing to climb, passing over the track level at 75 ft to reach its maximum of 100 ft, whilst the track's level remains constant at +50 feet. The contours' spacing on the left-hand side indicates rapid change in ground levels, whilst on the bottom right is a comparatively flat area, the contours being spaced wide apart.

Left Part of a map showing the levels of a drainage ditch above ground level. The water is raised from the −10 level to the datum zero level—compare the map and the drawing of the same area.

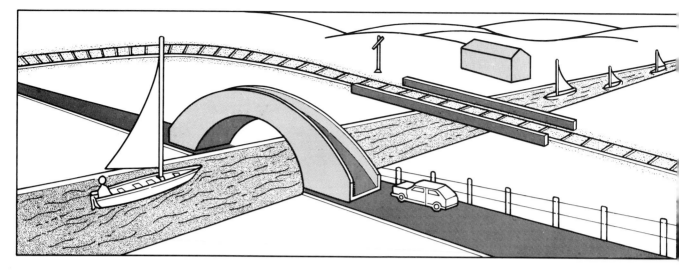

Above The unnatural situation above could easily be changed into a realistic setting by replacing the hump back and the railway bridges with 'swing out of the way' types. By combining the two bridges in one, a very elaborate 'lift up out of the way' type could be made.

Right This shows a railway over a road and stream, situated in Athlone (Ireland). The rail bridge over the road shows a 12 ft 11 in clearance. The Athlone west junction cabin is built on the side of the embankment.

Right A small lifting bridge over a canal. The bridge when raised is closed to road traffic by the gates on one side and on the other side by the bridge itself which, now being vertical, blocks the road.

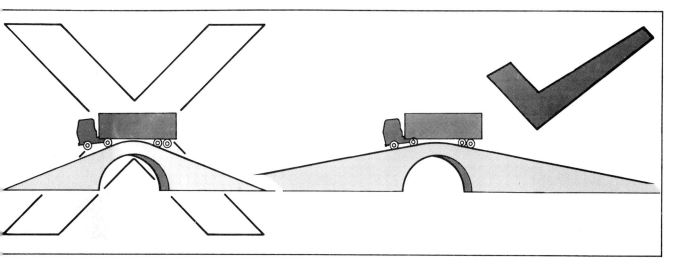

To avoid this type of situation careful planning of the layout is required and an understanding of the rules and regulations that have been laid down. These rules cover public road usage, they lay down maximum recommended gradients for the approaches to bridges and the radius of the bridge so as to provide clearance for traffic passing over the bridge or under it. Many hump-back bridges are still in existence today but their use has been restricted, in many cases to pedestrians only, or they have been considerably modified to meet the demands of today's traffic, but with restrictions on vehicle length, axle weight, etc. Roads are also built to regulations which govern the radii of bends, so that two-way traffic can negotiate them without using the other side of the road. Similarly there will be recommendations as to the maximum gradient of a hill, for the provison for emergency escape bays on the long downhill stretches of roads should the brakes fail, etc. Finally the width of the road will be regulated for the type and volume of traffic using it. In many countries the minimum width of a public road is the single width of a private motor car, and in country lanes, passing places must be provided at regular intervals, to allow traffic passing in the opposite direction to pass. When traffic constantly travels in both directions, the road will be wider and as the road width increases so does the radius of a bend in it. Thus small country lanes are notorious for their steep hills and sharp bends whilst motorways are noted for their billiard table flatness and gentle curves.

What actually happens in practice? The gradient of a hill can be reduced in many ways. Steep roads travelling up or down hills can be reduced in gradient by forming cuttings or embankments, the same as found on the railways. Roads (and railways) which travel diagonally up a hill are generally half excavated into the hillside, the earth removed being used to form an embankment on the other side of the road (or track). This also applies to roads (or track) travelling along a hillside which will be built this way for economy reasons, since it is far cheaper to half excavate and fill with the excavated material

(see illustration) on the other side of the road (track). The same form of economy measures are also applied to bridges and viaducts by redirecting the road to travel under the railway alongside a stream or river, thus building one bridge instead of two. The height of the embankment quite often equals the volume of the excavated material from the cutting simply because it is less expensive to transport large volumes of earth short distances. It is worth keeping in mind these types of practice whilst redesigning the layout to suit the base board as it also adds interest and realism to the model railway.

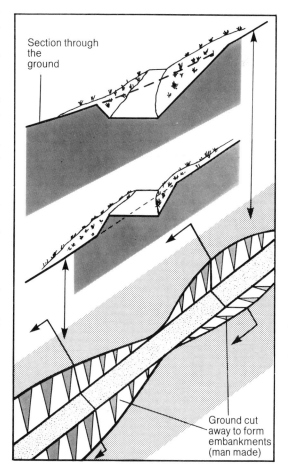

Section through the ground

Ground cut away to form embankments (man made)

Above The lorry going over the hump back bridge hits its chassis leaving its wheels airborne. This should be prevented by extending the approaches to the bridge.

Left The sections through the ground show a cutting for the road through a hillside. This keeps the road flat across its width and the gradient at a reasonable angle up the hillside. Note the way the embankment is cut away and shown with tapering arrows to indicate man-made earthworks on the plan.

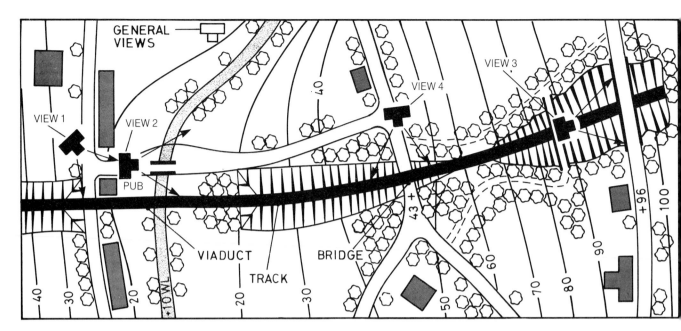

The photographs used in the making of this plan have their real locations miles apart from each other and by combining this real information and then using selective compression the baseboard's plan can be designed to look real yet meet the restricted size of the available space and the track shape. The unknown areas outside the photographs view are invented to suit the joining of each situation together.

Right Public house and viaduct (View 1).

RESEARCH AND COMPROMISE

If it was decided to try to make a true to scale layout which included every item modelled in great detail, it would require an enormous amount of research, time and effort, plus a very large space in which to assemble the finished layout. The involvement of making just one fully detailed model that is in fact a small part of the overall layout, requires a considerable amount of research from various sources. This will include plans, photographs, notes, etc, and each bit of information obtained will then need to be

cross-checked for accuracy, especially if a model is being made of a subject from the past, when authenticity of the information is doubtful. If the subject still exists, it can at times be far easier to make a visit to the place or subject to gather one's own information.

Say a particular situation is required, of a railway bridge over a road and stream. Start by studying a series of updated maps, following the railway lines, until a suitable bridge is found, then study the map's ground contours, as this will provide an indication as

Opposite page, top (View 1) Selection of photographs joined together to form an overall view. **Upper centre (View 2)** Bridge and ford, sited at Edenbridge, Kent. **Lower centre (View 3)** Railway cutting at Rochester. **Bottom (View 4)** Railway bridge over a road.

the setting. Finally, if all is still suitable make a site
sit.

Unfortunately at times the map will fail to show the
umber of trees surrounding the subject, which of
ourse one finds on arrival obscuring the majority of
ie bridge from view. In this situation all one can do
to make a series of sketches, take photographs of
ie bits visible and prepare notes, then at home
ece all the information together.

The important information to obtain is: the
earance between the road's surface and the
nderside of the bridge; the construction style of the
ridge, eg, stone, brick or metal, and its colour; and
1 estimate of the difference in the ground levels
ound the site. Finally take a series of photographs
oking away, from and around the bridge, so as to
ather all the reference material required for the
ridge and its setting.

Whilst it is also possible to work from photographs
f other people's models shown in books and
iagazines, one has to be very careful not to model a
iodel. Use the modelling techniques described but
:udy and work from reality, using notes and
iotographs, as the model shown could easily be
ie author's interpretation of what he has seen,
Japted to suit his layout.

A decision will be required at some time as to
hether the layout is going to be true to scale in
very way, or will it be a series of different
ell-researched and convincingly made buildings,
olling stock, etc, all made to the same scale and set
a realistic condensed situation to suit the layout's
ze restrictions. The latter type of modelling is
enerally referred to as 'being based upon', for
xample 'Little Bovington', and it allows consider-
oly wider scope with the design, also the content
id the interpretation of layout, as it uses real
tuations which are in reality miles away from each
her, but adapted to suit the layout with its
nitations of baseboard size and which must be
ractical to operate.

The plan illustrated shows how a selection of
fferent area photographs can be combined and
rmed into a layout plan, whilst each subject in real
e is miles away from the others. The way I have set
Jout this is to keep the track at a constant height,
stimated from the viaduct as being 58 ft above
ound level. Since the ground level at the stream is
ven as the height of +10 ft above sea level, this is
Jded to the viaduct's height, to total 68 ft above sea
vel. The rail bridge over the road is estimated at 25
above the road's surface. The track height is 68 ft
ss 25 ft, making the road height at +43 ft, to form a
oot height. The ground then has to rise to track
vel at 68 feet, then continue to around 100 feet, so
s to allow for the tunnel, through which the track
vel passes. This provides a series of heights along
e track's length. Starting at the water level of 10 ft
the highest level of 100 ft, it is divided up using
e heights established, into a series of levels to
it, these forming the contour intervals.

2. DESIGNING THE LAYOUT

LAYOUTS BOXED

Opposite page, top There is an extremely wide choice of pre-packed layouts, produced by numerous manufacturers. The very basic introductory set contains sufficient track to make a single oval, with some rolling stock to use. Any additional items required have to be purchased separately and generally from manufacturers specialising in accessories.

Opposite page, bottom The oval measures 7 ft × 4 ft but dismantles into convenient sections for storage.

Right and below The colour printed plan produced by Graham Farish is also available mounted on a board, complete with track. The stand used to support the layout is simply assembled using a hammer; its height is designed for convenient use by a disabled person. Since the completed layout is very small it can be stored away under a single bed.

In some ways the oval layout is ideal for both the beginner and the enthusiast and with this in mind Graham Farish have especially produced a colour-printed plan for the N gauge layout. The plan, in addition to the track, shows roads, paving, and housing positions, and at the time of writing Graham Farish are working on a second interlocking plan, for possible release in the future. The marketed plan is also available as a pre-assembled track mounted on a baseboard complete with a knockdown table, the height of which is designed to enable a disabled person to manage comfortably (baseboard panel size 5 ft × 2 ft 6 in (152 cm × 76 cm)).

It is the same with their buildings. The company has designed a very simple to assemble and robust range of buildings, using plastic blocks of assorted shapes similar to 'Lego', over which self-adhesive pre-printed building elevations are placed. The self-adhesive elevations are also used to hold the blocks in place so that no additional glues are used and a pair of scissors is the only tool required to assemble the buildings (being used to cut out the elevations). In this way children from the age of eight or so can start modelling their own buildings. Since the blocks are not glued together, at a later date the buildings can be stripped of their elevation detail and rebuilt using home-made elevations as described in a later chapter. It is this advantage that makes them ideal for the beginner to purchase, and they are very different from the hollow cardboard buildings, which are far more difficult and time-consuming to construct.

The storage of a layout after use is a common problem, but the Graham Farish layout, being complete and solidly constructed on a one-piece baseboard, can simply be picked up and stored away (eg, under the bed as in many cases the bedroom is used for the hobby room, or another good storage space is behind the wardrobe). Storage of the layout is one of the major problems of model railways, since the layouts require room both in use and afterwards and can force the decision of which scale to model in. For example, if one lives in a small flat and space is at the premium then one

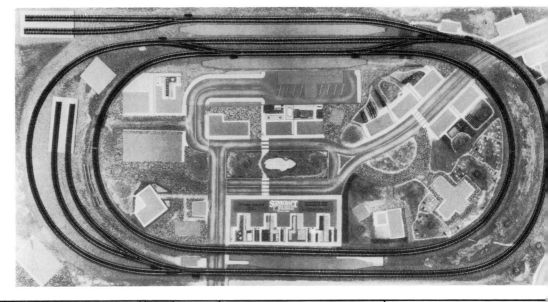

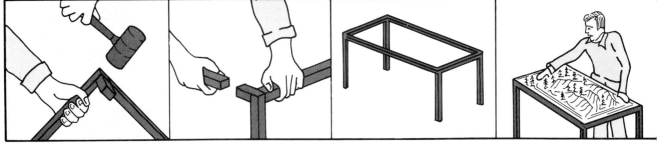

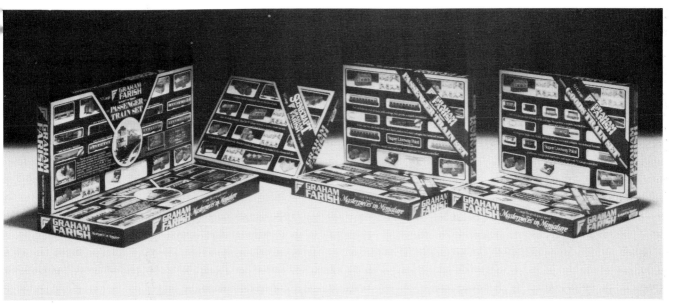

forced to build a small layout. Similarly, if one lives alone then one tends to put up with some inconvenience, but if one is married one's other half may not share these thoughts, thus requiring the layout to be put away after use, especially if there are little fingers about. The layout therefore has to be designed to get around these problems.

If one is a club member then the layout problem could be of less concern at home as one can help build and run the club's layout, and at home use display cases or even boxes for storage, requiring just a short length of test track so as to keep the rolling stock in good working order. Alternatively the layout could well be designed to fit into a piece of furniture, for example a long sofa which really is a disguised storage chest with cushions on, allowing two or three baseboards to be stored inside. Such a layout would necessarily have to be of a back and forth design due to its long narrow storage. If one has a larger house then the problems of storage are reduced considerably as many houses have a loft, cellar or garage, and these are points to consider when purchasing a house.

For an example of how the siting of the layout influences design, the loft could be converted by boarding it for use as a hobby room. The hatch size into the loft will then pre-decide the maximum size of baseboard, just in case one moves. The cellar cleaned out makes an ideal layout area especially if one has a lot of visitors. Failing this it's the garage, the layout being built around three walls leaving the door clear in the form of a big 'U', the car being garaged in the middle overnight. The height of the track will allow the bonnet of the car to go underneath the layout, and don't forget to leave sufficient room on one side for the driver to get out. Alternatively, you could leave the car outside!

Having a hobby room in a loft, cellar or garage gives one almost unlimited freedom in designing a layout, which is only restricted by the size of the room. However, there are other considerations than

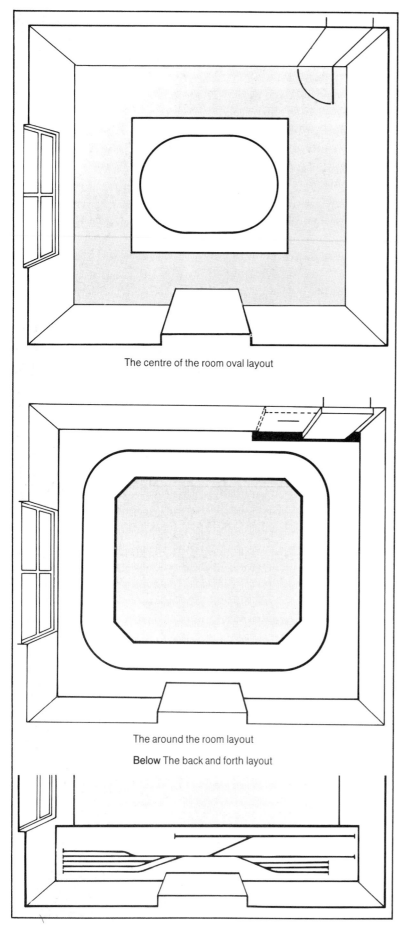

The centre of the room oval layout

The around the room layout

Below The back and forth layout

just those of space. Few people have unlimited money or time, so a small layout is often dictated by circumstances rather than choice anyway.

The self-contained layout under average circumstances can have many advantages, and a concealed fiddle yard greatly expands the layout's running programes for it allows one to undertake all the non-realistic situations; it is a behind the scenes operation and 'fiddled' so as to make the layout work conveniently in the minimum of space.

LAYOUT PLANS

The simplest form of layout for the younger modeller to build is a basic oval with a siding, laid out on a solid board, the standard track lengths being clipped together with fishplates. The manufacturers encourage this by producing various layouts to suit all budgets and prepacked ready for use. These 'train sets' generally consist of a number of lengths of track, a battery-operated controller and a simple locomotive, plus some carriages or wagons. The disadvantage of this type of layout is that it always uses batteries.

The first stage in expanding the layout is to purchase additional track, some points, a mains transformer and controller, then to carefully plan a layout and fix the track down permanently into position. The next stage is to paint the baseboard with emulsion paints to represent roads, paving, grass, etc, and by adding buildings and other structures, the expanded layout can be made to look more attractive. (All these are items that can be undertaken by the younger modeller under parental supervision.) These stages can be further expanded until eventually a large-scale layout is constructed.

Unfortunately, by building on a flat board the layout will not look as visually attractive as it might, being just a series of loops on a flat landscape. It can be made far more attractive by varying the levels, raising the track level above the basic baseboard level, so that a stream, for example, can be modelled at the lowest level, providing an excuse to build railway and road bridges over it. By similarly raising other levels to a sufficient height above the track, the landscape's shape suggests the reason for the building of tunnels, road bridges or viaducts. By now adding buildings, gardens, paving with kerbs, grass with texture and trees with various colours, the layout becomes even more visually interesting.

THE 'L' AND 'U' SHAPE LAYOUTS

These types of layout are ideal for building along the walls of a room and are generally modelled to represent a small terminus. The object of building this type of layout is to try to follow full size practice, by keeping the tracks, curves, distances, etc, as realistic as possible. This is impossible with the small oval layout, as a railway is in reality a route from A to B with stations along the way. All one can do with the oval layout is to try and disguise this fact as much as possible. The back and forth layout loses the continuous running facility, but the gain is the advantage of displaying a sky and landscape backdrop which considerably enhances the layout.

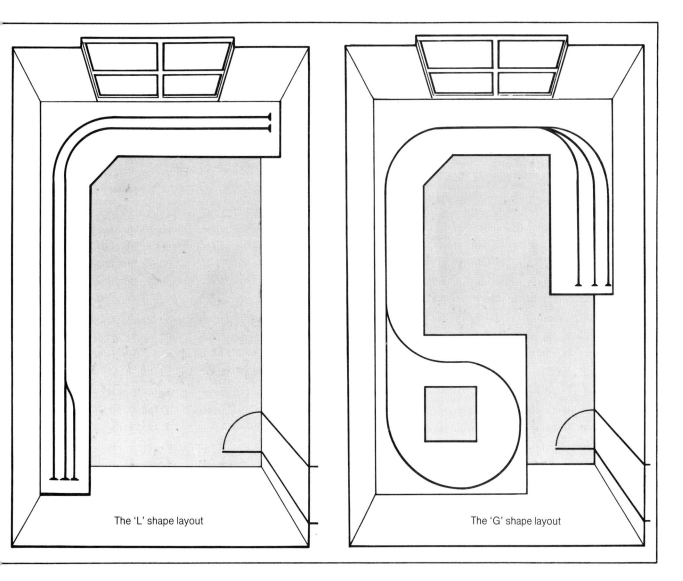

The 'L' shape layout

The 'G' shape layout

his again is almost impossible with the oval layout, ue to the fact that it requires access from all sides.

HE 'G' SHAPE LAYOUT

he 'G' shape layout is an extension of the 'L' and J' layout but has the advantage of a return loop hich allows rolling stock to depart and return coupled with a fiddle yard), the return loop generally eing disguised under a hill.

HE AROUND-THE-ROOM LAYOUT

he around-the-room layout really is the ultimate, he operator standing in the middle of the room urrounded by a panoramic view of railway. It has all he advantages of the oval layout's continuous unning facilities, large radius curves for fast nainline running programmes, provision for sidings, tations, fiddle yards, etc, and section control, nabling several operators to work the layout ogether, passing on each scheduled train to the ext operator just as happens in real life. The only isadvantage is that it requires a complete room to self.

The style and shapes of the layouts are endless, enerally only limited by the cost and space vailable. One way of reducing cost is to join a club and share in the facilities. Some clubs work on the principle that each member builds a baseboard to a specification. This standardizes all the key dimensions so that the baseboards become interchangeable, and on club nights the owners arrive with their baseboards and rolling stock and join them all together for running.

CHOICE OF SUBJECT

Railways run throughout the world which provides enormous scope for the modeller. Much will depend upon the modeller's skill as to whether he chooses to scratch-build or use commercially available rolling stock. Availability of stock will vary from country to country as will the scales in which it is produced. Each country tends to support its own type of outline, so that difficulties could well be encountered if the choice is foreign to one's own country.

The choice of country is very important, for not only is rolling stock of that country required, but information on buildings and scenery, which can be considerably different to one's own surroundings. Also, as previously mentioned the scales vary from country to country due to commercial influence, so that many factors now have to be taken into

Opposite page, top The layout in the centre of the room supported on a table.

Centre The 'around the room' layout, requiring the doorway to be converted for use.

Bottom The 'back and forth' layout along one wall of the room.

This page, above left An extension of the 'back and forth' layout using a second wall.

Above The return loop layout using three walls of the room. All of the around the room layouts use the wall to support the back and legs to support the front, spaced as required and at a suitable height.

Typical British terraced town houses, the layout of their interiors changing very little over a great number of years as the design worked so well.

A French variation on the same theme built much more narrowly so as to provide more dwellings per street. The windows are typically taller and more deeply recessed than British windows.

The majority of countries use wood to support the roof tiles. This photograph, taken in France, clearly shows the roof structure.

consideration—one of the key considerations being the local dealer. Fortunately many specialist dealers run a mail order service, so that if items are unavailable locally they could well be purchased through the post. This is a mixed blessing as one cannot inspect the purchase before paying, which sometimes leaves one a little disappointed but on the other hand has solved many a problem. One answer to this is to obtain a catalogue or hobby magazine from the country to be modelled. From this information can be gathered as to the following of the hobby, and an indication of trade support as well as some idea of the local scenery and stations. Since most magazine contributors tend to model subjects of their own country rather than from abroad, they provide all sorts of valuable information obtained locally or easily accessible to them. Thus, if an overseas modeller writes to the author of an article via the magazine, a contact may be made in that country and much useful information can be exchanged. Alternatively the name of a particular club or layout can be found that is of interest, and since most modellers enjoy the exchange of ideas a reply is generally given, especially if an international reply coupon is enclosed with the letter. One problem really does exist, and that of course is language, so that the country you are writing to really needs to be English-speaking. Fortunately English is understood in many more countries than, say, French or German are in the UK or America, as the residents of most European and Scandinavian countries tend to be multi-lingual. If you can read French, say, but not speak it or write it easily, a two-way correspondence can still take place with each person writing in his own language. When this happens it is a good idea to enclose plenty of photographs. If you are asking for information also offer a service in lieu of the inconvenience possibly caused to the person who has taken the trouble to reply.

RESEARCH

If one wishes to undertake one's own research there is a vast number of books, magazines and posters to call upon to aid this. For example, if one wishes to model a railway set in the south of England, a book on the subject can be borrowed from the local library, showing the type of countryside, housing, streets, and industrial areas etc. The book need not be about railways, but a general guide to the area, providing an idea of the locality, preferably with maps and colour photos showing a selection of very different types of locations, rather than for example a book on south of England churches, which is too specialised. What one is looking for is a selection of modelling possibilities showing how the towns and villages look, the materials in which they are built, the type of roofs, an idea of the landscape's contours and its ground cover, ie, what type of growth is shown in the way of trees and crops, etc, and how are the fields enclosed. The characteristic style of the roads and bridges can also be seen, so that one forms an overall picture. Once this is obtained and one is satisfied, then deeper research into the railway locations can be undertaken and having established an area of interest further specialized research can be carried out.

Since for practical reasons the layout will not be of true scale proportions, one can use artistic licence by moving situations around. An attractive village that is miles away in real life can be sited on the layout to suit, the same applies to the hillsides, landscape, bridges, roads, streams, all placed in appropriate positions to enhance the visual appearance of the layout and being designed to match the overall effect of the area as found in the general locations book showing the vicinity.

The amount of replanning now depends entirely upon the modeller. Some modellers prefer to try to keep the layout as realistic in terms of scale distance as possible, others just try to capture a feeling of the area, as the object in most cases is to landscape the baseboard so that it looks attractive, with a selection of carefully chosen subjects.

Having now researched into the locality and an idea formed of the buildings, one needs now to find out what kits are availabe of suitable buildings, stations, etc, so that an indication can be assessed of what is easily obtained and what needs to be

Below A selection of British-style builder-plus cardboard kits. This type of cardboard kit is available in most countries.

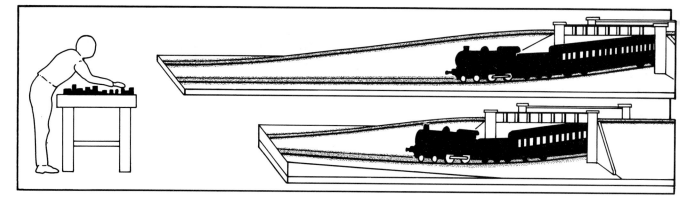

Above left Measure your comfortable reach and use this for the maximum width of a base, when the layout is to be situated against a wall.

Above right By splitting the levels of the track, one rising and the other descending, the overall distance required to allow the first track to pass over the other is shortened.

scratch-built. This information is required so as to decide the physical area that the buildings will occupy on the baseboard for design purposes, especially if one is planning a series of buildings going down a hill or along a main road with no front gardens. Careful planning will be required at this point so as to disguise the variations of levels, as kit cardboard and plastic buildings tend to have flat base levels which will require careful remodelling to fit the street's change in level. A point worth remembering!

DESIGN CONSIDERATIONS

Since the design of the layout in many situations is completely influenced by the restrictions on the available space, and since for practical reasons the building of the layout uses stock timber size sheets, why not design the layout from the very beginning as a series of separate interlocking baseboards? The finished size of each board can then be planned so that they are portable and will fit into the available storage space, can be manoeuvred through doors and are not too heavy to carry. There is also the possibility of moving home to be taken into

consideration. This factor can well be turned into an advantage rather than an inconvenient nuisance by making the baseboard sections in such a way that the layout is interchangeable. This gives more flexibility in the way the layout is arranged than does building a fixed one-piece layout which will be extremely difficult to alter at a later date without major rebuilding, during which time the layout is unworkable.

Most modellers find that their modelling skills increase as they work, so that as they progress around the layout, the first area to have been modelled does not look as good as later ones. Dissatisfaction with the early work may mean complete replanning and rebuilding, at the cost of considerable delay in getting the layout completed. This situation can be avoided by designing the layout in interchangeable sections in the first place, as then one area can be built and left and the second worked upon and built. Then at a later date a completely new first area can be built if required as a separate baseboard which completely replaces the old first one. During the construction time required

Right Use a pencil to mark out the carriage's overhang on bends and then space the tracks accordingly.

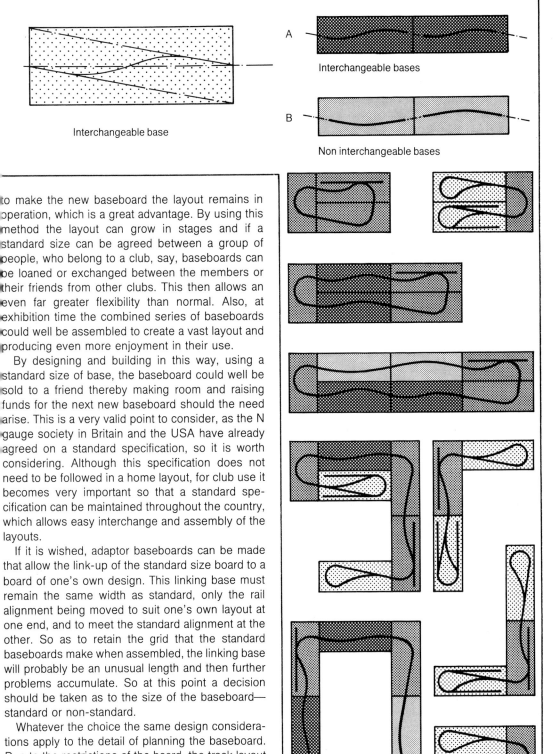

Interchangeable base

A
Interchangeable bases

B
Non interchangeable bases

Top far left To align the tracks' angle on the base, first mark out the centre line, then from the centre line mark out the two diagonal lines; this now forms the alignment angle used for all the bases shown. The tracks' curves are positioned along these two lines.

Top left Two bases joined together using an interchangeable hand (A), and two bases joined together using a reversed diagonal join (B) as on baseboards 6 and 7, which go together as a pair. The two interchangeable bases use the same diagonal angle therefore they can be interchangeable at either end or one base can be turned around at a time. The sequence of assembly of these bases is extremely flexible and designed for home, club, or exhibition use. The wiring to the bases is kept to the minimum. The track is on its own wiring circuit allowing zone control and the signalling on a second electrical circuit.

to make the new baseboard the layout remains in operation, which is a great advantage. By using this method the layout can grow in stages and if a standard size can be agreed between a group of people, who belong to a club, say, baseboards can be loaned or exchanged between the members or their friends from other clubs. This then allows an even far greater flexibility than normal. Also, at exhibition time the combined series of baseboards could well be assembled to create a vast layout and producing even more enjoyment in their use.

By designing and building in this way, using a standard size of base, the baseboard could well be sold to a friend thereby making room and raising funds for the next new baseboard should the need arise. This is a very valid point to consider, as the N gauge society in Britain and the USA have already agreed on a standard specification, so it is worth considering. Although this specification does not need to be followed in a home layout, for club use it becomes very important so that a standard specification can be maintained throughout the country, which allows easy interchange and assembly of the layouts.

If it is wished, adaptor baseboards can be made that allow the link-up of the standard size board to a board of one's own design. This linking base must remain the same width as standard, only the rail alignment being moved to suit one's own layout at one end, and to meet the standard alignment at the other. So as to retain the grid that the standard baseboards make when assembled, the linking base will probably be an unusual length and then further problems accumulate. So at this point a decision should be taken as to the size of the baseboard—standard or non-standard.

Whatever the choice the same design considerations apply to the detail of planning the baseboard. Due to the restrictions of the board, the track layout shape is the first to consider (the minimum radius guide will be found at the front of the book). Plan the layout starting from the outside and working inwards across the baseboard so that maximum radii of curves can be used. Make sure if laying two or three parallel tracks close to each other to allow sufficient clearance room between them, especially on the curves. The clearance necessary is best established by running the longest piece of rolling stock which

Right The use of the door hinge with a removable pin aligns bases well and is quick and simple to use, but the hinge needs to be recessed to 'lose' its thickness.

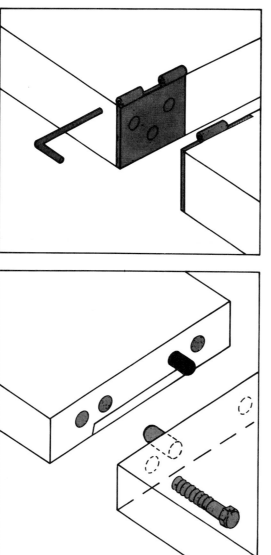

Right Bolting and using locating pegs firmly fixes the bases together, allowing foldaway legs to be fitted to the underside of the baseboard.

you plan to use around the smallest bend and drawing a line from the front outside overhang so as to establish its arc of travel; then draw a line from the mid-point, so as to establish its overhang inside the track's radius. These two lines inside and outside the radius of the track establish its clearance requirements (see illustration).

An additional point to be taken into consideration is the distance of the track from the edge of the baseboard, so that in case of a derailment you can easily reach to put things right; similarly, track should not be laid too close to the front edge of the board in case valuable stock falls on the floor after an accident.

Finally, if one is using a multi-level layout the angle of rise or fall in the track's gradient must be very shallow, approximately two metres length being required to clear a OO/HO gauge locomotive (10 cm high rise). Allow for a thin 10 mm track support under the bridging track for a single rise above a baseboard level. Halve this distance if using the split rise and fall method each side of the bridge, so that one track rises whilst the other drops in its level. This second method, whilst considerably reducing the overall length required, can sometimes cause other problems by weakening the support batten underneath the layout if it is not properly planned for.

THE COMPROMISE LAYOUT DESIGN

Using the information found in Chapter One and establishing the available room space for the layout, you could well by now have decided to work with a group of friends, all of whom have limited storage space and money. This really forces you to build a series of baseboards that plug into each other, and since each baseboard will be subject to a lot of carrying around, they will have to be light yet very sturdy and easily secured together.

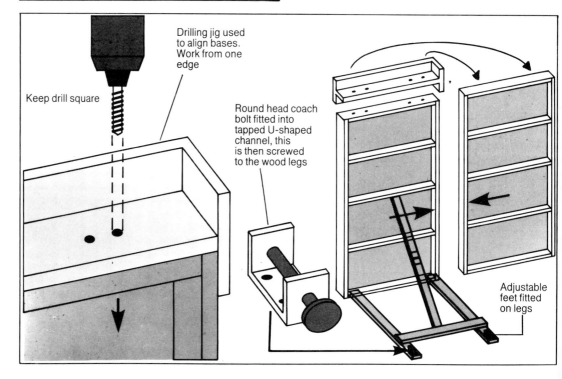

Drilling jig used to align bases. Work from one edge

Keep drill square

Round head coach bolt fitted into tapped U-shaped channel, this is then screwed to the wood legs

Adjustable feet fitted on legs

Right The jig is used on both ends of the base by turning over, therefore working from the same edge.

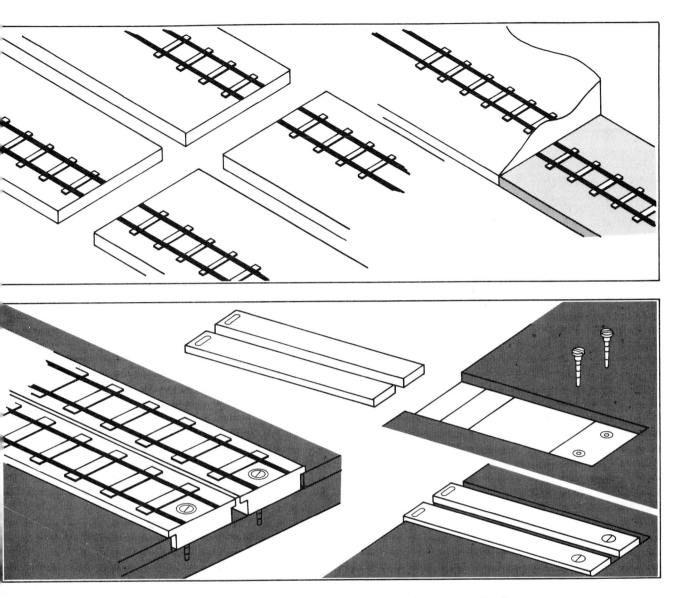

A ready-made basic structure will be required unless all the members of the group are capable of woodwork, and the answer to this problem could well be to purchase a series of lightweight doors, of the type that are hardboard-surfaced, filled with a criss-cross of cardboard and edged with thin batten, designed for domestic internal use. This now fixes the baseboards' sizes in a very convenient way which is easily added to. The track now needs to be designed; the most convenient practical way is to run the tracks in straight lines parallel to one edge, allowing for the scenery at the back. This unfortunately looks very uninteresting and considerably worse after several baseboards have been joined together. It also restricts assembly configurations as each board has a front and back.

This problem can be overcome by running the track down the middle of the baseboard so that the baseboard may be turned around and viewed from both sides. Now if the track is also built in a series of curves greater visual interest can be created, whilst maintaining the interchangeability of the baseboards. The next problem to arise is the joining of

the contours, as these obviously need to be at a common level at each end of the baseboard, so the track joins at a standard level and angle.

After taking all these factors into consideration you may well agree to forgo one or two points due to the problems and inconvenience they all cause. The baseboard size could be too big for N gauge or too small for OO/HO gauge, or laying the track in a series of curves could present problems in joining the baseboards together. So a compromise has to be reached, especially since carpentry is nearly always a stumbling block, due either to lack of facilities or skill. So even if you decide to retain the large door size as the basic baseboard size, you may decide to lay the track off centre, sacrificing the facility of turning the baseboards around but allowing a greater modelling area on the back edge, providing depth to the layout. The track can be laid as a 'home and away' configuration with a hidden return loop and a fiddle yard at the other end.

If the scale of the layout is to be N gauge, so as to allow maximum scenic modelling, the buildings, trees, hills, etc, will be proportionately smaller than

Top The tracks' level must align for obvious reasons! The same applies to the distance from the edge, for an off-centre track means that the base will only align one way around.

Above The track adjusters are made from strips of wood, of the same thickness used for the base's top, fixed with a single screw at both ends. The first screw allows the track to pivot, while a slotted hole at the other end allows room for sideways movement, secured by tightening the second screw.

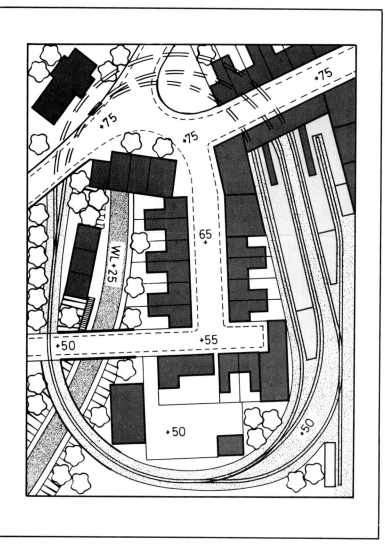

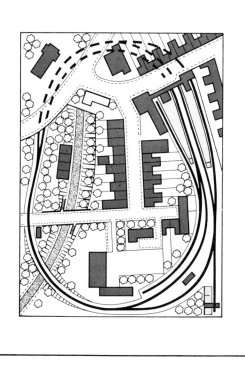

The OO or HO scale layout using the N scale design, condensed so that it is not twice as large but one and a half times. The N scale base is 4 ft by 3 ft, the OO/HO scale base is 6 ft by 4 ft 6 in. Notice the way the roads have been increased in their width and the way buildings have been removed on the HO/OO version.

OO/HO gauge, so you will require more of them to cover the baseboard—a real swings and roundabout situation, gain in one direction, lose on the next. However, an N gauge layout could be smaller and the baseboards thinner and lighter, so you can see there are many different valid points to consider when selecting the scale of the layout.

OO/HO SCALE BASEBOARDS

By using the 2 mm to the foot N gauge layout plans shown (base size 5 ft × 2 ft) and doubling up the size to 4 mm to one foot (OO scale) a new base size is formed of 10 ft by 4 ft (3 m × 1.22 m), or slightly smaller at HO scale. This is far too large to construct in one piece and remain practical, and is also unnecessary since a complete OO/HO oval layout can be constructed on a 6 ft × 4 ft 6 in (2 m × 1.5 m) baseboard including passing loops and sidings.

An easy way of reducing the area of the plans shown is to model the centre strip only on a 2 ft 6 in wide by 10 ft long base, which will remove a lot of the unwanted surrounding ground detail; alternatively selective condensing could well be used so that the base becomes 6 ft 6 in by 2 ft 6 in—again about the size of a standard door. This second method allows a similar type of layout to be built, but this time in greater detail, especially if you opt for narrow gauge modelling. This is much the same as running N gauge track width wise but the locomotives are at OO/HO scale and it is just the track width that is narrower. This opens up a completely new zone of modelling not discussed as yet and really provides the best of both worlds. Quarries, chalk pits, coal mines, etc, can now be modelled with their own working rolling stock, which can link up with the standard gauge at terminals allowing two types of layout to be run in conjunction with each other on the same baseboard. Although N gauge can be run on OO/HO layouts as a backdrop to create the effect of distance, this of course only really works when viewing the layout from ground level and not from the bird's eye view at which it is seen from most of the time.

The method used for condensing length is to widen the roads and increase the buildings' size to suit, working on top of the existing plans, in this particular case by half size (ie, a building or road width of 2 in (50 mm) becomes 3 in (75 mm). Where the buildings are too close together, to increase size, remove some of the buildings: compare the two oval layouts. This method effectively reduces the surrounding area to the buildings, making them closer together. The base drawing is then re-scaled so that the base becomes 6 ft 6 in instead of the 5 ft length and contour distances also become closer together so that the landscape becomes more hilly. The spacing of the contours 6 in (150 mm) apart means that scale distance 38 ft for a 10 ft road rise is the critical distance for the maximum 25 per cent gradient of road.

THE DESIGN MODEL

Some of the biggest problems facing the modeller are the changes required from reality to make the

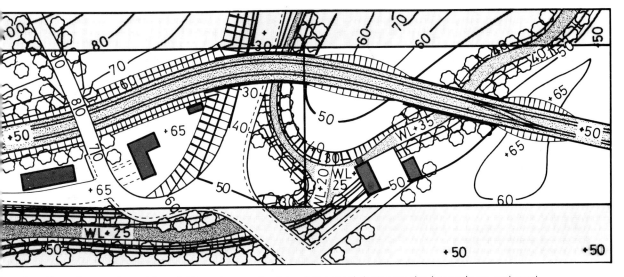

1 Modelling the centre strip· of this plan and doubling its size makes it 10 ft by 2 ft; it also puts the join of the track between the bases in an awkward position, being right at the back.

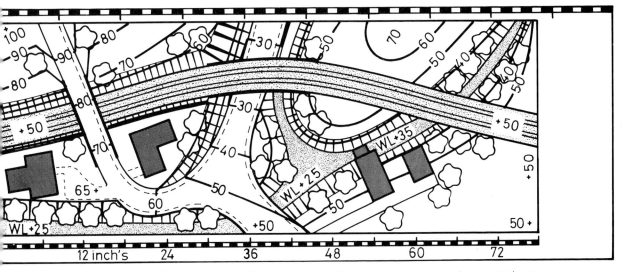

2 By rescaling the base and thickening up both the track and road width, the design and content of the base can be much the same. In terms of scale distance, items have moved closer, and are condensed.

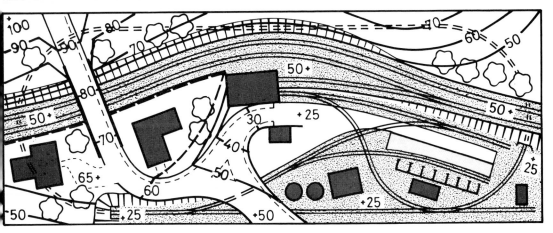

3 By reducing the tracks' radius, room can be created. The lower area ceases to be water, but now becomes a self-contained narrow gauge layout, built into one of the sections of the bases. Adding narrow gauge to a layout considerably increases its working potential.

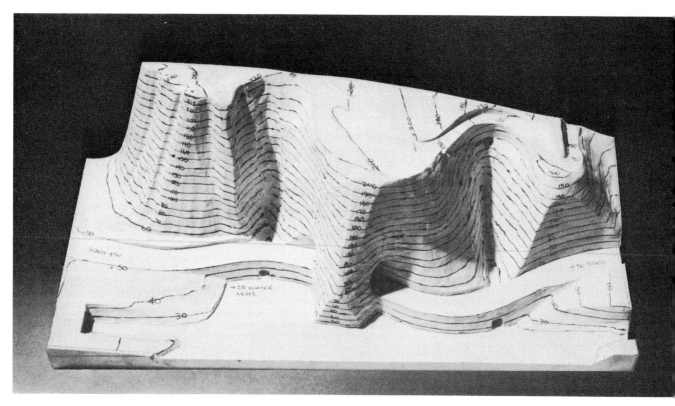

Above Base 7: Card and balsa wood were used to form the basic levels of the water and track, Plasticine then being used to model the rock face. See pages 38, 46 and 52.

Having drawn the lines over the mock-up models using the methods shown, I photographed them. The photographs were enlarged to a scale of 3 in to a foot. Tracing paper was used to cover the photographs and the detail was then drawn in as shown in the illustrations. These were then rephotographed on slide film and projected on to the 5 ft by 2 ft baseboard size paper, to make the full-size drawings from which to work.

Right Cardboard and balsa wood were also used to construct this model of base 6, Plasticine being used to shape awkward bits. Both models were then painted white and height lines applied using the height block and bridge method. See page 19.

layout work, not just in a practical sense, in that the tracks must line up and function well, but also in the overall visual effect of the layout, since the majority of its design is a compromise rather than reality scaled down. This is due to the restrictions of the baseboard's size which means the landscape, buildings, roads, etc, all have to be moved around and resited to suit the baseboard, yet at the same time need to look as natural and realistic as possible—just as if, in fact, it is modelled on reality and nothing has been changed.

This is a very difficult task to undertake in plan form alone, especially when the levels of the ground are constantly changing, and is one of the major problems of working from drawings only. Two-dimensional drawings are very difficult at times to mentally interpret into three dimensions. That is to say, it is not always easy to form a mental picture of what the drawings show; ie, how the contours and levels relate to each other. At times problems also arise within the design of the layout, when several ramps or levels all at different angles coincide with each other, all of which require clearance over each other and, due to the gradient angle required by the

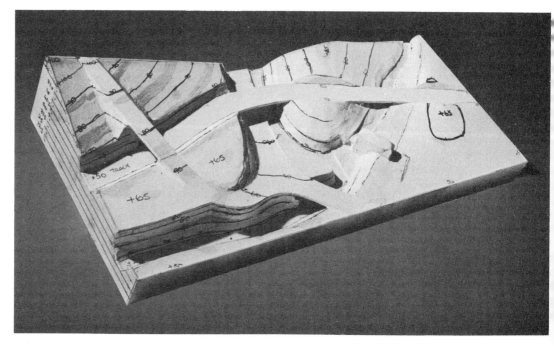

ack or road, are long in length, affecting an area a ong way away from the original problem zone. By olving one problem, a new problem can be created lsewhere. Unless it is very clear in one's mind recisely what is happening, mistakes can easily ccumulate, resulting in a lot of hard work and effort eeding to be altered all because a design point was verlooked and to much annoyance only discovered uring the construction stage.

Fortunately a lot of these design problems can asily be resolved in the design stage by making a nock model of the layout first. This mock-up design model needs only to be simple, but can assist the esign and visual effect immensely, since it gives ou a solid visual impression of the proposed layout or study and from which working dimensions can be btained. By simply producing the 'model' of the ayout using card, balsa wood, Plasticene or modelling clay, alterations can be quickly made as roblems are discovered during the design process tage.

The mock-up modelling technique used is to cut ut a piece of cardboard, scaled to a convenient ize. This is used to represent the plywood aseboard level; then, using card and balsa wood, dd the basic rail and road levels, the card being sed to represent the plywood and the hardboard, ne balsa to represent wood battens. The construc- on methods are the same as if it was the full size ase, including the building of the below-ground lab levels which the buildings are going to sit on (so s to establish the additional below-ground level equirements of the buildings). Finally fill in the gaps eft with Plasticene or modelling clay to represent ne contours, all of which can easily be changed round whilst undertaking the design process of the ayout. Each step or alteration can thus be studied or effect in solid form, rather than trying to form a nental picture allowing a much clearer interpretation o be made of the progress of the design. The utline of buildings and trees can be added in 'block nd blob' form so that a complete three-dimensional epresentation of the layout can be made for study.

On completing the design and being satisfied with ne overall effect, the model is painted using ousehold oil-based white undercoat, and when dry imensions and heights are taken from the model sing the scriber or depth gauge bridge method, so s to translate back into two dimensions or work om. The outside of the model can also be drawn round so as to obtain the baseboard's edge ontour levels, and by using the grid method these an then be enlarged to layout size. The use of roportional dividers and scale rules helps keep stimating to the minimum.

Alternatively, the design model can be photo- raphed on slide film in plan form and then projected n to the full-size baseboard, the lines as required hen being drawn in to suit. This method is a very uick, simple and accurate way of enlarging rawings or mock-up models to working size.

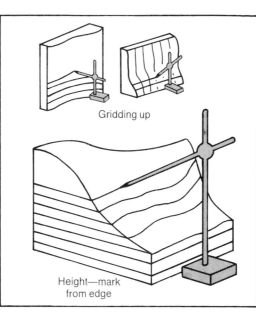

Gridding up

Height—mark from edge

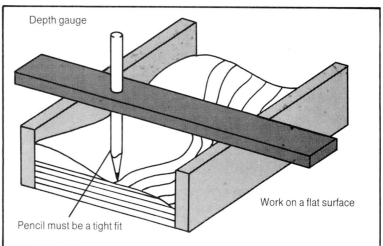

Depth gauge

Pencil must be a tight fit

Work on a flat surface

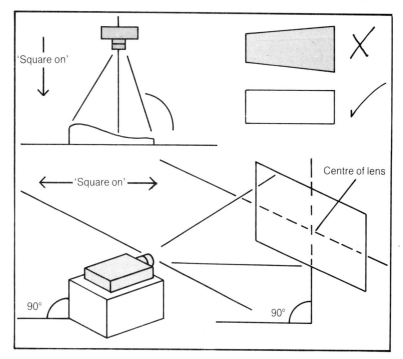

'Square on'

'Square on'

Centre of lens

90°   90°

Left An engineer's height gauge, used to mark out contours.

Below Using blocks of wood of the same height spanned by a strip of wood, the pencil is set to the required height.

Bottom It is important when photographing or projecting an image to keep 'square on' to the surface, thus preventing distortion.

3. CONSTRUCTING THE LAYOUT

THE BASEBOARD

The methods used for the construction of baseboards vary so much that the beginner, at first, finds it very difficult to understand. Just why is it that every time help or advice is sought on a particular problem, each individual asked resolves the problem in a different way? Well, the truth of the matter is that there is no 'fixed way' to model anything. Some methods just suit one individual better than another.

The reasons for this are: material preferences; available space (the vast majority of modellers being forced to work within a confined space, ie on the kitchen table, whilst others have garages or a room in which to work); available equipment (some modellers own hand tools only, whilst others in addition own a selection of power tools which allow them to work with a far wider range of material conveniently); finally, skills and experience, progressively developed over a number of years model-making.

These four infinitely variable factors are the reason for producing my selection of variable answers given to any beginner, simply because each person is inevitably at a different level of skill and knowledge.

KITCHEN TABLE MODELLING

This situation has gained enormous respect over the years. As previously mentioned, many modellers only have this facility at their disposal but, working at home with the minimum of tools, have devised methods and developed incredibly high skills. The newcomer to the hobby, I feel, should always keep this in mind.

CONSTRUCTION METHODS

So as to cover the wide range of construction methods used for the baseboards I advise the reader to read this entire chapter as a series of methods, all of which can be intermixed and applied to suit. My reason for choosing N scale as the prime example is the physical size of the baseboards, all of which have had to be constructed and photographed within my own limited available space. Secondly, N scale can be easily scaled up to HO/OO but the conversion does not work so conveniently the other way around, the reason being that the minimum radius of the track's curves become impractical when scaling down.

As an example of this, take the standard Peco OO/HO set track's minimum radius of 371 mm (14. in). If you halve this it becomes 185.5 mm (7.25 in). The minimum equivalent standard radius curve of N gauge track is 228 mm (9 in), which is well over half the size of the OO/HO dimension for scaling-down purposes. Working in reverse, ie, scaling up from N gauge to OO/HO gauge, a 228 mm (9 in) radius becomes 58 mm (18 in), an almost standard radius size. Finally, and very important, more problems could be encountered within each of the N scale bases and the reader should study these.

The construction methods for N, OO/HO and O scales, although progressively larger in physical size, hardly change, so that the methods shown can be used throughout these various scales. Large scales such as gauge 1 are too large in practical terms to have a baseboard of this nature.

ADVICE FOR THE BEGINNER

For the beginner building his or her first baseboard, recommend that a very simple layout is tried first

Below On a layout which uses woven card or wire to support the scenery over the track, it is necessary to provide access into the covered area via cutouts in the side of the base.

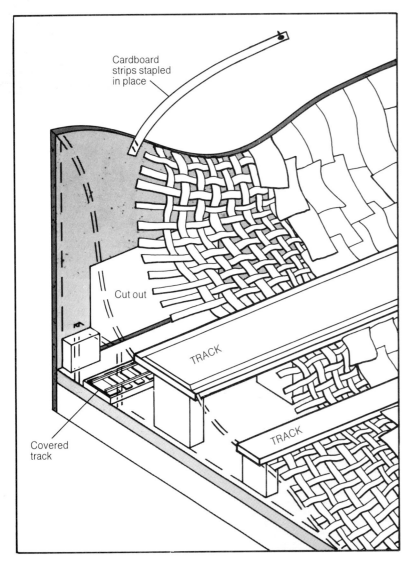

Cardboard strips stapled in place

Cut out

TRACK

TRACK

Covered track

This will allow you to experiment within the basic learning stage. Small separate samples can be made and if they do not work satisfactorily, these can be thrown away. By doing this, one is encouraged to try out different techniques, knowing that the outcome cannot damage the main layout. This is the procedure I still use today when trying out new methods.

The illustration on page 24 shows a simple layout built on a single flat board. It uses a single controller and the points (turnouts) are operated by hand. This type of layout is typical of the many boxed commercial 'railway sets', which simply have their track pushed together and dismantled after use. The design is known as a double loop, allowing two-train operation from a single controller. The oval layout (above) shows an extension of the double loop, an elaborate contoured single baseboard oval layout, complete with sidings, station, roads and other buildings. The points (turnouts) are operated electrically, the working signals correspond to the turnouts' settings. Two controllers are used to operate the selection of rolling stock and the entire layout becomes visually more attractive, due to its self-contained lifelike environment, complete with trees, cars and people. The illustration on the right shows a single baseboard which forms part of a series to make up a large layout when joined together, the construction of which is explained elsewhere.

Above The oval base has changing levels making for a more realistic setting. The points and signals can be operated electrically or manually and the track is split into electrical sections; by using more than one controller, several different rolling-stock movements can be carried out simultaneously.

Left The cliff baseboard, which forms part of a series, is a complex base to construct because of its changes of level.

HAND AND POWER TOOLS

Since the majority of the material used for the construction of the average baseboard is wood, this simply becomes a carpentry procedure, requiring the use of some woodworking tools, etc. These are easily purchased in any good DIY shop. Surprisingly, the selection of tools required need not be elaborate for a simple baseboard. If the wood is purchased pre-cut to size, then it just becomes an assembly job requiring the use of a hammer, some nails and woodworking glue. On the other hand, if the baseboard is of a complex design, additional tools will be required.

The choice of tools is quite important as cheaply priced tools, generally, are of a poor-quality steel which means they do not retain their cutting edges for very long. Chisels are particularly prone to this. Alternatively, over-purchase or the acquisition of more tools than are required is easily done. The newcomer to the hobby is recommended to purchase equipment and tools as required and as skills develop.

Fortunately the majority of the hand tools initially required will already be found in the home, so seldom does one actually start from scratch. But if this is the case then I recommend the purchase of the following: 9 in carpenter's square, 3 metre steel Imperial/metric tape, tennon saw, small set of twist drills, hand drill, counter sink drill, set of screwdrivers, hammer, small plane, 12 mm (½ in) chisel, HB pencil, Stanley knife and 300 mm (12 in) steel rule.

This is a minimum selection of tools that will enable a start to be made. The carpenter's square is used to square things up, a very important point to remember as assemblies out of alignment create all sorts of problems, especially when a series of bases are to be assembled together. It is also useful to have a Stanley knife, not only used for cutting things out but for marking out, as this provides a finer line to work to, again very important when a number of items have to fit together. For sharpening the knifes and chisels an oil sharpening stone will be required. For cutting large sheets of timber a ripsaw can be purchased, preferably Teflon-coated so that it cuts more easily, but if an old saw is available then it can be waxed with a candle to help it cut. Whether it is old or new this type of saw is only suitable for cutting straight lines and if one is going to the expense of purchasing a saw, then buy a more useful type which will also cut radii, ie, a power jigsaw (and knowing today's prices it wil not be very much more expensive).

I think the reader can quickly gather that it does not take long to acquire a basic selection of tools. My own choice of tools, remembering that I am a trained machinist, would further include a bandsaw and circular saw. The bandsaw is used to cut out curved shapes conveniently, the circular saw for machining material to size. In the professional world of modelmaking the circular saw is one of the most

Below A selection of my well-used hand tools. These have been acquired over the years as my skills increased and to meet a particular piece of work's requirements.

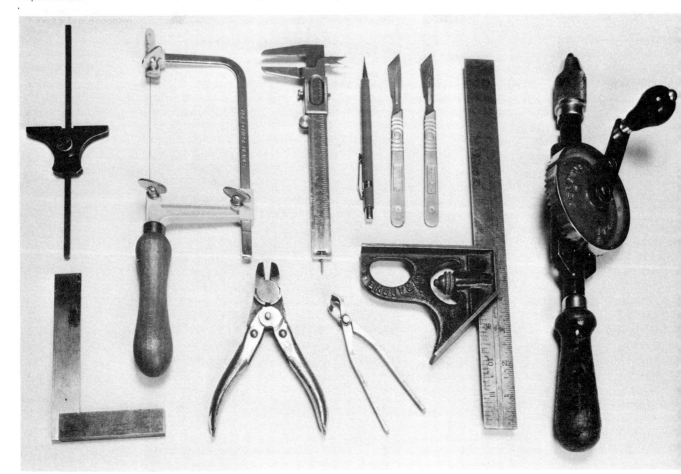

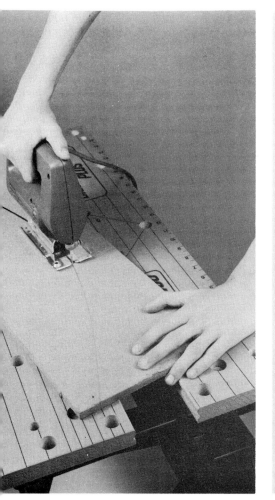

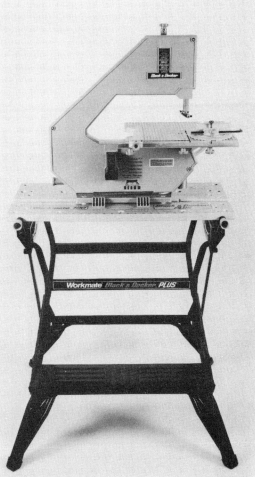

Far left The jigsaw is a very versatile power tool, extremely useful for cutting curves. By placing the timber to be cut on a partially open portable workbench, the material is supported on each side of the cut.

Left The bandsaw is extremely useful for cutting out small pieces.

Warning All power tools are dangerous so do not use them unless you have received proper instruction. Since they are an aid to convenient working I have shown them, but can take no responsibility for their use since it is beyond my control.

nportant machines to be able to use, as the majority of all the materials used are cut on this machine. But for the home user of power equipment a bandsaw is a reasonably safe machine provided it is used sensibly, not only within the machine's working limits *but within the individual's working limits.*

To use a bandsaw safely—and this applies to all power equipment—the machine needs to be set up properly on a firm foundation. A good method for this is to mount the equipment on to a thick board and clamp it down on to a solid workbench. Black and Decker make an ideal portable workbench known as a Workmate. This bench is ideal for mounting a bandsaw, plus many other uses when awkward jobs need to be secured.

A Disk sander is one additional machine that I would be lost without as it enables the trimming of materials, especially squaring up of ends when the material has been rough-cut or difficult to cut. Unfortunately this machine creates dust so that an extractor needs to be fitted; a domestic cylinder vacuum cleaner is ideal for this but the bag needs to be changed regularly.

THE OVAL LAYOUT

The self-contained layout is in many ways the easiest to build since it does not join on to other baseboards, it can be constructed as simply as one wishes or built as a multi-level complex layout with its tracks at various heights. For the beginner building the first base I recommend retaining a constant track level, then to contour the landscape above and below it. By doing this the layout will still look interesting, but it avoids all the problems associated with, for example, a curved track with gradients. The first illustration (overleaf) shows a simple track layout plan with passing loops and sidings, designed to be constructed using this method.

The second illustration shows how the series of levels work. Starting with the track level, this remains flat throughout at a constant height of +50 ft, the lowest area being the canal support level at +25 ft, the highest of the areas being the road bridges and surrounding ground over the track at +75 ft. To make things easier the bottom edge of the baseboard is counted as zero. The high areas over the track are constructed on top of the track level and have removable panels. These are to allow room for access down to the track level should a derailment occur within the tunnel, created by having higher ground over the track, which disguises the track's oval shape. This access into the tunnels is a very important point to remember. The levels of 25 ft, 50 ft and 75 ft are derived from converting (N scale) 2 mm to 1 ft into standard wood size (ie, scale 25 mm multiplied by 2 mm to 1 foot equals 50 mm actual size). Finished timber batten

Note Read the text and illustrations on the next few pages as a series of methods; by combining them, any base can be constructed to any design.

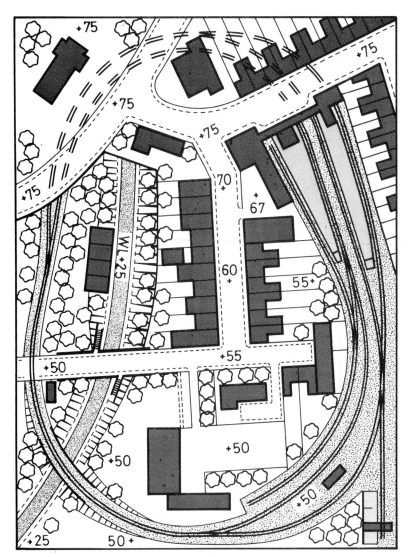

Above The plan for the oval base uses variable levels. The spot heights on the base show the ground's level (ie, + 50). This is 50 scale feet from the bottom edge of the base, which is counted as zero.

standard plywood unit is 2 ft wide but, since th edges are added to the outside of this, they increas the size of the base to a true finished width of 63. mm (2 ft 1 in) by 1,155 mm (5 ft 1 in) long.

By looking at the second illustration showing th basic levels the cutting programme of the base ca be worked out, any part of the base less than +5 being removed and lowered, levels above +5 being added as separate overlays of wood. You ca use either ply or hardboard, the hardboard havin the advantage of its flat smooth surface, which w require little finishing. However, the standard siz most easily available is only 3 mm thick, so it ma need packing with 2 mm card. Difficult areas of th layout such as embankments are filled with ex panded foam then carved to shape. The surface the foam is then covered with rag or paper square soaked in a white woodworker's glue (PVA) dilute 50:50 with water so as to form when dry a har surface over the expanded foam and make it mor durable.

The reason for using a split level base instead building up directly from the lowest level (ie, +2 ft—the canal level) is to allow access directly to th track support structure (+50 level) so that poir motors, signals, etc, can be easily installed. If th base was built up from the canal level access hole would need to be cut into the low level of +25 allow access to the +50 track support level. Th supporting and stiffening batten should be pos tioned so as to clear point motors or othe miscellaneous items so that they are spaced approximately 300 mm (12 in) centres. Due to th cutting out of the track level, the canal's water lev will be cut into sections so it will need to b completely re-cut out, using a new single piece material. A strip of hardboard is best suited as it ha a smooth surface; unfortunately this raises the wate level by the thickness of material being used, but this case it does not matter so can be ignored.

The second illustration shows the cut out lines the overlays, the term overlay referring to anythin that is applied on top of a surface, which in this cas is on top of the batten used as a support. The mos efficient way of cutting overlays out is to use a powe hand-held jigsaw as it involves a lot of curved cut The cutting of the supporting batten is best done b using a tennon saw and a jig to produce a squar cut.

The third illustration shows how the levels wor and although it looks very complicated it is in fact straightforward procedure, and the following page show this in greater detail with other bases.

LAYOUT CONSIDERATIONS

The colour photographs overleaf show the one piece oval layout and the oval layout as assemble by using baseboards 01, 02 and 03. These ar designed to join on to the baseboards 4, 5, 6 and (extension bases) so as to form a very large ov layout. Bases 01, 02 and 03, since they form complete layout within themselves, are recon mended to be constructed first, followed b

size equalling 45 mm in thickness plus 5 mm ply totals 50 mm. 50 mm equals a 25 ft contour change interval and this multiplied by three equals 150 mm (6 in), a standard 'Contiboard' size, suitable for edging the base.

The 'Contiboard' material is easily obtainable from DIY shops and is used for shelving, the home construction of furniture and available in various widths, etc. The material itself is a chipboard covered with a thin layer of compressed resinized paper which has been finished smooth. It is this smooth finish that makes it ideal for edging the bases and since it can be cut easily with the aid of a wood saw and can be glued and screwed in the usual way, it is a useful general-purpose material to add to the list of readily available items, so that the majority of the base's construction uses standard size material as much as possible.

It can now be seen just how much available material sizes can influence baseboard construction, scrap material in many cases influencing a particular part of a base's construction. The overall sizes of the bases shown on the following pages are also influenced by this: the base widths for practical terms cease to be exactly 2 ft wide as the available aseboards 4 and 5 to extend the basic oval layout. ases 6 and 7 are built last as these two link gether to form a long non-interchangeable sec- on. Baseboards 8 and 9 are designed to assemble n to any of the bases so as to form an end return op and fiddle yard, which provides a condensed et self-contained layout. In other words, base- oards 8, 01 and 9 form an 'L' shape (see the page n layout variations) to provide the builder with ultiple choice on the configuration of the layout.

The colouring of the bases is extremely important; y own colours are chosen to represent late ummer, when the trees are fully matured with all eir foliage and are just beginning to turn in colour. he same applies to the colour selected for the rass; instead of a rich green which would dominate e landscape, a browny-yellow is used which omplements the trees and allows them to stand out their own colours.

The overall colour of both trees and grass has een taken into consideration in the colouring of the uildings, roads and paving. (Since I have used raham Farish buildings the tone of all the urrounding colour is almost predetermined by the uildings' colouring so that they work in a har- ony—a point to remember with other manufactur- rs' products.) Finally cars and people are added to ring the model to life.

The plans for the layouts shown can easily be hanged. When the choice of the layout is solely for e owner then the modelling scale and baseboard ze can be chosen upon their own merits, but do emember it does require a reasonable amount of oom if an acceptable realism is to be achieved. isguise the basic track shape, especially on an oval yout, by using a long tunnel, the train momentarily

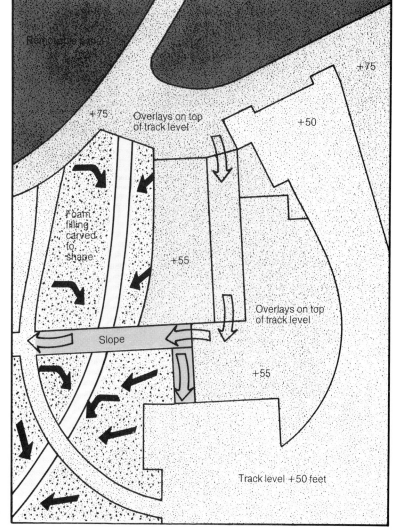

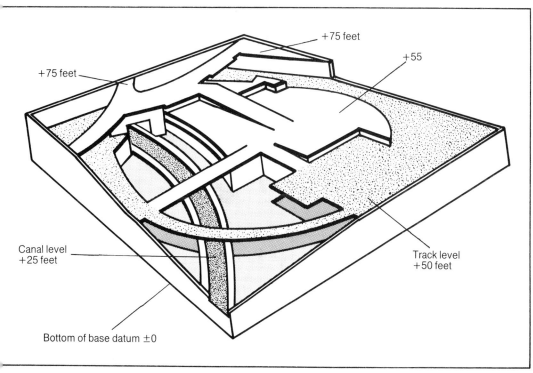

Above This shows the different levels in plan form.

Note It is recommended that the beginner build the layout plan shown on p 147 on a flat board and wire up as shown.

Left An angled view of the same drawing to help explain the levels.

I have numbered the interchangeable bases as follows: 01, 02, 03, 4, 5, 6, 7, 8 and 9. The first three make up the basic oval, bases 4 to 7 are interchangeable. Base 8 shows the plan of a return loop, and base 9 the fiddle yard. By using these plans and modifying as necessary a wide selection of variations can be made to suit the particular situation of an individual (see page 31).

The levels are shown in scale feet heights, so that no adjustment is required between the various N, HO and OO modelling sizes.

Base 01 This has all its levels at +50, the buildings resting on this level; the loading platform is built from card.

Base 02 This introduces levels above the +50 level, (built on top) to form raised areas for bridges.

Base 03 The return base uses raised levels to disguise the return of the track. Access into the lower level is obtained by lifting off panels over the track. See photograph on p126.

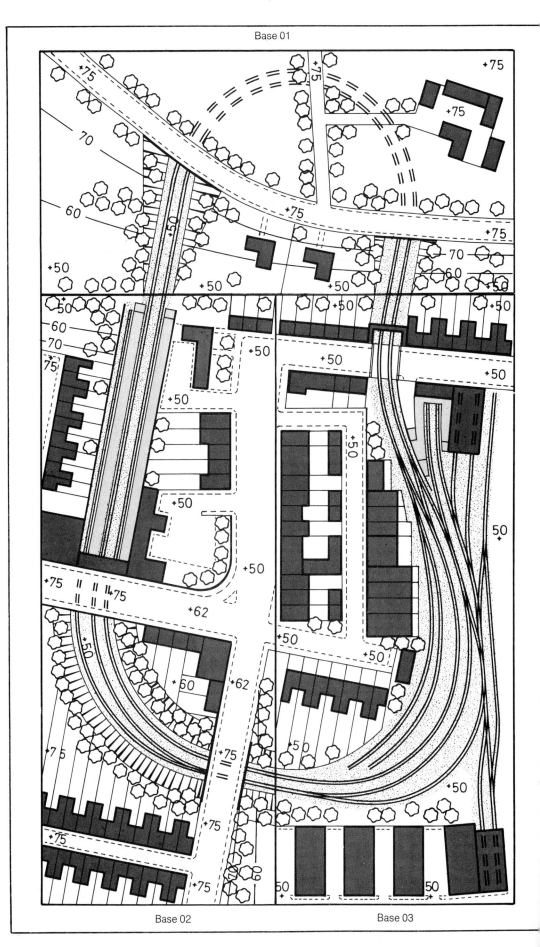

Base 01

Base 02

Base 03

Above *Bases 01 and 02 adjacent to 4 and 7. Compare 01 and 02 with the plan.*

Below *The self-contained oval layout which is contoured to make it look more natural.*

Top *Bases 01, 02 and 03.* **Centre** *Bases 7 and 4 with 01, 02, 6 and 7 alongside.* **Bottom** *Bases 01 and 03.*

The seven baseboards when joined together form a layout size of 17 ft by 4 ft providing a running track length of approximately 34 ft in an oval shape. The arrangement of bases 01, 02 and 03 (layout size 7 ft by 4 ft) provides a running length of track of approximately 13 ft. By placing baseboards 4 and 5 between bases 01 and 02 at one end and using base 03 (the U-shaped return), the layout's running length becomes approximately 23 ft (layout size 12 ft by 4 ft).

The content of each of the bases covers a particular construction problem in a progressive way. For example, base 01 is flat and simple to make whilst base 7 contains a cliff face rising some 200 scale feet above track level, therefore is far more complex in its construction. For the beginner, the construction sequence is designed to allow the easiest bases to be made first, that is bases 01, 02 and 03, as these cover the basic construction methods; they are kept simple by building from the track datum level, a well tried and tested standard method of construction which will allow any type of layout to be constructed.

The history of the ideas behind the base-

Top *Bases 4, 5, 6 and 7.* **Centre** *Bases 5 and 6 with 03 alongside.* **Bottom** *Base 5.*

boards uses a method which will suit any design of layout. Lengths of track were studied many hundreds of miles in length using a map. Points of interest were noted and the most interesting places were visited, photographs taken and notes made. Local guidebooks were obtained which contained aerial photographs to provide and build up an overall idea of the locality. The next stage was to plan out the track's position to suit the baseboards, the

ground then being contoured to suit each locality being modelled. In the end, despite the places being miles apart, the situations were joined together by inventing surrounding areas and adjusting the real places to suit the restrictions imposed by the bases.

Bases 01 and 02 are typical town areas, while bases 03, 4, 5, 6 and 7 are countryside. During the remainder of 1987 and 1988, the layout will be on permanent display at Merley House Model Museum, Merley Park, Wimborne, Dorset (entry off the A31 Wimborne bypass). It will be in running order and visitors are welcome; the author himself will be in attendance on specific dates which will be announced in the modelling magazines.

Above *Bases 4 and 5 joined together with 01, 02 and 03.*

Below *Base 03 joined together with 01 and 02 (se plan).*

vanishing from sight and then when it re-emerges it appears to be a second train following the first. If the tunnel was not there, it would be chasing its own tail! The tunnel can be made to fool the eye with even greater effect if a storage loop is concealed within the tunnel and a second train emerges.

BASEBOARD CONSTRUCTION

The construction materials used should be of good quality, the plywood that forms the top should be 3/8 in thick (9 mm) and supported with cross battens. Plywood has the advantages over chipboard that it is stronger and it does not warp by absorbing moisture. The batten timber should be carefully selected so that it is as straight and knot-free as possible. The edging material 'Contiboard', which is of a wood chip base, does not warp either provided the edges are sealed, as its surface is covered with a resinized layer. The assembly method of the base 01 shows the basic construction of all the baseboards.

Baseboard 01

1 Cut plywood to the size of the base including provision for track aligners.

2 Cut batten and fix into position by glueing and screwing.

3 Trim the baseboard to the finished dimensions using a hand plane and keeping edges square and straight.

4 Edge with 'Contiboard' fixed by screws from the inside.

5 Sand and fill as required to make good.

Baseboards 02 and 03

1 Make as baseboard 01 excluding the instructions for parts 4 and 5.

2 Draw out the layout on to the top of the plywood board.

3 Mark out the positions of the raised area of roads and high ground.

4 Mark out the heights of the raised levels on to the batten.

5 Join the heights together, radiusing the change in levels if required to look natural, the same way as edging.

6 Cut the batten out to shape using a jigsaw or bandsaw and fix the batten into position on the base.

7 Repeat with all other height-battened levels.

8 Mark out hardboard covering with roads and paving, etc.

9 Cut out hardboard along the change in level lines or in places not required.

10 Overlay hardboard on to base and check that it fits.

11 When satisfied that cut-outs and changes in levels work correctly glue into position by using PVA glue and hardboard nails.

12 Fill in difficult areas of embankment with polyurethane or expanded polystyrene foam or use cardboard cut to shape.

13 Trim foam to shape allowing for the thickness of surfacing.

14 Cover foam with newspaper or rag dipped in PVA glue to form a hard surface over the foam.

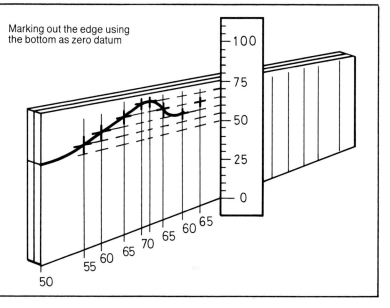

Marking out the edge using the bottom as zero datum

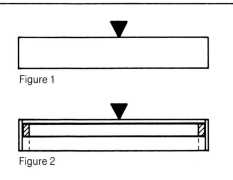

Figure 1

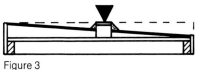

Figure 2

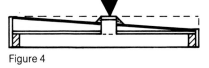

Figure 3

Figure 4

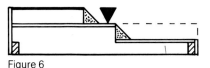

Figure 5

Figure 6

Figure 7

Above The bases' levels start by using the bottom edge as zero datum and then scaling up from this. The term scaling is used as this dimension either in metric or Imperial will vary depending upon the scale used. If the base is at 2 mm to the foot the 50 ft will measure 100 mm; if it is at 4 mm to the foot it will measure 200 mm. In the latter case the 200 mm thickness of the base could be too high for convenience, so that 50 m is removed or 12.5 scale feet making the bottom edge a new datum of +12.5. This dimension is then subtracted from all other spot heights.

Note Mark out two sides together where two baseboards join (one for each). See p 55 for more details.

Left The tracks' levels are indicated by the inverted triangle. *Fig 1* Typical end section. *Fig 2* Typical section of base 01. *Fig 3* Track level built up on top of ply base. *Fig 4* Track level cut out of ply base and supports extended. *Fig 5* Road over track built up from ply level. *Fig 6* Split level base. *Fig 7* Track below base top level.

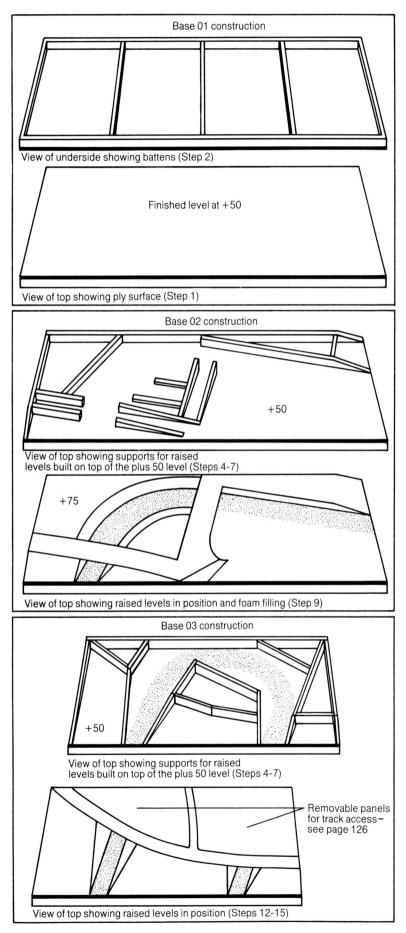

Base 01 construction

View of underside showing battens (Step 2)

Finished level at +50

View of top showing ply surface (Step 1)

Base 02 construction

+50

View of top showing supports for raised
levels built on top of the plus 50 level (Steps 4-7)

+75

View of top showing raised levels in position and foam filling (Step 9)

Base 03 construction

+50

View of top showing supports for raised
levels built on top of the plus 50 level (Steps 4-7)

Removable panels
for track access—
see page 126

View of top showing raised levels in position (Steps 12-15)

15 Trim off surplus material used for surfacing whilst still wet with a sharp knife.

16 Allow to dry.

17 Plane edges of base to size keeping square and straight.

18 Edge with 'Contiboard', fixing by screwing into positon from the inside; sand and fill as required to make good.

Baseboard 4 Extension to 01, 02 and 03

I have numbered the first three bases starting with an 'O' as they are the basic 'oval'. The following bases are extensions to this, with bases 4 and 5 designed to be built first as they interlock sideways to form a double extension. Bases 6 and 7 then form a further extension.

Baseboard 4 is a split level base which uses a single sheet of ply cut along a contour line to form both the +25 level and the +50 level.

1 Mark out plan on to the plywood.

2 Cut along the +25 to +50 change in contour line, following the track's edge right along the base.

3 Cut up lower shorter batten (five pieces) slightly wider than the water level's plywood width.

4 Cut up two standard long lengths of batten and fix front batten to underside of water level.

5 Fix shorter cross batten to underside of water level.

6 Cut up two full width end battens.

7 Fix end battens on top of water level.

8 Fix long batten on to the short cross battens so that it touches the underside of the standard width cross battens (the top of this batten should be level with the water).

9 Cut up two more long battens.

10 Fix one long batten on top of the construction described in 8 above (to align with batten on water level).

11 Cut up three variable length battens.

12 Fix the last long batten and three short battens in position.

13 Fix the +50 level plywood into position on top of the raised batten.

14 Mark out hardboard and cut out around lake.

15 Cut out as required hardboard supports to height and length and fix on top of +25 water level.

16 Fix hardboard into position with glue and hardboard nails, warping hardboard to suit.

17 Cut out ground level over canal and supporting pieces of batten and fix into position.

18 Square up edges of baseboard using a hand plane and size the base to correct dimensions.

19 Cut out edging for all sides and fix into position.

20 Sand and fill as required to make good.

Baseboard 5

(Sunken road and raised track.)

1 Cut out battens as base 01.

2 Mark out layout plan on to ply top.

3 Cut out track level the entire length of base.

4 Cut out sunken road along the +50 contour level.

5 Cut out canal along +50 level.

6 Fix battens together to sides of base.

7 Fix the +50 plywood on top of battens (five pieces of ply).

8 Cut out and fix batten to support lowered canal level including cutting through long batten (re-support with scrap wood).

9 Cut out hardboard road level and supporting battens then fix into place.

10 Cut out raised track supports for track level and fix into position (track level with base at each end).

11 Fix track support level into position.

12 Fill in and shape the embankments then surface as per base 02.

13 Cut out edging and fix into position.

14 Sand and fill as required.

SELF CONTAINED OVAL LAYOUT CONSTRUCTION

It can be seen that by using parts of the instructions for building the other bases, the smaller self-contained layout can be constructed as it uses the same techniques. For example, see the instructions for base 02 part 2. Draw out the layout on to the top of a plywood board. Mark out the positions of the raised area of roads and high ground. Alter base 4 part 2 instructions to read: cut along +25 to +50 change in contour line *as required to follow* the track's edge. In effect the areas of ground below track level are cut away and lowered, the track level being kept in one piece as higher levels are added by using further material. This additional material over the track level then traps the track's surface in a sandwich situation, the contents of which can be difficult to get at unless provision for access is made. Since the road and kerb lines make good joint disguise lines these can be used to get at the track level and a small number of lift panels can be used, which are easier to handle. This also means that you can design your own layout plans and use the construction techniques as required.

PLANS FOR BASEBOARDS 4, 5, 6 AND 7

Since in reality the landscape existed first, the railway being an afterthought, the levels of the track are a compromise which had to take into consideration the limits of the pulling power of the locomotives. This placed a very restricted angle of gradient upon the track both up and down, so as to retain a reasonably flat surface for the rolling stock to travel upon and allow a single locomotive pulling its load to manage the track's gradients without additional help. This factor applies to the layouts at model size since the model locomotive also has a limit to its pulling power before wheel spin occurs and it cannot pull its load.

The track layout plans shown take this into consideration, the level of the track remaining constant and the surrounding ground levels or contours changing in height above and below the track's level. This is a very important part of the layout because in reality the embankments and tunnels form a major part of railway construction, as these features enable the levels of the ground supporting the track to be maintained within an acceptable incline. From the modelling point of view,

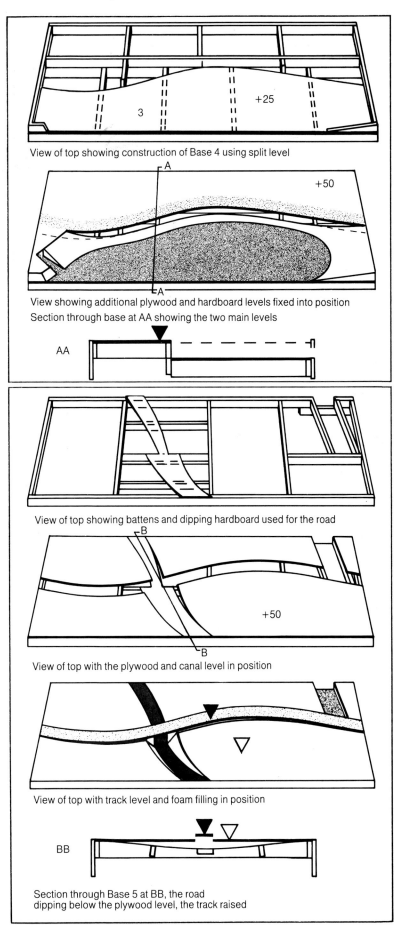

View of top showing construction of Base 4 using split level

View showing additional plywood and hardboard levels fixed into position
Section through base at AA showing the two main levels

AA

View of top showing battens and dipping hardboard used for the road

View of top with the plywood and canal level in position

View of top with track level and foam filling in position

BB

Section through Base 5 at BB, the road
dipping below the plywood level, the track raised

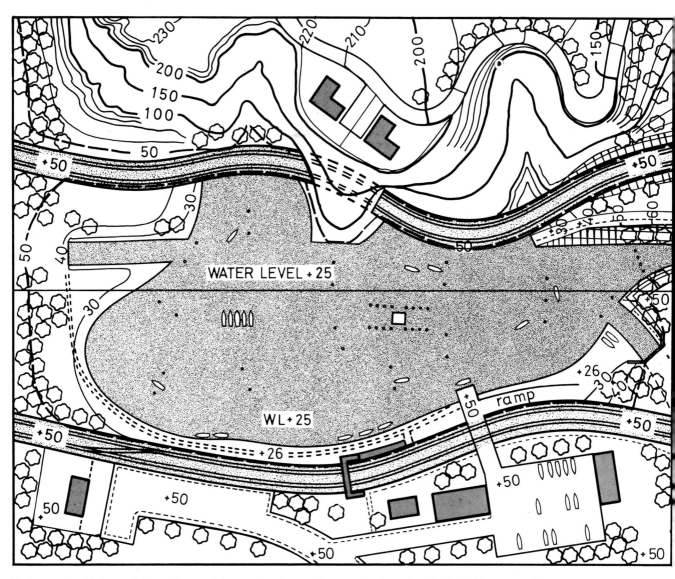

Top Plan of base 7, the cliff face. This can be constructed in various ways. The method that I have used is chicken wire and plaster, alternatively expanded ridged foam could have been used. This base shows construction of mountain and rocky situations.

Above Plan of base 4. This shows the application of split levels used to reduce the construction materials required. Level 25 is water, level 50 is raised ground ramps and slopes are used to link the two.

this can be used to an advantage as it provides the excuse to design and build tunnels, bridges, cuttings, embankments, etc, to use the hillside for hidden sidings and return loops, all to help the overall running efficiency of the layout. This factor can also be used to enhance the visual appearance of the layout so that the ground contours vary in an interesting way and are covered with roads, buildings, trees and grass, etc, the railway running through this setting.

Baseboard 01
This uses a completely flat base at the +50 ft level, the height being measured from the bottom of the base (see illustration), the road crossing the track via a level crossing.

Baseboards 02 and 03
Both of these bases retain the track level at +50 ft, the additional baseboard levels being built from this basic level.

Baseboard 4
This uses a two part split basic level base, the first part of one level being at +25 ft, used for the water level, the second level at +50 ft being used for the track and scenery. This base and base 5 can be

interlocked sideways to form an extension of bases 01, 02 and 03.

Baseboard 5
This base uses a series of levels, the basic level at +50 ft, the track gaining height from +50 to +55 ft in the middle and then returning to the +50 ft level. The road starts at +50 then reduces in its levels so that it passes underneath the railway track and then increases in its levels until it rejoins the +50 level.

Baseboard 6
This is the most complex of baseboards, as the contour levels around the track's level of +50 ft constantly change above and below the track's level. The height of the water is also at three different levels and the road constantly changes in height, being at one point below track level, the next above it. This base and base 7 are designed as a pair of handed bases which interlock at one end with each other.

Baseboard 7
This base, despite its change in levels, is in many ways an easier base to construct. It starts with a split level of +25 ft for the water and +50 ft for the track, the cliffs above the track allowing considerable

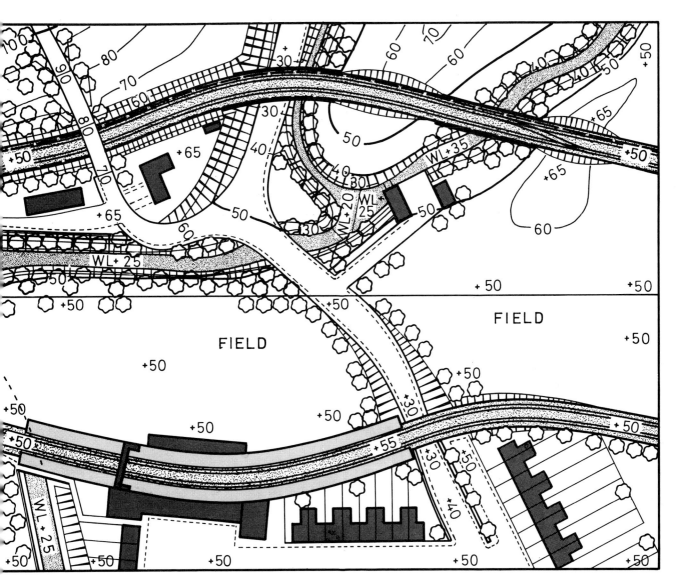

scope for artistic licence in their shape, or they can be built to follow the contour lines precisely.

Baseboards 6 and 7

Baseboards 6 and 7 are designed to be a pair of bases that have a contoured join in the middle. The reason for this is to demonstrate within the construction of baseboards, how to make this type of join, and the landscape formations.

The track and the contours of these two bases pre-decide the join and that they cannot be interchangeable. Secondly, bases 4, 5, 6 and 7 when joined together must have the visual appearance of being part of the same landscape, yet not be repetitive in their track shape.

Baseboard 6

All the methods used for the construction of this baseboard are a natural progression from techniques required on the earlier bases, but taken a stage further. (Note: The plywood level of this base is at +25 and all other levels are constructed from this, above or below.)

1 Cut out plywood and battens (as per baseboard instructions 01).

2 Draw out layout plan on to plywood including contour lines.

3 Cut out in plywood for the lowest water level of +20.

4 Fix batten in place (as base 01).

5 Insert +20 water level using scrap ply to underside of +25 level.

6 Cut one full length and one width batten and fix on top of water level.

7 Trim base to size using hand plane, keeping square and edges straight.

8 Mark out and cut out edging from 'Contiboard', copying the edge of baseboard 5 along the join, and allowing for the track adjusters.

9 Fix edging in place, keeping square and true.

10 Mark and cut out the roads using hardboard or thin ply (3 mm).

11 Mark out and cut out the track level from 9 mm ply.

12 Cut out the track supports and fix so as to bring the track support level up to the +50 level from the plywood level of +25.

(Note: 'S' equals scale height difference of 25 ft. 2 mm to 1 ft equals 50 mm true dimension, less 9 mm track support thickness, total 41 mm (LT equals less

Top Plan of base 6. This is the most complex of the bases to construct, as the contours constantly vary although the construction technique is reasonably simple, using rigid foam as necessary. The ply level is +25, construction being above and below this level.

Above Plan of base 5. This uses the plywood level as +50, the track level raising and returning to this level.

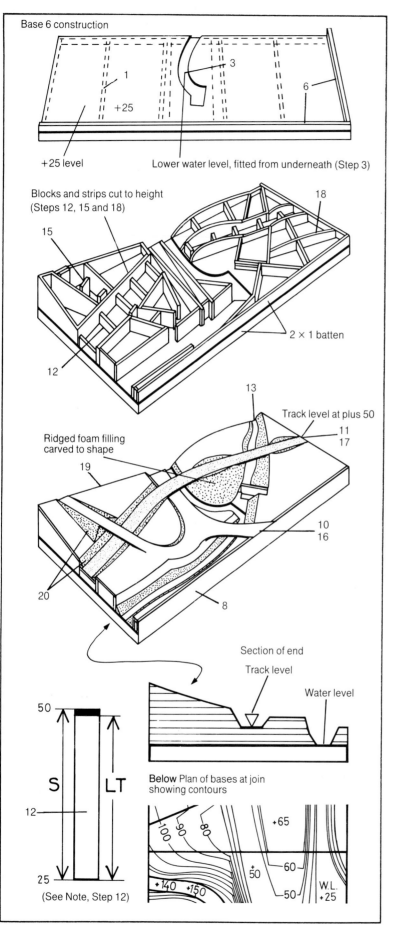

Base 6 construction

1
+25

3

6

+25 level

Lower water level, fitted from underneath (Step 3)

Blocks and strips cut to height
(Steps 12, 15 and 18)

15

18

12

2 × 1 batten

Ridged foam filling
carved to shape

19

13

Track level at plus 50

11
17

20

10
16

8

50

S

LT

12

25

(See Note, Step 12)

Section of end

Track level

Water level

Below Plan of bases at join
showing contours

100   90   80

+65

+50

60

+140   +150

50

W.L.
+25

thickness.) This is the track support height (see
illustration).

13 Cut out the stream at +35 level from 3 mm ply or
hardboard.

14 Cut out and fix stream water level support blocks
to bring the stream up to +35 level allowing for the
thickness of material (ie, material thickness 3 mm,
stream level +35, plywood level +25, gives a scale
difference of 10 ft. Multiplied by 2 mm to 1 ft (N
gauge) this equals a 20 mm rise, and 20 mm less 3
mm thickness of material equals 17 mm block
height).

(Note: The difference in the material thickness
used on top of the blocks is subtracted from the total
height required which is variable depending upon
thickness used.)

15 Cut out and fix the various height supporting
blocks for the roads allowing for road thickness
material by using the spot heights on the roads.

16 Fix roads into place.

17 Fix track level in place allowing for track
adjusters.

18 Cut out and fix supporting structure for landscape
using the contour lines drawn on the plywood, to
provide the heights and allowing for the thickness of
covering.

19 Cut out and fix hardboard covering material for
landscape.

20 Fill difficult areas of hillside and embankments
using expanded foam and surface (as base 02 parts
13-17).

21 Fill and make good as required in preparation for
painting.

Baseboard 7

The construction of this base allows a great deal of
artistic licence and could be constructed in several
ways depending on the final effect required.

1 Cut out plywood and battens (as baseboard
instructions 01).

2 Draw out layout plan on to plywood and include
contour lines below the +50 level only.

3 Cut out the track level of +50.

4 Assemble the base as per base 4.

5 Mark out the edges and assemble, taking care to
align the end of the base which joins on to
baseboard 6.

6 Cut assorted battens which fit on top of the +25
plywood level.

7 Cut out the formers as required and fix on to the
batten (see illustration).

8 Fix formers in position and then fix track support
level into position on top of the extending batten.

9 Cut and fix supporting material for the hardboard.

10 Mark and cut out the hardboard for the levels
below the +50 level to the shape of the water line.

11 Cover the formers with chicken wire.

12 Fix road in position on top of chicken wire using
hardboard cut to shape.

13 Fill difficult areas with expanded polystyrene, and
landscape as described in the Section on rock faces
and cliffs.

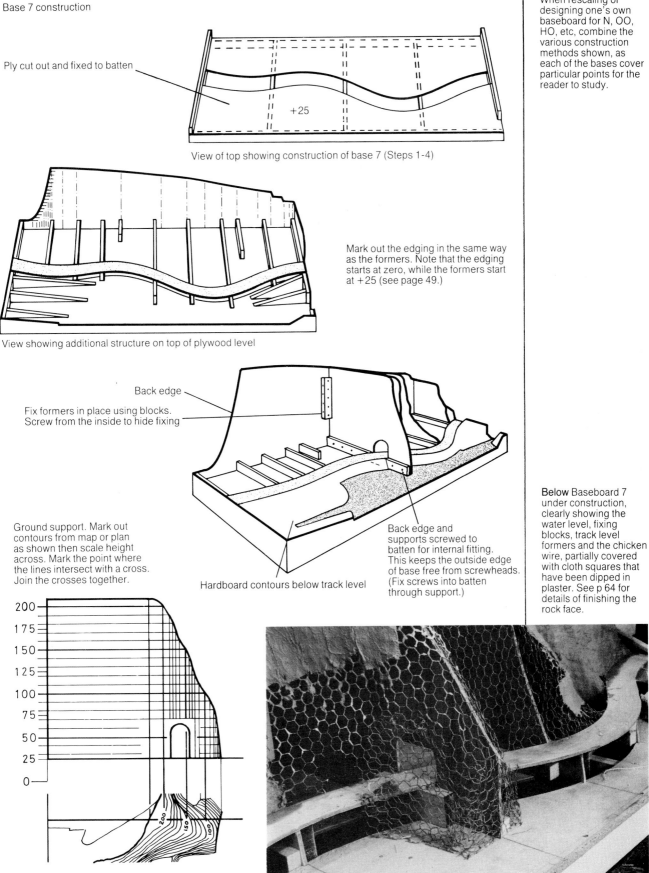

Base 7 construction

Ply cut out and fixed to batten

+25

View of top showing construction of base 7 (Steps 1-4)

When rescaling or designing one's own baseboard for N, OO, HO, etc, combine the various construction methods shown, as each of the bases cover particular points for the reader to study.

View showing additional structure on top of plywood level

Mark out the edging in the same way as the formers. Note that the edging starts at zero, while the formers start at +25 (see page 49.)

Back edge

Fix formers in place using blocks. Screw from the inside to hide fixing

Ground support. Mark out contours from map or plan as shown then scale height across. Mark the point where the lines intersect with a cross. Join the crosses together.

Hardboard contours below track level

Back edge and supports screwed to batten for internal fitting. This keeps the outside edge of base free from screwheads. (Fix screws into batten through support.)

Below Baseboard 7 under construction, clearly showing the water level, fixing blocks, track level formers and the chicken wire, partially covered with cloth squares that have been dipped in plaster. See p 64 for details of finishing the rock face.

200
175
150
125
100
75
50
25
0

Mark out position from plan.

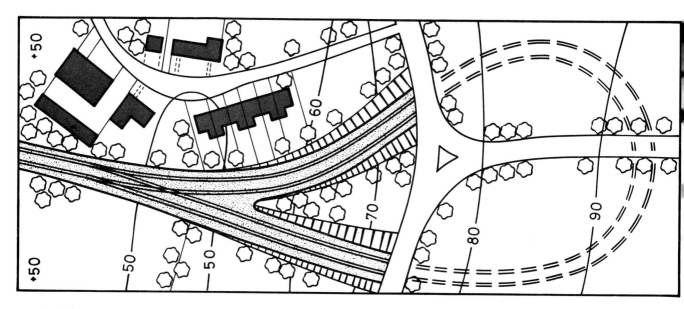

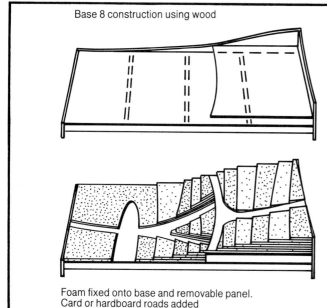

Base 8 construction using wood

Foam fixed onto base and removable panel.
Card or hardboard roads added

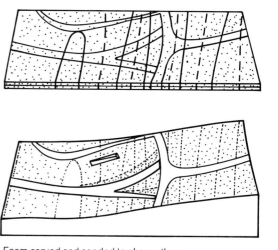

Layers of ridged foam cut out on the contour lines

Foam carved and sanded to shape, then
covered with surfacing material

The construction of base 8 uses methods previously described for the wooden part of the structure. The contours this time use expanded rigid foam (polyurethane or polystyrene) carved to shape, covered with paper, rag and plaster or 'Modroc', etc. The ground covering the return loop track is removeable in case of a derailment.

RETURN LOOPS, TUNNELS AND FIDDLE YARDS

The 03 baseboard and the self-contained oval layout as well as this baseboard number 8 use tunnels to disguise the tracks' return. The length of the tunnel is important if its effect is to work satisfactorily, the ideal length being slightly longer than the longest length of rolling stock configuration to be used, so that the complete length of train disappears from view within the tunnel. When it re-emerges it appears to be a second train, the tunnel being used to fool the eye with even greater effect if a storage loop or sidings are concealed within the tunnel and a second train emerges.

This 'fooling the eye' can be taken further by using short lengths of rolling stock, three carriages instead of six, for example, and reducing the platform length accordingly. It is even better still if the platform and tunnel join each other; this way, six carriages can still be used although the platform is

only three carriage lengths' long as the rest of the train's length can be hidden in the tunnel whilst it is in the station.

The same effect can be created with buildings; instead of using one large structure, use a number of small buildings to create the illusion of distance. In this way you give an impression of greater variety within the same space.

Baseboard 8

The construction of the return loop base uses the instructions for base 03 as its track level is at +50, but this time expanded polystyrene or polyurethane is used to form the contours, laid in flat sheets and glued into position with suitable adhesive, then carved to shape. The surface is prepared by covering it with newspaper dipped in PVA glue or rag and plaster (see the section on landscaping).

The fiddle yard

This base uses the construction methods of base 01, but for effect the baseboard top could utilize the

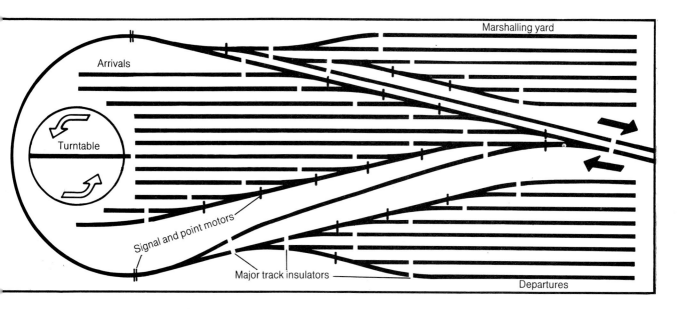

Marshalling yard

Arrivals

Turntable

Signal and point motors

Major track insulators

Departures

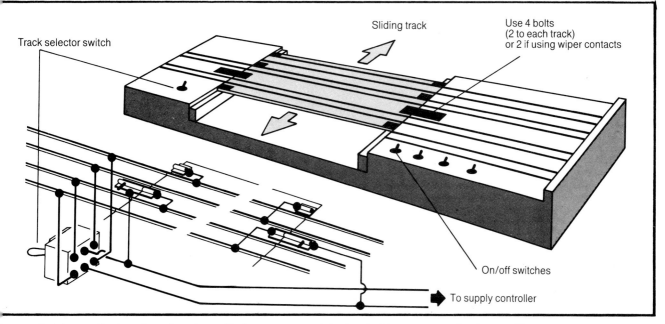

Track selector switch

Sliding track

Use 4 bolts
(2 to each track)
or 2 if using wiper contacts

On/off switches

To supply controller

ame material as on the baseboard's edge, with the ack laid directly on top of this (making allowance for e thickness of the cork which is used as an nderlay to help reduce noise).

urntables

urntables enable the rolling stock to be turned round either in single items, or as complete train ngths, and is very much up to the individual as far s choice and size are concerned. The manufactur- rs produce a number of different types, all of which ave different fitting instructions.

liding fiddle yards

his method of fiddling the rolling stock to work onvincingly uses parallel tracks which are pushed ack and forth by hand so as to align with the coming and outgoing tracks. The rolling stock is ssembled on this in running order and is released s required on to the main layout.

The main use of this method is for large scale olling stock or when space is at a premium, as it saves a lot of valuable room on the layout. The disadvantage is that the rolling stock cannot be turned around, but it is ideal for the branch line layout when this is not required.

The construction of a sliding fiddle yard is very simple, as it can all be made from plywood, stiffened as necessary with batten, then glued and screwed together. The tracks' alignments are secured into position at each end by brass bolts. These are wired up as shown, as they are also used for an electrical contact. The other side of the bridge, used for storing the rolling stock which is assembled in ready-to-run lengths, is switched on or off as required.

'L' GIRDER CONSTRUCTION

This method of construction relies on a basic open framework, similar to a table, and is constructed using two inverted 'L' girders. These are the weight carriers of the layout to which the legs are attached (see illustration). The cross members are fitted on

The construction of the fiddle yard shown on the plan uses the methods for the 01 base. Note the numerous track insulators used to electrically separate the sections (additional switches will be required). The construction for the sliding fiddle yard will vary to suit individual needs. Electrical contact is made through the bolts, plug in connectors or other suitable items. In practice spring contacts are preferred and easier to use. The sliding bridge uses three tracks to help prevent the accidental arrival disappearing off the end into space!

The open framework used on the girder type of assembly enables track levels to be altered easily during construction. The disadvantage with this method is it is difficult to move easily, as it is not very rigid.

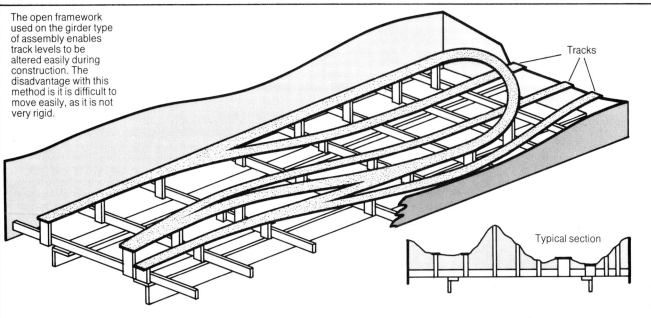

Typical section

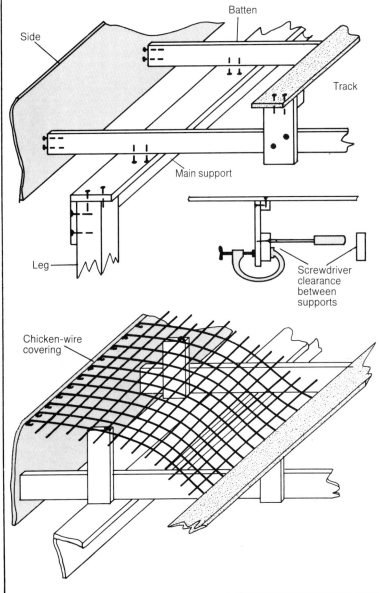

Side

Batten

Track

Main support

Leg

Screwdriver clearance between supports

Chicken-wire covering

top of these inverted 'L' girders. These are spaced at a suitable distance which allows a screwdriver to be inserted in between for the fixing of the uprights. The uprights support the various track levels. The track supports are cut out of ½ in ply shaped to suit the track plan and are wider than the track (see illustration). The exact width required is determined by what is necessary for the fixing of the scenery supports, which can be chicken wire or canvas. This is used as a base to support the actual scenery, additional supports being placed as required to help hold up the scenery, or to create an effect.

The advantage with this type of construction is that it allows limitless adjustment to the track levels so that the track layout can be in full working order before landscaping. In addition, most of the timber used will be short offcuts, which helps reduce cost. Finally, because the parts are all screwed together, they can be dismantled and reassembled in a different way, remaking the scenery to suit. The only real disadvantage is that once built, the layout is extremely difficult to move due to the lack of cross bracing.

TUNNELS, EMBANKMENTS AND WATER CULVERTS

The construction of the scenic setting would not be complete without roads, embankments and tunnels. The last-named are very easy to construct as a number of manufacturers produce tunnel portals made in card, plastic or resin. A length of cardboard is used to form the actual tunnel. On a short stretch of tunnel it is recommended that you take the cardboard right the way through. The track is laid first then the tunnel is built over it, but do save the track from damage whilst doing so by covering it with a suitable protective material. The same method is used for a rock cutting.

In reality, when a tunnel has been drilled out of solid rock (eg, a cutting situation through a rock

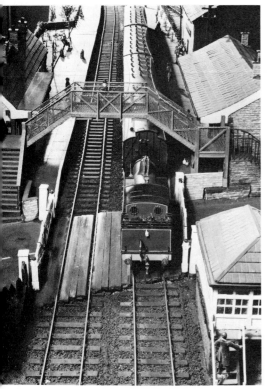

The 'Helmshore' 0 gauge (7 mm to 1 foot) layout shown was built by 'Pemberton Engineering' and is based on part of the East Lancashire railway line running from Accrington to Bury. Unfortunately the real line closed in 1966 but some of the stock remained and is on show in the Bury transport museum. The layout has a good running length of track, which was built in sections. Each base measuring 5 ft by 2 ft 6 inch (10 bases equalling 50 ft running length.) and their construction is similar to the methods that I have shown in this book, for further details of this magnificent layout see 'Your Model Railways' magazine September 1984 (*Brian Monaghan*).

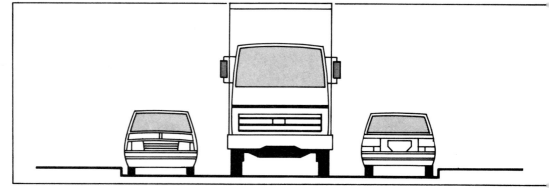

Right The road widths in a town vary so much that no hard or fast rule can be applied. The illustration shows a typical back street, cars parked on both sides of the road with just enough room for a lorry to pass down the middle.

The construction of a tunnel and its portal will vary from layout to layout. The technique shown is a typical method of construction when using expanded rigid foam which is cut to shape using a bread knife or hacksaw blade, the blade of the latter being wrapped at one end to form a handle.

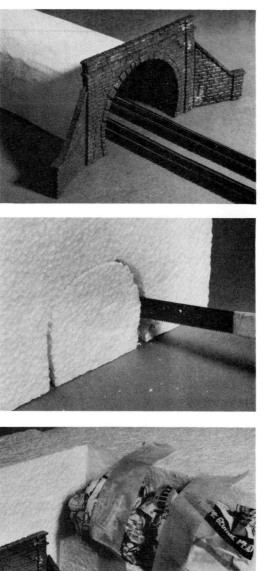

outcrop as modelled on baseboard 7) a portal would not be used, as the rock would be sufficiently strong to support itself. In a soft soil or chalk situation however, portals would be used to secure the surface at the entrances of the tunnel and the tunnel itself would be supported by a brick or steel tube. On the model a short length of cardboard is used behind the tunnel entrance to represent this.

On longer tunnels access to the track will be required in the form of a lift-off hatch. In this situation it is easier to build the basic hillside first, leaving room to position the tunnel entrance, the track and a short length of card. Then fill around the tunnel entrance with foam polystyrene, shaped to match the back of the tunnel entrance. Gaps can be filled with plaster and painted to suit. This method allows a small amount of track adjustment should the building of the tunnel be slightly out of alignment. The embankment around the tunnel is constructed from foam polystyrene cut to suit and glued in position with PVA or ceiling tile cement (don't use solvent glues or it will melt) then plastered, so as to form a hard durable surface which will finally be painted and textured (see the section on landscaping).

Roads can be modelled by using good quality thick card or hardboard cut to shape with a sharp knife or jigsaw. Don't try to slice through the card in one cut but use several lighter strokes; this gives more control over the cutting and is also safer as it reduces blade breakage. Keep the knife blade sharp by using a slip stone to resharpen it regularly and cut on to and old piece of linoleum or hardboard (not chipboard as it quickly blunts the blade). Cut hardboard with a coping saw, fretsaw, a powered jigsaw or bandsaw. Use a metal cutting blade when using powered tools, so as to produce a clean cut, and also take care when cutting with the jigsaw not to cut through the power cable.

It is very important to support the hardboard firmly whilst cutting to prevent accidents so support the hardboard on both sides of the cut. The Workmate portable bench makes this extremely simple because its top can be opened so there is a large gap between the vice jaws, forming a working surface. The hardboard is placed on this working surface and the cutting is carried out over the gap, thus supporting the hardboard each side of the cut. Use the road width guide shown for planning and cutting the roads.

Left A 125 emerging at speed from the finished tunnel.

Left A close-up of base 6. This has three bridges each built using the same method. The road/track surface is laid first, followed by cardboard walling painted to represent random stone. The water effect used on all the bases was obtained by first stippling thin Polyfilla with a brush on the water level, then painting with emulsion paint, and finally varnishing with clear high gloss polyurethane using several coats.

Left Water culverts add interest to river banks. They can be made from scrap tube and matchsticks. Add sections of walling to help support the banks or embankments when the angle is very steep.

4. CONSTRUCTING SCENERY

Previous page View over bases 4, 5, 6 and 7.

Opposite page The rock face on base 7 was modelled using the tin foil method and coloured with emulsion paint. Whilst still wet stones and grass texture were applied.

Below, top Rag, plaster, and kitchen foil method.

Centre Plaster and cork method.

Bottom Plaster and coal dust method.

ROCK FACES

Rock, whether naturally exposed or cut by man, produces various types of surface so that each type will need to be modelled in a slightly different way to look realistic. Well-washed boulders, for example, found in a stream, tend to be rounded whilst loose boulders exposed to the elements through a landslip or excavation tend to have hard edges. Also, no two areas are alike, some contain rocky outcrops with no vegetation, some just boulders mixed with grass, whilst vertical cliffs are reasonably smooth but with a texture of a random pattern. Cliff ledges will generally contain some plant growth, thus adding colour to their otherwise barren surfaces. The angle of the rock face will also vary depending upon its

hardness. Granite and other hard rocks tend to form almost a 90 degree sheer drop, but loose sandy bouldery surfaces about 45 degrees due to their self stacking properties. This is easily demonstrated by pouring out some household salt into cones of approximately 3 cm high and noting the angles of the cones. Very dry salt will form a shallower angle than damp salt. It is the same with cliffs since hard rock faces tend to be sheer whilst softer surfaces become shallower in their angle. This is the reason for the various embankment angles used on railway cuttings, and also explains why plant life is encouraged to grow on the embankments as it helps to hold together the topsoil, thus preventing the ground being washed down by the elements.

MODELLING

We have at our disposal several different types of modelling materials, all of various weights. Much will depend upon the use of the layout, expanded polystyrene is extremely light compared to plaster for example, but plaster is tough whilst expanded polystyrene is somewhat fragile and easily damaged. On a layout which will not need to be moved I prefer the chicken wire and plaster method of modelling rock faces. The chicken wire is stapled to the framework of the baseboard and shaped, then covered with a series of small cloth squares soaked in a mixture of builder's plaster (not Plaster of Paris it sets too quickly) and PVA white woodworkers glue, thinned down with water to a 25 per cent glue to 75 per cent water mixture. (This I have found helps prevent cracking of the plaster.) After covering the chicken wire framework with these presoaked cloth squares and waiting for them to have hardened, I then mix up a thicker mixture of plaster and place this in to crumpled-up tin foil, of about 30 cm square in size. While the plaster is still soft it is applied over the base layer of plaster-impregnated cloth, foil uppermost, the cloth squares preventing the plaster going through the chicken wire. The edges of the tin foil are pressed to shape to meet the contours of the adjoining surfaces. The plaster is then allowed to harden in place covered with the tin foil. When the plaster has almost completely set the tin foil is removed, exposing a random rockface-like texture. This procedure is repeated along the length of the surface being modelled slightly overlapping each join. The joins are carefully knifed away to match the previously modelled surface, so that the join line becomes lost. This produces a very hard and realistic surface ready for painting, the texture of which can be varied by the amount that the tin foil is crumpled.

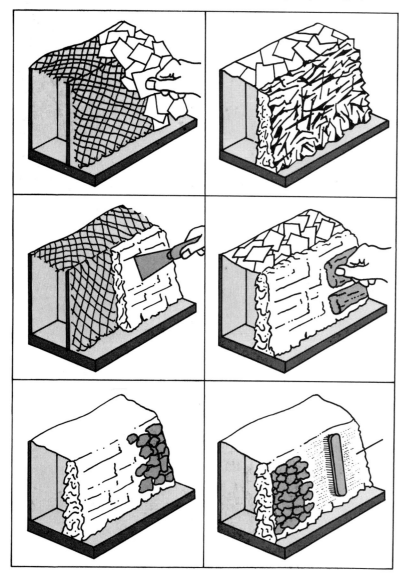

ORK METHOD

second method is the use of cork bark, which can
fixed on to either the chicken wire and cloth base
on to expanded polystyrene, glued and pinned in
ace with white PVA woodworker's glue. The joins
e filled with plaster or other household equivalent
olyfilla, etc). Don't get the cork too wet or it will
pand then shrink on drying out leaving more gaps
be filled. Cleaned and prepared cork can be
tained from local modelling shops or bark can be
tained from local woodland. This will require
aning to get rid of unwanted insects, etc, and
hough saving some money is a long messy
ocedure. The cork or bark must be thoroughly
ied before it is ready for use.

OAL AND DUST

al and dust can produce a very effective
dscaping medium which is ideal for modelling
ge areas at a time. Shaped polystyrene is used as
e foundation and primed with PVA white glue
thinned). The small coal lumps are scattered over
e surface of the wet PVA followed by a sprinkling
the fine coal dust or plaster powder which is
owed to dry. When completely dry the baseboard
turned upside down to remove the coal that has
t adhered to the surface of the polystyrene. If the
yout is large, it can be hoovered off with a vacuum
aner fitted with a new bag so as to recover the
al dust mixture. The coal glued to the baseboard is
w ready for painting.

Above A typical chalk embankment and weathered locomotive.

Right Base 03 has a rocky embankment, made by sprinkling stones then adding grass texture.

Opposite page Base 7. The cliff was modelled using the kitchen foil technique, then painted and textured as described within the text.

Opposite page, bottom A typical construction sequence shown in stages.

CHALK FACES AND EMBANKMENTS

here are several ways of making chalk faces, one
ing to use the plaster rockface method, painted
ite over the chicken wire/expanded polystyrene
se. For a very light structure to minimize
seboard weight when expanded polystyrene is
available, woven cardboard strips can be used,
pled in place at the top and bottom of the cliff or
tting. These woven cardboard strips form a base
which screwed/rolled/crumpled newspaper is
d (sticky taping it in place). This crumpled
wspaper in turn is covered with small flat strips of
wspaper, pre-soaked in a mixture of white glue
d water at the ratio of half glue to half water. Take
re when overlaying the strips not to flatten the
umpled newspaper underneath but overlay them
that they produce an uneven surface. When they
ve dried and hardened, the newspaper is painted
ite using emulsion paint. When the first layer of
int is completely dry, apply a second coat and
ilst this is still wet thinly sprinkle it with white
aster of Paris powder through a sieve to form a
xture. When dry and set add a third coat of white
ulsion paint and this time sprinkle with stones
d grass to form the finished texture. The wet paint
lds the texture permanently in place when dry.
ee chapter six for further information on painting,
c.)

MALL HILLSIDE EMBANKMENTS

any materials can be mixed together whilst
nstructing baseboards. The important thing to
member is which glue or solvent dissolves certain
terials. For example, UHU or Evostick dissolve
panded polystyrene but do not dissolve expanded
id polyurethane (the type of material used in the
ilding industry for heat insulation). Similarly,
rtain paints dissolve some plastic materials but will
t stick or adhere to other plastics. So care must be
en in the choice of glues and paints. Fortunately
ulsion paint (being water-based) does not cause
ny difficulties. If in doubt, though, make a test on
material being used before involving it in any

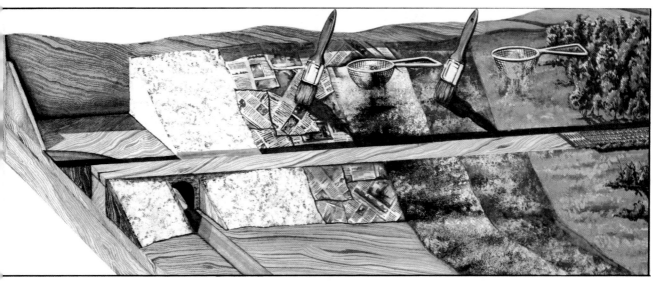

The rocks at Lands End jutting out into the sea meet a mixture of cross currents from the sea, causing tidal swirls. This makes the water foam as it meets the rocks above and beneath the water, creating a white line. The sea is not blue, but a reflection of the sky. Also notice the weathering of the rocks.

Note Since expanded polystyrene dissolves on contact with cellulose thinners, it can be used to etch and shape the material. Use a paint brush dipped in thinners; do not use a lot, or the polystyrene will vanish!

mixed construction method.

The rigid expanded polyurethane material, although expensive, is an ideal material for filling in awkward areas, being easily cut with a bread knife, using a sawing action. It also carves and sands extremely well and accepts all types of paints and glues without dissolving.

The mixed method of constructing baseboards allows for large areas to be covered in solid sheet form so as to quickly obtain a finished surface whilst the tricky contoured areas are filled in with a safer and more easily worked material, painted and textured to suit.

SEDIMENT FACES

These type of faces are the result of the different layers of soil being formed over thousands of years of time, and through changes either made by man or nature becoming exposed as a cross section. The layers each have their own weathering characteristics. The harder the material the longer it takes to break down. Soft sand, for example, is very easily eroded away by the wind and rain emphasizing the

harder material underneath. The sediment laye within also vary themselves, quite often being mixture of hard and soft materials. The soft mate again erodes away more quickly than the harder, each layer has its own characteristic of erosion a colour. Alum Bay on the Isle of Wight, as example, has 21 clearly definable different colo within a very short length of cliff face contain black, white, red, yellow, grey and a mixture of so tones in between. This, of course, is an exceptio case and far from normal, most areas having predominant colour. Devon, for example, is no for its reddish soil, whilst in other areas it is darke lighter in' colour depending on the chalk or c content of the soil. If one is modelling a particu area research will therefore be required into the soil and sediment layers.

From the modelling point of view this allows c to use different layers and colours to enhance layout so that the scenery becomes more intere ing, and by the careful selection of materials, r rocks and sand can be used rather than trying

SEDIMENT FACES 69

aint a representation of the material. Nowadays
vailable on the market are various types of
repacked textures replacing the old outdated dyed
awdust method. These new textures are produced
rom dyed cork granules, ground up foams and
atural selected materials. But of course one is not
estricted to pre-packed materials as stones and
ifferent soils abound around us, all of which can be
ery easily gathered up and prepared for use. The
method that I use is to collect a couple of jam or
coffee jars full of each different type of soil or stone
hat I am going to use, then to spread out the
collected materials on newspaper so as to allow
hem to dry out. Then I sieve the gathered material
hrough different hole-sized sieves, so as to obtain
arious grades of texture, working from the largest
o the smallest size of particle. These sorted grades
re now placed into self-seal plastic bags with the
ocation, the type of material and a number written
n, for identification at a later date. This is important
o one can rematch the various grades together, as
fter modelling for a number of years one can very
asily gather several hundred sample bags, all of
vhich are slightly different. If you later require more
f a particular material you then know where to
egather it should the need arise.

The basic structure of a sediment face can be
vood, chicken wire/plaster or polystyrene depend-
ng upon the baseboard. Broken up fibre board and
polystyrene ceiling tiles work well but both are
difficult to vary in their thickness. In reality the
sediment layers rarely maintain a consistent thickness or run in a straight line, so to help overcome
his particular problem I use pieces of wood at
different points so as to jack up and vary the
sediments' contour levels. Alternatively I use a solid
block of expanded polystyrene and etch the
contours in as required using a paintbrush dipped in
cellulose thinners to melt the expanded polystyrene
o shape. To guide the brush strokes I use a piece of
cardboard cut in an irregular line which also helps
plan out the contours. When the etching is finished
or the fibre board is fixed in position I then paint the
surface using matt oil or emulsion paint similar in
colour to the natural texture I am going to use. This
first coat I allow to dry out completely and form a
base coat. The second coat is now applied, oil paint
now becoming more useful than emulsion as it
remains wet longer and is more 'sticky'. On to the
wet paint surface sprinkle the textures, starting with
the coarsest granules which form the rocks, then
adding the medium textures followed lastly by the
finest dust-like texture. The dust helps to fill in all the
gaps between the larger stones. After a day or so,
when all of this has completely dried out, the excess
materials are removed either by turning the baseboard over or by the vacuum cleaner method. In
each case the excess materials are regathered,
re-sieved then stored away for the next project. A
realistic, naturally-textured sediment surface will be
revealed, requiring no further work and which is also
quite hard-wearing and easily repaired.

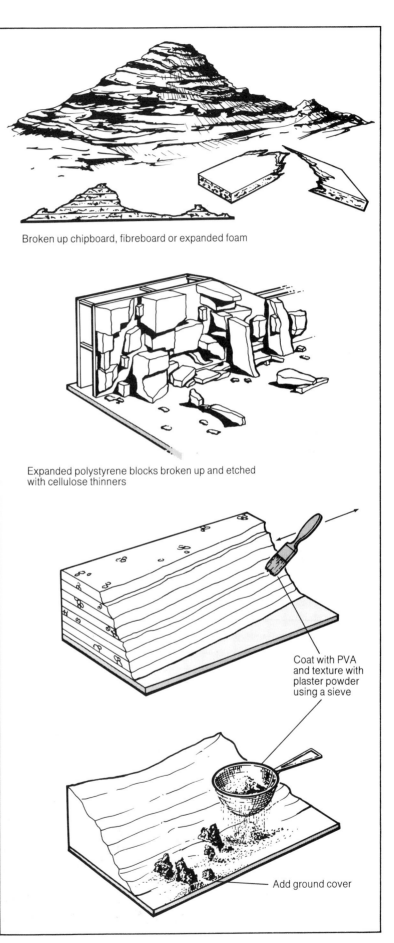

Broken up chipboard, fibreboard or expanded foam

Expanded polystyrene blocks broken up and etched
with cellulose thinners

Coat with PVA
and texture with
plaster powder
using a sieve

Add ground cover

For the ploughed field effect (above) cut a piece of plastic with grooves as shown (right). Spread plaster thinly over the surface and then shape with the grooved plastic and allow to harden. Paint the surface basic ground colour and when dry apply PVA glue with a stiff brush or a flat sponge so that only the tops of the ridges have glue on them. Then sprinkle on foliage texture to represent growing crops. Allow to dry and clean off unwanted material.

Right Add grass stubble using sisal string or natural materials. Hair from an old brush makes good grass as the hairs are tapered. Plant by drilling a hole and secure in place using PVA glue, then paint to suit.

Right Rubberized horse hair cut in lengths and sprayed with clear matt varnish, then sprinkled with pre-coloured cork granules, makes very good hedges.

PLOUGHED FIELDS, GRASS AND HEDGES

The furrows and planting of ploughed fields are very simple to reproduce in model form. The technique is first to cut a piece of plastic into a comb-like shape using a knife or file, to the scale that one is using. Secondly one mixes up builder's plaster to a butter-like mixture with water and white glue at about 50:50 glue:water ratio, adding plaster to suit. This is then spread over the baseboard's surface and, using the comb, is moulded to shape, the comb forming the small ridges and valleys and, at the end of each straight line, being pivoted around to represent the turning of the tractor and plough and repeated alongside the previous ploughed line, until the field is finished.

Finally, when the plaster has set and dried, the 'field' is painted with emulsion paint of a colour to suit the location being modelled. This first coat is allowed to dry out, then a very thin mixture of paint of the colour used plus some white is applied in a wash-like form so that it runs down into the 'valleys' and is allowed to dry. White glue is now mixed up with some of the ground colour paint to colour it. This is applied with a stiff brush to the tops of the plough marks. The glue is then sprinkled with foliage material, and when dry you remove unwanted foliage.

RIVERS, STREAMS AND PONDS

There are three basic ways of producing 'water'. The first is just to paint the flat surface area of water being modelled with a mixture of muddy tones. Then you apply several coats of clear varnish to the water area, stippling with a sponge or brush to represent the ripples on the water. Each coat of varnish must be allowed to dry before applying the next until the desired effect is obtained.

The second method is to use a sheet of clear plastic material, this being laid over the model river/stream bed and the banks, the clear plastic being varnished to represent the ripples on the water's surface, and streaks being added to represent weeds, etc.

The third method is the use of clear casting resin, building up the depth of water in thin layers, otherwise it cracks and shrinks badly. This method is a very long process but carefully done allows reeds, etc, to be placed at various levels throughout the water which looks more realistic. Care must be taken when making the resin to obtain the exact mixing ratios otherwise the resin will not set or alternatively ends up with a sticky surface. If this happens, with luck one can varnish the surface and save the situation. Around the water's edge reeds and grasses can be planted either by glueing or drilling holes and inserting long plants glued in place.

TREES

Trees form a major part of a scenic setting by helping to provide a scale to the layout. A fully grown tree is very large, quite often exceeding 75 ft (25 m) in height, or 12 in (30 mm) model size at OO/HO scale. Although trees vary in types and age, which affects their size, on average the majority of trees seen are mature and at their full height. One of the reasons so many modellers make under-size trees is the difficulty of constructing big trees and the time they consume, especially when one considers a small layout can easily require fifty trees.

The easiest of trees to make are the small scale, small in size Z or N gauge type, which are simply made from lichen or rubberized horse hair (used as a branch shaping material) cut into small pieces and glued on to a cocktail stick, long small-headed nail or length of wire, which forms the trunk. The branch material is then trimmed to shape with a pair of scissors, forming the basic winter tree shape. Then, by holding the trunk and dipping the 'branches' into

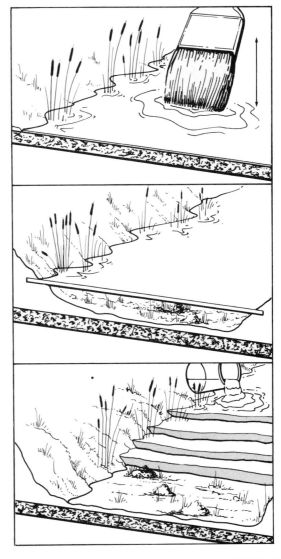

Left Water can be made in several ways. The first method uses a flat surface stippled with thin Polyfilla, painted and varnished as described earlier.

Alternatively, clear plastic or glass can be embedded in the banks, the underwater level being prepared and painted first. The above-water level is then modelled and painted to suit.

Finally, clear casting resin is poured on to the stream bed in a series of layers and each layer allowed to harden, until the required depth is obtained.

Left A corner photograph of the oval base showing bridges, canal boats and people, all helping to build up a busy scene. It is the small details and people that help to bring the model alive.

clear matt varnish (allow excess varnish to drain off) the summer foliage can be applied on to the 'branches'. Once this has dried, the unwanted foliage can be trimmed off. This method is ideal for making trees up to 3 in (8 mm) in height.

For the construction of larger-size trees requiring thick trunks the easiest basic material to use is welding rod, as this material is available in various thicknesses and in convenient straight lengths. Depending upon the size of the tree, between three and six lengths of rod can be bent to suit so that they form a series of prongs. The prongs are bound together at the base to form the trunk of the tree. Ideally, copper wire should be used for the binding (removed from old household power cable), then soldered to prevent movement. Binding tightly with strong twine will, however, suffice as on top of the binding is applied car body filler mixed with some glass fibre resin to thin it down. Alternatively, acrylic paste could be used or pre-coloured plaster mixed with white glue can be applied. The idea is to thicken up the trunk and cover the binding, so that the trunk looks natural. When this has been completed the basic trunk is painted, and the finer branches added. Rubberized horse hair is the ideal material to use, as it can be purchased in large sheets approximately

2 in thick, from good furniture or bedding repair specialists. The rubberized hair is cut up into small random pieces and glued on to the prongs of the trunk. From experience I have found that UHU (yellow tube) is the best glue to use as it is easy to apply and holds the rubberized horse hair firmly in position.

When the prongs of the trees' trunks are completely covered with the horse hair and the glue has hardened, the next stage is to trim the tree to shape using scissors to cut the horse hair in a typical winter overall shape as found on the real tree being modelled. When this is finished the trunk and branches of the tree are sprayed a suitable colour with a matt oil-bound paint. Since trees vary in their basic colour this method works extremely well as the foliage for each is applied separately, allowing choice of colour for each individual tree.

COMMERCIAL TREE KITS

A wide selection of various types of tree kits are available today, ranging from the 'Britains' all-plastic kits to the more realistic cast metal and etched ones. John Piper of 'Scale Link', Jack Kine and Isabel Fisher of 'The Factree' are all British specialist manufacturers whom I have known over a long period of time. In the United States the American

Below Adding a considerable number of trees to a setting makes it more realistic. This part of bases 01 and 02 contains 28 trees.

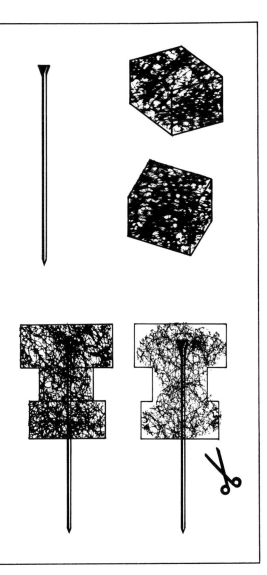

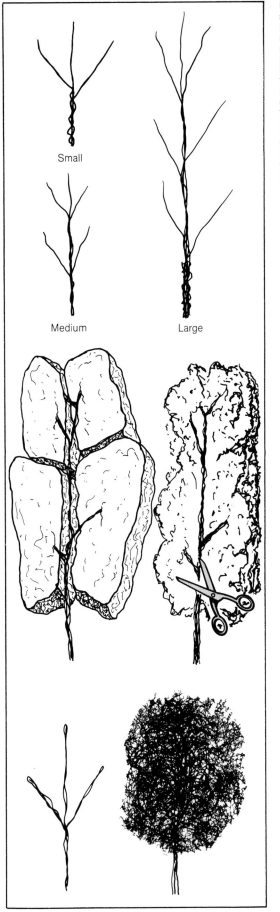

Small

Medium

Large

Far left One of the simplest types of tree to make uses a 2-3 inch nail as the trunk and rubberized horse hair or lichen as branches. The branches are glued on to the pre-painted nail using UHU clear adhesive and when dry trimmed to shape. Finally they are dipped in clear varnish and textured with foliage material. The majority of trees on these layouts use this method.

Left By extending the type of trunk used the shape of the tree can be improved upon. Cut stiff wire into a selection of lengths and twist to form three to seven prongs so that one prong always stays straight; this forms the top. Rubberized horse hair or lichen is glued on to the prongs using UHU and when set trimmed to shape. To make the tree more solid in its shape when using rubberized horse hair the material can be covered with wire wool, secured in place with spray adhesive. The trunk is covered by binding with masking tape or plastic tubing.

Note If foam rubber is used, pick bits off with tweezers for a more realistic effect.

Firm of 'Woodland Scenes' produce kits which are from time to time imported into Britain. All of these companies produce an excellent range of texturing materials suitable for both ground cover and foliaging, nowadays used by both the amateur and professional model maker. Jack Kine, who runs his own shop has also produced a video on his products and methods, which I feel is worth watching.

All the tree kits contain the basic materials, but exclude glue and paint. Their construction varies only slightly since the techniques have not really changed for a considerable number of years, so the methods shown in this book are time-tested and found to be extremely reliable.

Actual construction is dependent upon the type and size of the kit, as is the need for soldering during the kit's construction. Small trees are cast in one piece, and are ideal for Z and N scale layouts. For OO/HO scale, the trees obviously have to be considerably larger and to overcome production problems, the trunks are produced in sections and joined together by soldering, rather than glueing as a

Right It is very important to study the overall shape of a tree, as each type has its own particular shape and colouring. Winter months are an ideal time to obtain photographs of the basic shape and spring or autumn for the tree with some of its foliage missing. Modelling trees in spring or autumn conditions makes them look light and airy which is visually better than a solid lump. The model shown uses metal etched branches and leaves.

Opposite page Start by binding a number of wires together, using a single strand of wire and threading into the main bundle. Twist and separate the wires to form branches. Twist these again until they become single and separate strands. Trim as required, bend and shape the trunk and cover the lower part to thicken it; paint as required and add foliage as described later.

Note For the construction of larger trees of 6 inches (150mm) and upwards, use thicker wire and solder finer wires to the ends. These are then twisted in the same way as for making a trunk, and form the finer branches. Cover with foliage material or use wire wool and pre-coloured large cork chips, fixed in place with sprayed on clear matt oil-based varnish.

glue joint always seems to break when shaping the tree. The soldering is carried out with a large hot iron using just the tip to melt the metal of which the tree is made. Since the metal used in the trees' construction is very similar to solder, care must be taken not to melt everything, just the points that the soldering iron touches, to form the join.

Once this has been completed the trunk and branches of the tree can be bent into the required shape to form the type of tree being modelled. Finally at this stage the tree is thoroughly washed to remove all traces of grease, etc, and when dry painted with cellulose or oil paint to the desired colour. This forms the basis of the tree ready for the application of rubberized horse hair or pre-prepared foliage material.

The brass metal etched kits are constructed in a similar way. The etching is removed from the fret and a wire stalk is soldered on to the trunk so as to extend the base. Brazing rod is ideal material to use for this as the rod is of a constant thickness. This provides an advantage when planting the trees, as the same drill size is used so you don't constantly have to change the bit's size. When the stalk has been soldered in place the tree is bent to shape and then car body filler of the resin type or an acrylic paste is applied to thicken up the trunk. The trees' finer branches are modelled from wire wool, rubberized horse hair or pre-prepared foliage material.

WIRE WOUND TRUNKS

Wire wound tree trunks are very simple to produce and the method has the added advantages that any variety of tree can be modelled and that they can be made at any scale.

The basic construction material consists of a bundle of soft iron wire, the type used in flower arranging, which is available in various thicknesses. Rose wire is ideal for smaller trees. For the largest trees brass picture wire or wire cable can be used, but is very hard to cut and shape. The technique is to bind a series of wires together at what will be the base of the tree's main trunk. The wires are then unwound, one of the easiest methods being to place the bound trunk into a hand drill's chuck and clamp the drill in a vice. Next you hold on to the other end of the wires with pliers and rotate the drill to unwind the wire.

The number of wires used will all depend upon the type of tree being modelled. A silver birch, for example, will require less wire because it is tall and slender whilst the oak's trunk and branches are considerably thicker, requiring far more wire (probably four times as much for the same tree height than for the birch), so it can be quickly seen that the number of wires used is very important in order to capture the overall feeling of the tree's shape.

The unwound wires are now rewound using the drill, vice and pliers method, and always with the same direction of twist, to form the branches. Separate a small bundle of wires out, folded through the middle as if plaiting, to trap the selected bundle,

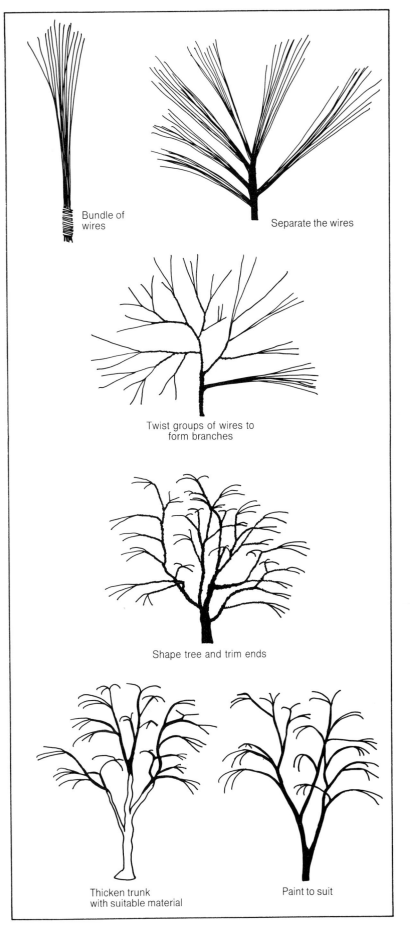

Bundle of wires

Separate the wires

Twist groups of wires to form branches

Shape tree and trim ends

Thicken trunk with suitable material

Paint to suit

The wire and string method requires two people to work satisfactorily. One person twists the wires, the second aligns the lengths of sizal string between the wires as the twisting is started. Once the wire is partially wound the pieces become trapped. Having done this the strands can be shaped and trimmed. By pushing the strands upwards poplar trees are formed and by pushing downwards conifer trees are made. By dipping the tree in clear matt oil-based varnish or spraying, it can be foliaged either by sprinkling on or by rolling the tree into the foliaging material, so that just the outside edging becomes textured.

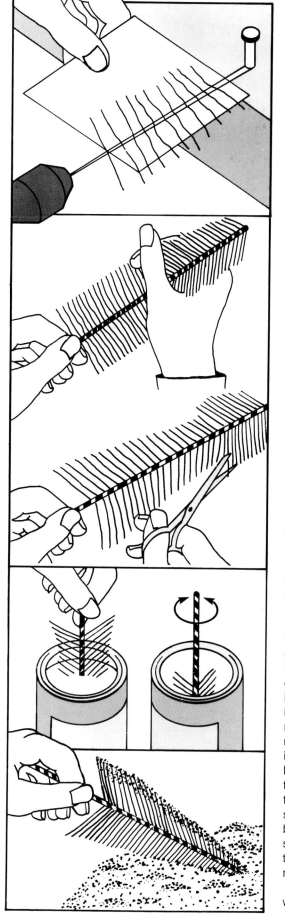

as the main wires are twisted. These separate lengths are also twisted to form the smaller branches until one ends up with two or three prongs of wire at the end of each length of twisted wire. Repeat this procedure until all the tree's wires are twisted.

Finally the tree can be shaped by spreading the wires out to a typical shape for the type of tree that is being modelled, then trimming off unwanted lengths of wire with cutters. Remove the tree from the drill's chuck and embed the base of its trunk into a block of Plasticine or modelling clay. The wire armature forming the tree is now ready for its application of filler. This can be pre-coloured plaster mixed up with white glue or acrylic paste or car body filler. The car body filler is of the paste type used for repairing dents in automobiles and thinned down to make it runny with glass fibre resin. The selected mixture is applied to the trunk of the tree and allowed to run down the trunk so that it smooths itself out, rather than being applied in blobs which of course will require cleaning up and shaping when the material has set hard.

WIRE AND STRING TREES

Trees can also be made of wire and string, a method probably dating from the bottle cleaners used to make conifer trees and developed further. By using this technique a mixture of materials can be used to form the branches, ranging from the stiff bristles found in a yard broom to sisal string, the type used for tying up parcels, white in colour and very much like thin strands of wood. The sisal string needs to be unwound so as to separate the strands. These are then cut in approximately 3 in (8 cm) lengths and are laid in between two wires which are pulled tightly together by clamping one end in a vice, the other end being secured in a twist drill pulled to keep the wires taut. A second person is needed to pass the separate strands through the two wires then they are twisted together using the drill, thus trapping the strands in place. A good length to produce is 3 ft (1 m) in one wire twisting session. The length of wound wire complete with its bristles is cut into smaller lengths to suit the height of the tree, allowing an additional length of approximately 1 in (3 cm) which is used to fix the tree into the baseboard. The trunk of the tree is formed by using a drinking straw which is pushed over the bottom part of the tree and glued in place (some of the bristles may need to be removed to make it fit). The main part of the tree is now trimmed to shape using scissors. This is an ideal technique for producing poplar trees, as the branches can be bent upwards. Alternatively the tree can be trimmed to form a conifer shape and textured. The tree can also be trimmed to a different shape and wire wool applied to form the outer branches, the wool being secured in place by spraying with oil-bound matt paint. When dry further trimming to shape is carried out, so that it is ready to receive its foliage.

This technique of applying wire wool can be used with other trees as it enables the production of dars or scotch pines, the foliage on these types of ee being very different from the types found on the k and plane tree. The foliage of the scots pine and dar is very flat on the branches, forming layers, hilst the foliage and branches of the oak and other ees are more bushy. The wire wool can also be ased out very thinly, making it an ideal material to se on silver birches noted for their fineness of liage.

OLIAGING

ere is a wide range of foliage materials available the market, ranging from wood chips, flock, anular cork, rubber and foam, all pre-coloured. atting is also produced by 'Woodland Scenes'. part from wood chips, in my opinion these are all eal foliage materials. The 'Woodland Scenes' mat aterial is the simplest of all to use as it is simply illed apart and laid over the branches, using a nall blob of glue to secure into position. When the liaging of the tree is finished, scissors are then sed to trim off the untidy bits.

The 'Woodland' scenic material is a textured e-coloured material ready for use. It can also be sed in many other ways, for instance low ground over, hanging foliage on walls or over rocks, etc. A milar home-made matting material can be pro- iced by using wire wool teased out and cross laid rubberized horse hair. The basic material is rayed in the appropriate colour then clear varnish rayed over it to form a sticky surface (oil-bound rnish is used as it remains sticky longer). On top this sticky surface is sprinkled the coloured xture materials, cork, rubber, foam, etc. The clear rnish acts like a glue and bonds it to the base aterial. When dry the excess foliage material is moved by shaking. This same technique is also sed for applying the foliage to trees, the model eing sprayed the correct colour for the tree being onstructed. Then it is sprayed with the clear matt l-bound varnish used to bond the foliage in place. e foliage is sprinkled on with a sieve while the rnish is still wet and a dry paint brush is used to move unwanted foliage from the lower branches d the trunk. Since clear matt varnish is used evious colours applied are unaffected in their matt ish. Also, since the varnish is clear it does not ain or discolour the foliage material.

Lichen can also be sprayed and textured, or flock aterial can be applied to conifer trees to represent e needles, using this spray method. Finally, small ees can be dipped into a tin of varnish, spun etween the fingers to remove excess varnish, and en textured. These small trees make ideal hedges r the larger layouts, planted tightly together in a w.

WORD OF WARNING

ubberized spray mount is toxic, both in fume and ontent and it should only be used in an extremely ell ventilated place. For personal protection a mask hould be worn at all times. As with all pressurized ans, the empties should never be disposed of in an cinerator or burnt on an open fire.

Top The illustration shows the tree being sprayed with matt varnish or rubberized spray mount, the type used for permanently mounting photographs or displays.

Centre The dip in a tin of matt varnish method, the tree then being spun between the fingers by its trunk to remove excess varnish. The prepared foliage material is then sprinkled on to the tree, the unused material being gathered for re-use by collecting in a container or on newspaper.

Bottom 'Woodland Scenes' or Jack Kine prepared foliaging material being glued into place on the tree using UHU glue (yellow tube).

Right Cork granules can be recoloured very easily by putting a small amount into a tin and adding emulsion paint. Only a very small amount of paint is required as the colour is smeared over the cork (not soaked) so that the granules do not stick to each other. They are then laid out on newspaper to dry.

Right Plastic foam can be ground up in an old mincing machine or coffee grinder to size.

Right Wire wool or a material available from Jack Kine called 'Postiche Rope' which is teased out and laid on a sheet of white polythene (bin liner will do) and then sprayed with spraymount or matt varnish. The texture is applied on top of this through a sieve.

SOFT TEXTURES

The selection of textures forms an important part scenic modelling as coarse over-scale or unde scale finishes look very wrong. Wood chips have long spiky texture whilst granulated foam has a s rounder shape, for example. The colour of t texture is also critical as this controls the over effect, each colour having to work in harmony w its neighbouring colour to please the eye. The ran of precoloured textures are vast but the dyes us to colour the materials leave at times something be desired. This can easily be overcome re-colouring the texture. Emulsion paint wor extremely well for this. An old tin can with the t removed by one of the modern openers provides good mixing vessel as the sides are smooth all t way down. (Do not use a jam jar as the lip around t top prevents proper mixing of the materials.) This important as, when re-colouring the granules of t materials, only a small amount of emulsion paint used so that the paint is smeared over the surface the granules by stirring and working the colour rather than soaking the granules with paint. T method, by using the minimum amount of pai prevents the granules from sticking together a they dry quicker. The drying is carried out on a she of newspaper at room temperature.

Textures can be home made by grinding up foa natural rubber foam producing a very differe texture from synthetic polyurethane foa Polyurethane foam dyed in small squares usi cellulose paint becomes brittle and grinds into dust-like powder, whilst dyed in emulsion pa forms rounder shapes. The round shapes are ide for small ground cover and the dust texture grass. An old mincer or coffee grinder works well shredding the foam into textures. The mince handle is rotated by hand and as the foam emerg from the machine it is sieved through various si sieves so that a selection of granular grades can obtained. Material which is still too big is return into the mincer for further grinding down. The coff grinder works in much the same way, but only sm amounts can be prepared at a time. Care must taken in the choice of material to be re-colour because the 'flock' texturing type of material or 'c litter' does not re-colour, it only forms a sticky mes Cork granules and stone which are non-dissolvat re-colour easily.

HARD TEXTURES

Hard textures like stone and brick are very use because they are natural materials. This natural lo is very difficult to reproduce by painted artwork ov other surfaces alone. For example, when a surfa is painted to represent another material, the additi of the natural texture carefully applied can enhan its appearance. Similarly, a derelict cottage usi natural small stones typical of the cottage's co struction looks far more convincing than trying paint pieces of material to look right.

Garden soil, dried out and sieved, provides easily obtainable material suitable for many applic

ns. The commercial market packages many types
 hard natural materials. 'Cat litter' designed for a
 t's toilet tray or 'Vermiculite', a material used for
 sulation, are good sources of small boulders
 itable for glueing together or scattering around,
 -coloured by painting. 'Vermiculite' has a very
 od texture, and also compresses so that it can be
 essed into shape. Unfortunately neither of these
 aterials are found in hobby shops, like the majority
 hard materials. Hard materials are worth gathering
 d storing in a self-seal plastic bag when making a
 ld trip to a location, so that an example is kept of
 e soil and stones found in the locality. From these
 thered samples coloured paints can be mixed to
 atch the stones and soil colour. The technique is
 st to paint the area being modelled with a base
 lour to seal the surface, then apply a second coat,
 rinkling on the texture over the wet paint. The wet
 int bonds the stones or earth to its surface.

The self-manufacture of natural materials in
 anular form is a long laborious business. Brick
 st, for example, is obtained by breaking up bricks
 th a hammer. This is dangerous and it is extremely
 portant to wear safety goggles to prevent being
 ruck in the eye by flying particles. Alternatively, a
 sit to a demolition site could well be fruitful in
 taining this material. Broken up plaster dyed to
 lour also works well and is very easily obtainable
 crumbling up half set plaster as one works. These
 nall irregular shapes are suitable for scattering
 ound the bottom of chalk embankments and
 ttings rather than using natural chalk, which is
 ry soft and becomes a nuisance rather than an
 dvantage.

HRUBS AND FLOWERS

 e planting of back yard or garden detail either in
 bs or around lawns forms an important detail that
 t only provides colour but creates the feeling that
 e buildings are occupied.

Planting flowers and shrubs to look convincing is a
 rprisingly time-consuming business as a garden
 n contain numerous plants, all of which have to be
 odelled somehow. Time can be saved by using
 nall natural foliage, grass seed heads dried out and
 coloured look very convincing mixed with yarrow;
 th grow wild and are easily obtainable. Flowering
 rubs can be made by using lichen dipped in clear
 rnish, first being sprinkled with a small amount of
 e-coloured course granules, to the colour of the
 wers then with green foliage-coloured finer cork
 anules. By applying the flower colour first, control
 er the amount of flowers can be obtained. If you
 verse this process all the green sticks in place and
 e flowers fall off! Reeds and other long plants with
 ads on can be made from single strands of wire,
 e wire being stripped of its plastic coating apart
 m a small piece at the top. The reed is painted and
 e top colour changed to show slightly differently so
 to represent the bloom. Alternatively, using
 e-coloured wire a thin layer of glue can be applied
 ong one side of the wire at the top and sprinkled
 ith a flower coloured texture. This technique

75%
water

25%
PVA

Glue/water mixture

Left By breaking up
plaster with your fingers
as it hardens, whilst
cleaning out the mixing
container, a selection of
random sizes of rubble
and rocks can be
obtained. Sieving the
material then provides a
selection of sizes,
which can be stored in a
plastic bag or glass
container when dry.
When required these
can then be pre-
coloured using
emulsion paint to suit
the situation. The
sequence and method
of applying the rocks to
the base is to first paint
the area with a suitable
colour, then repaint with
PVA glue. Whilst the
glue is still wet apply the
largest of the rocks in
prominent positions as
required, then the
smaller sizes until finally
the texture is like dust,
used to fill the nooks
and crannies. When dry
clean off unwanted
material. Alternatively
the rocks can be applied
in the same sequence,
but unpainted. This time
the finer texture plaster
powder is used over the
wet glue, sieved on and
allowed to dry. Then the
base is painted and
whilst it is still wet
further pre-coloured
textures are sprinkled
on, tufts of grass added,
etc.

produces gladioli-type plants which bloom on one side only. Glue all around the wire obviously produces other plants. For plants with larger heads ground-up foam, pre-coloured, can be used by simply glueing in place on a length of wire, other leaves being made from pre-coloured paper cut to shape. The detailing of plants can continue until the complete flower is built up of individual leaves, the sunflower being the biggest and most popular example. The petals are applied around a disc of paper and the leaves applied one at a time along its stalk.

For super-detailing of gardens etched plantation is available, or one can make one's own. This involves drawing up the plant's leaves and flowers on a sheet of shim copper, which is an extremely thin copp[er] sheet the back of which will require to be complete[ly] painted with acid resistant. The front of the sheet [is] painted with acid resistant to represent the leav[es] and flower detail. All the painted components w[ill] have to be linked together so that they sit on [a] spider's web which holds them in place (like t[he] 'sprue' in plastic kits). This is then immersed in ac[id] available from DIY radio shops for circuit makin[g.] *Always take great care when using acid.*

PALM TREES

Palm trees are one of the simplest types of tree [to] make, requiring paper, wire, glue, drinking stra[w] and scissors. A real whilst watching TV job! Th[e] technique is to pre-coat a sheet of writing paper wi[th] UHU glue, spreading the glue with a piece of plas[tic] to form an even thin coat over its surface. Then y[ou] pre-cut lengths of wire and insert them into the tu[be] of glue's nozzle so as to coat their surfaces. Th[e] glue-covered wire is then laid down on the pape[r] surface so that it sticks to the paper, leaving a g[ap] between each length of wire. A second fresh[ly] coated piece of paper is now glued in place over th[e] first sheet of paper, trapping the wire in between th[e] sheets of paper. The leaves are now ready f[or] cutting out with a pair of scissors in a typical pa[lm] leaf shape. Having completed this the leaves are c[ut] across to form the individual leaves typical of a palm[,] the wire in the middle preventing one from cuttin[g] them in half. Keep the cuts close together; the be[st] technique for this I have found is to hold the sciss[ors] steady and pass the leaf through the scissors as on[e] finishes the cut and opens the scissors, rather th[an] moving the scissors along the leaf. This way you ca[n] estimate the amount of cut rather than looking to se[e] how much has been cut. On completing the leave[s] they are bent to shape, the wire holding them [in] position. The stalk of each leaf is inserted into [a] paper drinking straw with a blob of glue to secure [it.] The easy way is to force some glue down th[e] drinking straw and push a number of leaf stall[s] down it (approximately nine to twelve) so as to for[m] the top of the tree. The trunk of the tree is no[w] covered with further drinking straws, cut along the[ir] length so as to open them out. Then cut acros[s] completely at an angle, these separate pieces [of] drinking straw being glued to the trunk of the tr[ee] starting from the top and working down, overlappin[g] each one so as to lose the gap formed by cutting th[e] straw in half along its length. This is continued dow[n] until the trunk is completed leaving a short length [at] the bottom for planting into the base.

A second method for making small palm trees [is] by using feathers. The feathers are cut to shape ar[d] glued into position with car body filler or epoxy res[in] on top of a large nail. The resin being a thick or st[iff] glue holds the feathers in place without droppin[g.] Alternatively the feathers can be bound to the na[il] and the trunk covered with paste to disguise th[e] binding. Finally, metal etched leaves can be use[d] soldered in place on a length of wire, sleeving bein[g] used to thicken up the trunk.

Top to bottom: Tubing glued onto wire to form reeds, or paper glued to wire to form flowers. Natural foliage coloured to suit makes good small flowers. By cutting a matchstick and then reworking the middle long-leaved ground plants and flowers can be made.

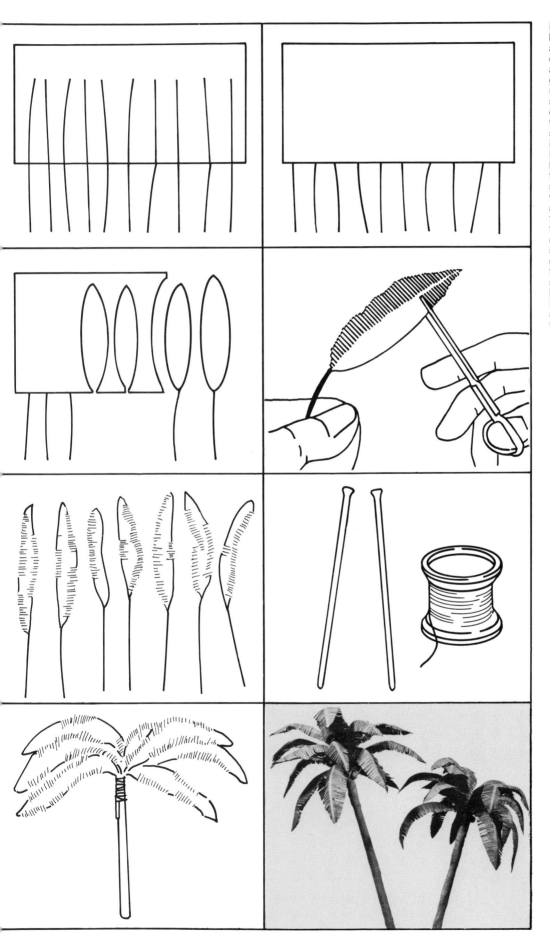

Palm trees. Top to bottom: Cut out paper and glue lengths of wire on as shown; cover with a second piece of paper glued into position; using scissors cut as shown to form the outline of the leaf and then cut across with scissors to form the individual fronds of the leaf. The distance between the cuts varies from type to type. For small palms push the wire into drinking straws and glue in place. For the larger types bind on to a suitable round stick, covering it with segments of straw by glueing in place to form the bark of the tree. The segments are formed by cutting a straw down its length and then at an angle diagonally across with scissors.

5. CONSTRUCTING BUILDINGS

Buildings produced to scale, either from kits or scratch-built, then painted and weathered, help to produce the feeling of reality within the layout as the eye observes every detail. The model on the previous page is built as described from the OO and N scale drawings.

PLANNING A TOWN BASEBOARD

If a study is made of a town or city map, it will be found to show a random arrangement of roads and buildings. Time has produced this, due to the changing situation of its history over hundreds of years. The original buildings in many cases no longer exist, but the roads or foot paths remain, and in many cases the actual name. For example, 'Moorland Road' could well be found now in the middle of the town, but once it led directly to the moors.

By studying the true to scale map shown it can be seen that it contains approximately 200 houses, a selection of shops, offices, factory sites and a railway. Quite a lot of modelling potential. Unfortunately for us, though, the size of a moderate town built at OO scale is enormous, even at N scale it is still very big. Just to build the area of the map shown at N scale layout would require a baseboard 6 ft by 5 ft in size. The railway's layout would also be impractical for our use.

By reducing the town and making the railwa curves smaller than in real life, an acceptable part it can be modelled, the number of houses reduce and the eye can also be deceived allowing the mir to be fooled into thinking things happen that in fa do not. For instance, part of a large station can b built, the roof used to cover a track return loo designed so that it emerges at a lower level to rejo the main line which apparently goes into the larg station. This redesigned town baseboard now form a return loop for practical use of the track.

The arrangement of the roads and building should also be aligned with the baseboard edge s as to avoid as much as possible cutting off building in half, yet the roads and buildings should portra the feeling of 'being there first', ie, before the railwa rather than as a backdrop for it.

The redesigning of a township is very much compromise. Although track radii are variable, as al the widths of roads, pavings, and house sizes, et there are minimum sizes that cannot be reduced ar still look convincing. Buildings require certain hea room inside, also the floor area that they occup cannot be reduced beyond a certain size. This als applies to roads and footpaths. Towns occupy a

The planning of a town is very complex as it is a mixture of old and new buildings, winding roads, twisting footpaths and various greenery. The best view of this is from an aircraft, failing that use the top floor of a tower block of flats that is situated in a mixed development area. Take a good look and a lot of photographs and use these coupled with the maps of the area to base the model upon. A good book to refer to is *Above London* by Alistair Cooke and Robert Cameron (The Bodley Head, 1980).

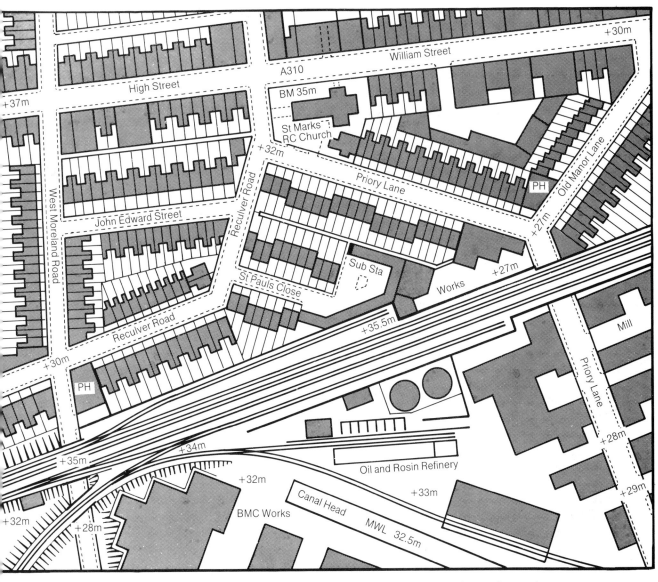

space. For instance, 67 houses in a row, each house 15 ft wide, equals 1,005 scale feet. Built at N scale (2 mm to 1 ft) this is about 2 m (6 ft) in length at model size, yet only portrays reality of less than one fifth of a mile—the length of 14 carriages and one locomotive.

Above *A typical map of a town showing a mixture of roads, paving, houses and factory sites, with the railway running through the middle.*

Below *A modified plan of a town suitable for model railway use, creating the feeling of being possible due to its design.*

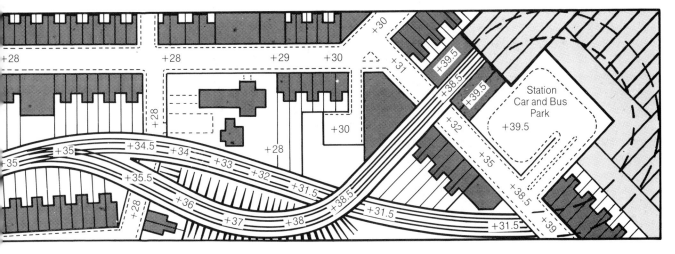

Right Sections from front to back through typical terraced houses and plans and cutaway sections through the buildings. The left-hand side shows the long ridge house and the right-hand side shows the London roof.

Bottom left The walling arrangement of the long ridge terraced house.

Bottom right The walling arrangements of the London roof terraced house. Compare the two buildings shown with each other, and then with the illustration on the opposite page.

Opposite page The left-hand and top side of the road shows the long ridge terraced house from front and back. By looking at the front it can be seen that the building is handed; this means the front door is on the left-hand or right-hand side looking at the front of the building, forming a natural pair of houses. On the right-hand side of the illustration, however, the front doors are all on one side of the building which means these houses are not handed, the back extension confirming this. Compare the backs with the handed houses. Also notice the different chimney arrangement between the designs, and the number of flues per chimney stack. The long ridge building has six flues per building, indicating six rooms, whilst the London roofed house has five, despite having six rooms, in this particular case. (The buildings were surveyed in Greenwich, London and still exist.)

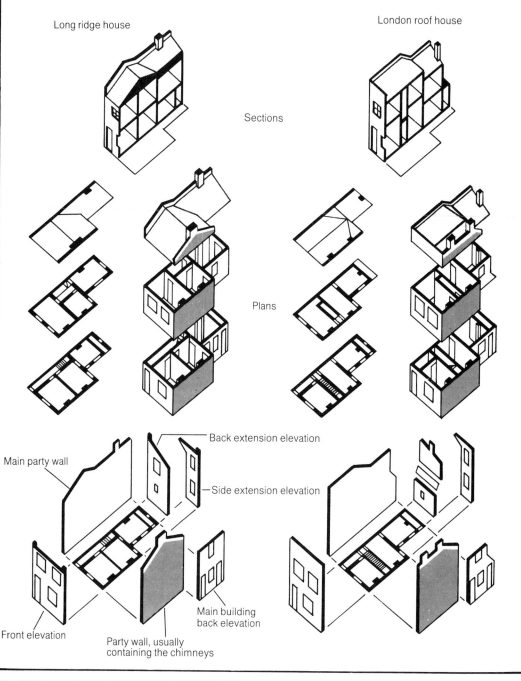

Long ridge house

London roof house

Sections

Plans

Back extension elevation

Main party wall

Side extension elevation

Main building back elevation

Front elevation

Party wall, usually containing the chimneys

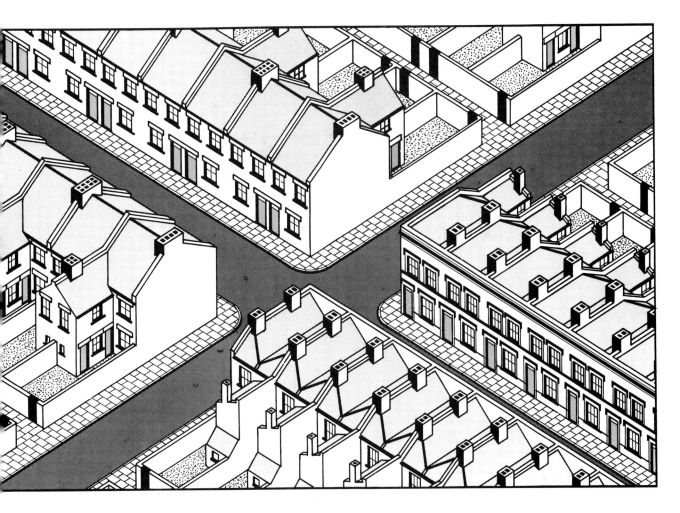

UNDERSTANDING DRAWINGS

When plans of buildings are first encountered, it is like looking at a new and foreign language, and these plans or drawings can be extremely difficult to interpret especially if the design is complex. Fortunately outline architectural drawings are basically easy to read, except when dealing with the finer points of the builder's instructions such as damp courses, etc. Since in model form this information is not required it can be ignored, the basic outline information is all that is needed, and this can be obtained in the form of floor plans, sections and elevations.

The floor plans will clearly show the layout of the internal walls and the positions of doors and windows (see illustration). By placing the drawings on top of each other and in the order of the ground floor, the first floor, etc, finally the roof, the planning arrangement can be quickly followed through and understood. By looking at each plan in turn, down through the building, a mental picture of the walls can be formed. Then, by looking at the sections the floor to ceiling heights can be established, together with the thickness of the floor slabs. Finally, one looks at the outside elevations so as to establish the positions of the doors and windows, their heights and sizes, etc, and even the style of glazing.

The buildings illustrated can be found in many countries and are typical of the terraced design when the buildings share a common frontage and consist of two party walls, these being shared with the adjoining building on each side. Some are 'handed' so each alternative house is a mirror image, to form left- and right-handed houses (see illustration).

By 'exploding' the house as shown in the illustration, it can be seen that the elevations comprise: main building front elevation; main building first party wall and extension; back extension elevation; side extension elevation; main building back elevation; and main building second smaller party wall. In practice, when sections through a building are shown on a drawing, they generally cut through it in a straight line at any point across or along the length of the building, but sometimes a staggered section is shown which can be very confusing.

The illustration above left shows the arrangement of a long ridge right- and left-handed door house, and the way it adjoins its neighbours, also its mirror imaged back elevation detail. Note the way the chimneys are arranged on the main building, being on the second smaller party wall, a point often missed. The lower right part of this illustration shows the 'London roof' terraced house, which in this case is all right-handed! The building is situated on the right-hand side of the doorway.

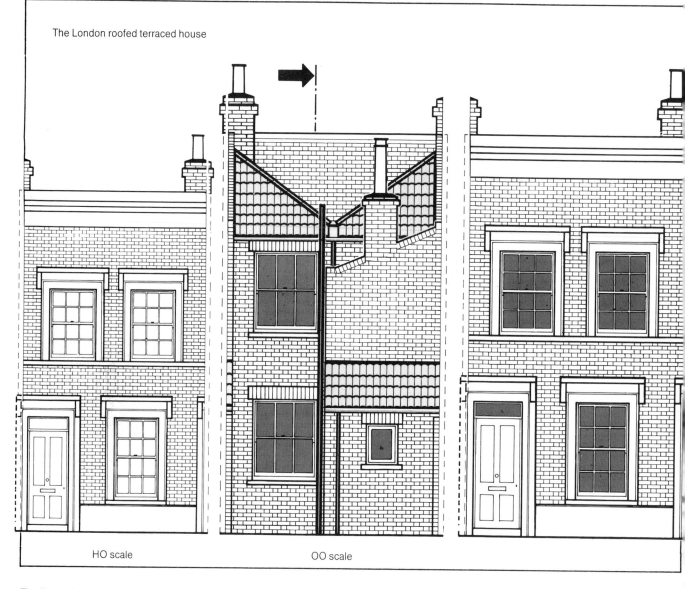

The London roofed terraced house

HO scale

OO scale

The illustrations show the difference in scale sizes between OO scale (4 mm to 1 ft), HO scale (3.5 mm to 1 ft) and N scale (2 mm to 1 ft). This vast difference in physical size influences the amount of detail practical to model or show. HO scale is smaller than OO scale although the track gauge is the same. For this reason HO and OO scale buildings should not be placed alongside each other.

STYLE OF BUILDINGS

The style used in modelling buildings must be consistent. This is very important in order to retain visual harmony throughout the layout. Other points to consider are: the available room on the baseboard; the total number of buildings; the style of the buildings, as each country has its own form of architecture; the number of repetitive buildings as this influences the method of model construction, and the number of self-contained separate buildings; the overall size of each building (ie, a small cottage or a large factory building); the availability of information to allow a reasonable representation of the building to be made; the availability of suitable materials commercially produced; and finally the modelling style, as the scale of the building influences the amount of detail that it is practical to model.

So as to provide an indication of model size, the illustrations shown are produced to three popular modelling scales.

The first elevation only is at HO scale (3.5 mm to 1

ft). The back, front and section are to OO scale (4 mm to 1 ft). The dimensions are: frontage 13 ft 6 in (54 mm model size), depth 34 ft 9 in (139 mm) and ridge height 23 ft 3 in (93 mm)—a typical London roof terraced house. Six houses of this type total 324 mm (13 in), almost the same length as the Hornby *Flying Scotsman* locomotive and tender. Thus it can be calculated quickly that a baseboard of 1,950 mm (6 ft 3 in) in length at OO scale can only contain 36 terraced houses along its length, but at N scale (2 mm to 1 ft) 72 houses. This is not many when one considers the normal number of houses in a street or road.

The last illustration shows at N scale a typical long ridged roofed house. This time the roof pitch runs towards the road and to the back of the building unlike the London roof which runs across the building, to form a gully in the middle of the roof.

TOWN HOUSES

By changing the ground floor but repeating the middle floor's plans, the terraced house becomes a series of dwellings above a lock-up shop. The back

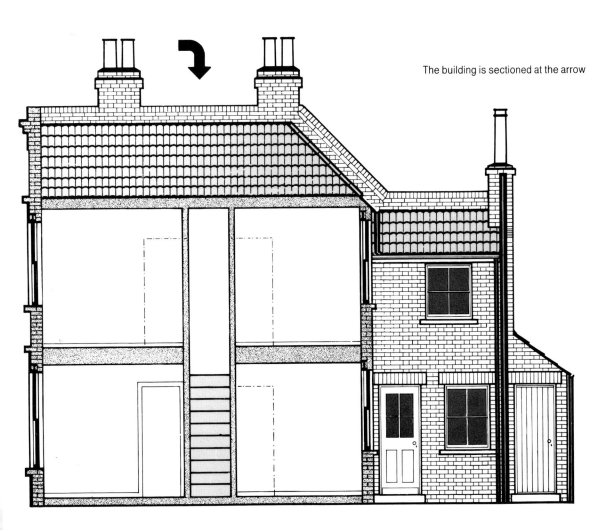

The building is sectioned at the arrow

N scale

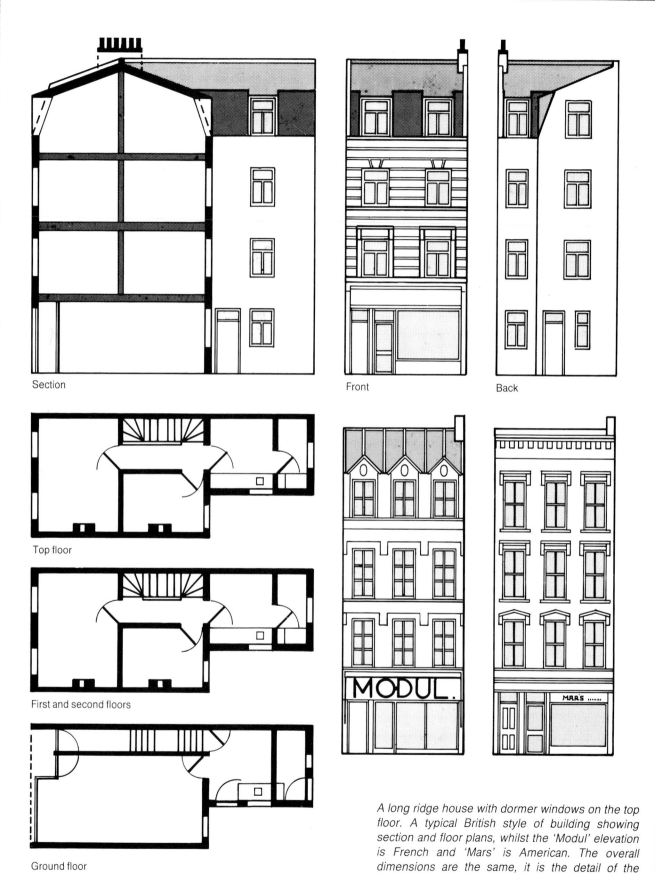

Section

Front

Back

Top floor

First and second floors

Ground floor

A long ridge house with dormer windows on the top floor. A typical British style of building showing section and floor plans, whilst the 'Modul' elevation is French and 'Mars' is American. The overall dimensions are the same, it is the detail of the elevation that has changed.

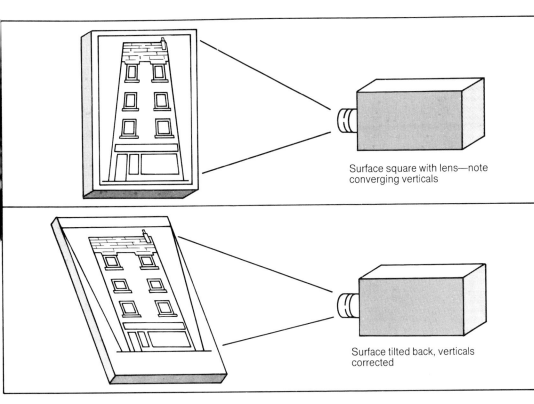

Surface square with lens—note converging verticals

Surface tilted back, verticals corrected

By photographing a building using slide (transparency) film the picture can be projected on to a board. By tilting the board backwards at the top, the converging verticals can be corrected. By varying the projection distance the building can be scaled to size, then drawn on to the board using pencil and ruler. If the board is replaced by a sheet of glass covered with tracing paper the photograph can be projected on to the back. This makes it easier to redraw.

Below A variety of buildings on bases 01, 02 and 03. The town-like appearance is enhanced by cars, people, road markings etc.

elevation of the building remains the same apart from a minor roof detail change. This is typical of high street architecture and it is found in many countries. It is in both the design and treatment of the elevation's detail that changes in character are achieved. For example, by altering the size and adding heavy mouldings around the windows, fitting shutters, using a different style of dormer window at roof level, and selecting pantiles instead of slate, a French style of architecture is portrayed. The three elevations shown are of British, French and American origin, but the overall size of the building remains the same. When surveying and information-gathering include if at all possible roof photographs. These will explain all sorts of peculiar roofing situations and clearly show the assortment of heights to the back of the building.

Architectural designs of buildings vary so much throughout the world that it is impossible to describe them all, so I have concentrated on one basic type. The library is a good source of additional information and a good book on town and country houses will include photographs, scale drawings and can well save a lot of hard work. Unfortunately, not all buildings are listed, so at some time or other one is forced to undertake one's own surveying.

SURVEYING

The recording of information on a warm sunny day is one of the delights of surveying. The equipment required need not be expensive—pen and pencil, a rubber, a tape measure, a few sheets of graph paper, a straight edge and a good eye for counting bricks will suffice, but in addition I have found useful a measuring pole. This I stand alongside the building when taking photographs. It is marked out in feet on

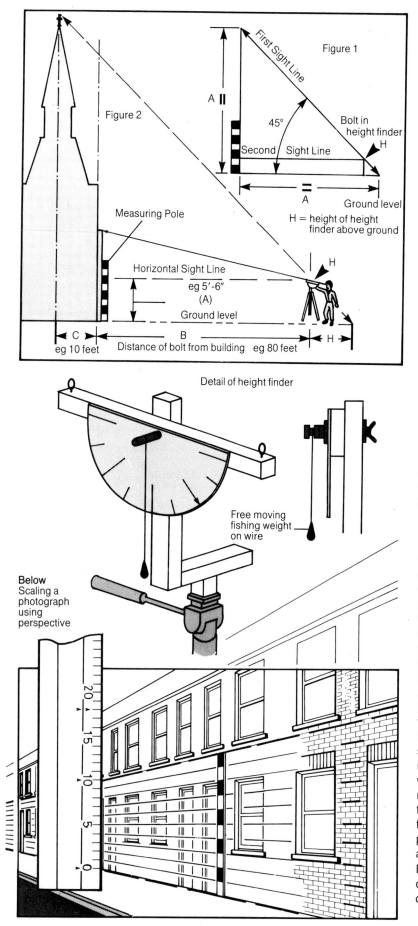

Figure 1

First Sight Line

A ||

45°

Second Sight Line

Bolt in height finder

H

=

A

Ground level

H = height of height finder above ground

Figure 2

Measuring Pole

Horizontal Sight Line
eg 5'-6"
(A)

Ground level

C
eg 10 feet

B
Distance of bolt from building   eg 80 feet

H

Detail of height finder

Free moving fishing weight on wire

Below
Scaling a photograph using perspective

one side and metres on the other and is 10 ft long made from 2 in × 1 in wood, hinged using bolts fitted with wing nuts so as to allow it to fold down into a portable 3 ft 6 in length. I also use a protractor, a 35 mm camera fitted with a 35 mm wide angle lens and loaded with colour print film, and finally my homemade height finder which fits on to the camera's tripod. Although the height finder (see illustration) looks difficult to make and use, it is in fact very simple. It is fabricated from a length of 1 in square hardwood fitted with two screw eyes, which form the sights. Also screwed to this wood strip is a big home-made protractor used to measure the angle. Then, passing through the centre is a long bolt, on which is first threaded a piece of wire shaped with an eyelet at one end and with a fishing weight firmly attached to the other, followed by a nut and locking nut then a washer.

The bolt then passes through the 1 in hardwood and protractor and a second washer is fitted. The bolt continues through the support followed by a third washer and a wing nut. This final wing nut is tightened against the support to lock the device, adjusting the first nuts until the weighted wire moves freely, as gravity is used to keep the sight line wire vertical so that various angles can be read off from the protractor.

By setting the height finder at 45 degrees to the wire, then moving away from the building until the sight aligns with the top of the building, you can easily measure the distance (the distance away equalling the height if the building has a flat face, when the sight line is taken to ground level (Fig 1)). Resight the device to zero (horizontal) and take a second sight line on the measuring pole (A). If it is above ground level use the measuring pole and take a reading to ground level. It may, for example, read 5 ft 6 in above ground level. Now measure the distance from the bolt in the height finder from the front of the building (B)—say 80 ft. Add the two together—total height (A) plus (B) equals 85 ft 6 in. If the top is set back you need to add together (B) distance from building, plus (A) height above ground, plus (C) distance set back—say 10 ft. The total now supplies the height of the building (95 ft 6 in). Measure and draw this out on graph paper to scale then take intermediate angle readings and project these across at the indicated angles given on the height finder. These supply further heights. Re-check these dimensions and angles from a second position in the same way, averaging out any minor difference. I find this method works extremely well for large tall buildings, when the brick-counting method (see later) cannot be used. The use of the tape measure re-checks the site plans obtained from maps, etc. In Britain, Ordnance Survey produce maps at 1:500 scale which are extremely accurate but unfortunately expensive to purchase. For a simple building these are not usually worth the cost, as it is far cheaper just to measure out and draw.

The second method of surveying (see illustration

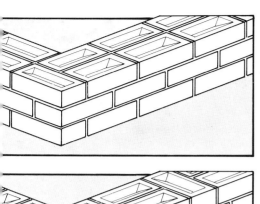

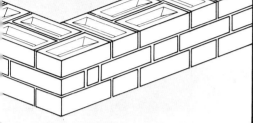

⊓p *English bond brickwork.*

⊓ove *Flemish bond brickwork showing a cut brick ⊓ centre course.*

Above *Typical terraced house built using Flemish bond brickwork. The brick courses are easily seen and counted. When calculating chimneys (top right), project lines along the brick courses then count the layers of bricks.*

Below *By counting the bricks and drawing on a sheet of metric graph paper, the elevation of the building can be scaled to size.*

⊓ow left) is by using the measuring pole and ⊓otography. By simply drawing lines to find the ⊓nishing point on the print, then placing a suitable ⊓ale rule across vertically and drawing a line at the ⊓int it aligns with, measured heights can be ⊓tained directly from the photograph. A different ⊓ale rule will give a new position on the building. ⊓e building scales 18 ft high and the brick count ⊓nfirms the pole to be 10 ft high at four bricks to the ⊓t). Finally, you can use the brick-counting method ⊓her from photographs or reality. Just count the ⊓cks but be careful of the way they have been laid, ⊓cause there may be cut bricks in the courses.

⊓NSTRUCTION OF CARDBOARD BUILD-
⊓GS

⊓e easiest and quickest building kits to construct ⊓ without doubt the Graham Farish N gauge range ⊓ the only tool required to construct them is a pair ⊓ scissors, used to cut out the pre-printed, ⊓f-adhesive elevations and roofs. Each kit contains ⊓ number of plastic blocks which are covered with ⊓e self-adhesive elevations which themselves ⊓cure the blocks in place.

⊓Unfortunately the Graham Farish system is not as ⊓ available in OO/HO scale so the majority of ⊓ildings at this scale will have to be built up using ⊓e hollow construction method. This is far more ⊓e-consuming as the OO/HO scale cardboard ⊓ildings are produced by printing on medium ⊓ckness card, so that they have to be cut out if they ⊓ve not already been pre-cut. Superquick and ⊓ilder Plus are two examples of pre-cut kits. As ⊓ays, the kit's instructions should be thoroughly ⊓died before starting construction. A most impor-⊓t point, do not remove any components from the ⊓e-cut sheets until required as pieces that look like

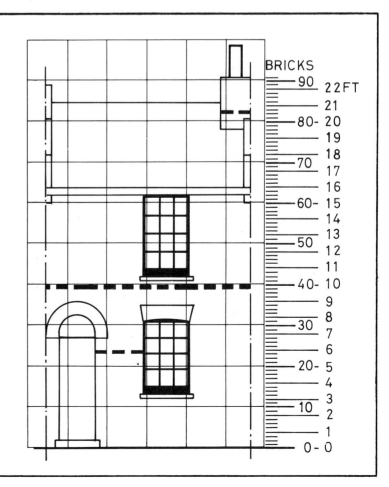

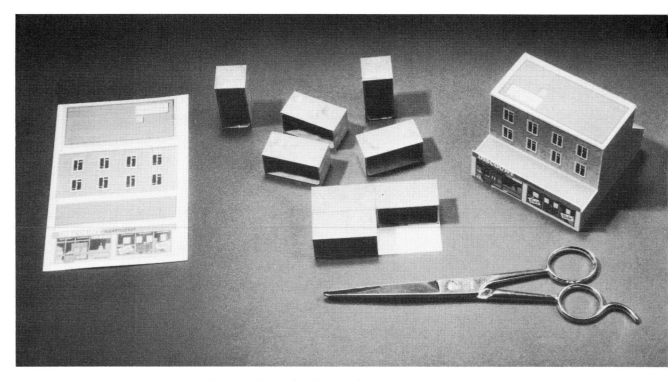

scrap are often used as bracing and corner strengtheners.

After reading the instructions detach each component as required using a very sharp knife (Swan Morton produce excellent scalpel knife handles which have replaceable blades suitable for modelling) and trim as required. Cut along a steel rule so as to keep the line straight, and cut out on a scrap piece of card, hardboard or linoleum so as to protect the knife blade's tip and the table's surface.

Assemble the building on a flat piece of chip or blockboard, which should be sufficiently large to

also allow the use of metal engineer's squares, the walls of the building can be held upright whi the glue dries (alternatively, use cardboa squares).

Start construction by using the largest wall a corner first. Pre-glaze the windows during constru tion and do not forget to touch-in the cut bare ed of the cardboard around the windows with colouring crayon of a suitable colour. Idea purchase the water-soluble type which are li colouring pencils but turn into water colours with t aid of a wet paintbrush.

Left For the beginner it is recommended that a small simple building is chosen as the first model and on starting it's construction try out one of the small assemblies. The illustration shows the covered entrance porch complete with steps which is ideal and on completing this successfully, then continue with the main building. The glazing can be added during or after construction. I prefer to glaze when the basic 4 walls are constructed, positioning the glazing from the back, but viewing from the front so that I can see clearly the position of the glazing bars within the cutout.

The window glazing only needs to be lightly ⬛cked in place, which will prevent excess glue ⬛mearing the window glazing. This also applies to ⬛e main corner joins, as I have found that to use a ⬛t of glue on a corner makes a messy join. I now ⬛refer to tack join the corners and brace them using ⬛ small square strip of balsa wood to form a fillet ⬛hich strengthens the corners. After the first corner ⬛ue has dried continue construction by adding the ⬛ther walls. If the walls are long and without further ⬛upport (ie, kerb or base) it is best to fix further balsa ⬛ form internal bracing along the inside of the

building, continuing the construction in this way until the model is completed.

The choice of glues for construction is important, my own preference being a mixture of white PVA woodworker's glue and clear UHU. PVA glue is easy to remove with a damp cloth should it accidentally come in contact with the printed elevation and is ideal for applying the balsa strengtheners. UHU is used very sparingly for general construction and window glazing, also for laminating card together when the use of PVA (which is water-based) would warp the card.

Left The finished building.

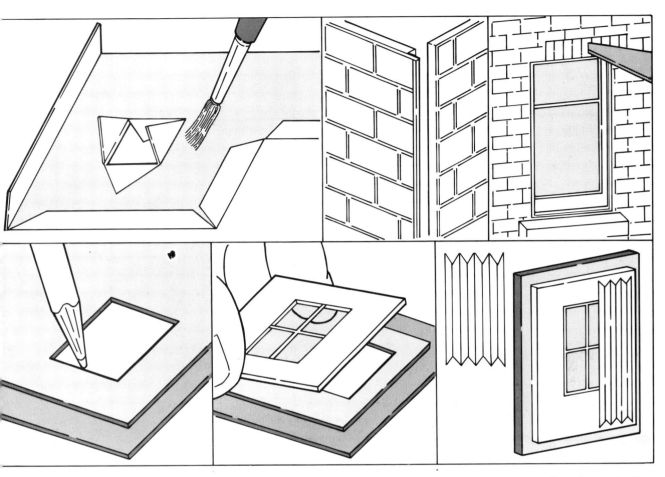

DDING DEPTH AND DETAIL TO ELEVA-
IONS

s produced, the thin card on which cardboard kits
e printed is much too thin at OO/HO scale to
present the thickness of the walls, and much the
ame applies to the N gauge range of buildings. By
arefully selecting additional cardboard backing,
ese elevations can easily be made thicker and
uer to scale.

The Graham Farish range of N gauge buildings
e among the easiest to change, as the majority of
e buildings are on a modular system which makes
e interchange of elevations easy. To add depth the
odeller simply applies the self-adhesive elevations
a sheet of suitable thickness cardboard. The
echnique is first to cut out the windows and doors
aving in place the backing that protects the
dhesive. These doors and windows are now placed
one side, then the protective backing to the
evation is removed and the cut-out elevation is
tuck on to a sheet of card, being careful to avoid
rinkles. This now forms a thicker laminate.
arefully apply double-sided sticky tape to the back
f the card, again taking care to avoid wrinkles. You
ow have a thicker elevation with an adhesive on its
ack.

Cut out the window and door openings again so
s to remove unwanted card and paint the exposed
ard edges to suit. On completion, stick the
elevation in place on its plastic blocks by removing

the backing to the double-sided sticky tape. This
gives you an elevation with a recess around its
windows and doors. Remove the protective backing
from the previously cut-out windows and doors and
replace them in position in the deeper door and
window openings.

Repeat this around the building as required,
disguising the cardboard's edge by using spare
brickwork saved by not using it in areas where
buildings join on to each other, or paint to match. Do
the same to the roofs and paint the edge as
required. Finally, paint thin strips of card pre-backed
with double-sided sticky tape for the protruding
window sills and place them in position. This all
produces a building with depth to its elevation.

Normally the cardboard kits produced have their
detail printed flat on their surfaces so that window
sills are non-existent in three-dimensional form.
This unfortunately looks wrong when viewed from
any angle other than square-on as there is no recess
around the window or a protrusion from the window
sill.

Other manufacturers' kits can be modified as
described but are more complicated to undertake as
they are produced as hollow models. The technique
for these is to use thick card or balsa wood to back
the thin cardboard elevations. This must be done
very carefully, so as to avoid complications in the
later part of the building's construction, unless one
is good at mitring corners. (Mitred corners are

Opposite page top By
carefully saving bits and
using pieces cut out
from magazines a
completely new building
has been created of a
Barclays Bank.

Opposite page bottom
Cut out the windows
and doors first, then fix
the elevation on to a
piece of card,
previously backed with
double-sided sticky
tape. Then recut out the
windows. The double-
sided sticky tape is
unpeeled, the elevation
is fixed on to the blocks.
The windows and doors
previously cut out are
fixed into the recesses.

Above By applying pre-
printed brickwork to
home-made cardboard
elevations and allowing
the brick paper to
overlap, the join is lost.
The window frame is
made from a separate
piece of white card
marked out through the
window opening. The
glazing bars are marked
out on clear plastic, then
assembled as shown,
adding curtains from
folded paper. The
outside of the building
then has its brick lintel
and window sill applied.

Above The model of 'Minden Mill' built by Martin Nicholls is cleverly constructed using card and is complete with the sagging roof on the out buildings. This adds age and realism to the model. The brickwork is modelled using computer chads, unfortunately these are not true to scale as they represent bricks 9 in long by 4 ½ in high. The normal modern brick is 8 ½ in long by 4 in wide by 2 ½ in high, but as Martin is very careful to point out his buildings are constructed using a special (but not unknown size) of brick produced by a local company, when there was a brick tax and manufacturers increased the size of brick. For further details of this model see 'Your Model Railway' June 1985.

produced by cutting a 45 degree angle cut along the two corners to be joined together (see illustration). Once perfected this method can actually speed up construction but the beginner is recommended to keep to straight square cuts using a metal ruler or metal engineer's square, and cutting the backing card less its thickness at certain points (see illustration), so that it does not interfere with the construction of the kit.

Start by pre-coating an elevation on its back with glue, UHU is ideal as it can be spread out thinly across a surface. Then, by pre-coating the second cardboard/balsa wood backing surface, the two surfaces can be joined as if one were using an impact adhesive. Since the bond of the join is made on contact, great care must be taken to correctly align the surfaces before pressing them together as you cannot rely on sliding the pieces into final position. Note, do not use water-based glues such as PVA for laminating or it will warp or twist the cardboard.

Having completed the first elevation lamination, cut out the door and window recesses as required. If the model is a Tudor type of building, cut out additional overlays of thin card and apply these over the timber areas so as to raise these from the main surface (as would happen in reality). Alternatively, purchase two identical kits, cutting one up to provide these timbered overlays. Cover the back of the

second kit with double-sided sticky tape and after removing its backing, place in position over the original kit's timber framing. Alternatively, to avoid having to buy a second kit, carefully cut out a piece of card to the size of the elevation then copy the timber framing, using tracing paper and redrawing by using carbon paper to transfer the lines on to the card. Glue down using spray mount or double-sided sticky tape. If this method is used the entire back of the card should be covered.

The latter method needs to be completed with great care so as not to distort the size of the elevation. The use of double-sided sticky tape has an advantage over conventional glues in this particular situation, as with a lot of small joins on one piece it is difficult to apply the glue in such a way that it has not dried at one end whilst one is still applying it at the other end. An alternative to double-sided sticky tape is to place the cut-out elevation face down and spray it with display mount so the back receives an even coat of adhesive in one application. Then, when the overlays to the elevation are completed, paint around the window and door recesses with the appropriate colour.

During construction always glaze the difficult areas of windows that cannot be conveniently reached when the building is completed and add the curtains, etc. Curtains can be made by using coloured photographs from magazines cup up and olded to suit (see illustration). Repeat as required, by working around the building and assembling it as each elevation is completed. Remember to cut the backing card to suit for width and length as necessary, so that the kit's true elevation size is not distorted. Brace the building internally as necessary to strengthen it and also fix a baffle in the middle of the building, otherwise you will be able to see right the way through it. Finally add the roof and chimneys as per the kit instructions to complete the building.

SCRATCH-BUILDING IN CARD

Scratch-building in card is the natural extension of card kit modelling, this time the modeller having to prepare his own detailed elevations. By copying the construction of a kit, many of the techniques as to the way the components should be designed and overlaid with colour can be learned. A small cottage, for example, will require four detailed elevations (front, back and two ends) plus roof, whilst a terraced house will require more detailed elevations, consisting of front, back, side extension and back extension elevations, plus one long party wall and one short party wall. (The party walls will require no detail unless they are at the end of the terrace). Finally, you need three pieces of roof, these nine components forming the basic external structure of the single terraced building.

To make a row of buildings easier and more robust to construct, use floor slabs and internal walls. These form a core which also prevents light passing through the building. Then mark and cut out the elevations, noting how they are aligned by deliberately marking one out upside down. Complete each elevation's detail such as glazing and curtains before applying it to the centre core. The length of the elevation will depend upon the number of houses that are modelled and its height upon the number of floors.

A second technique is to cut out the doors and window openings, but not to glaze the windows at this stage, and to assemble the shell of the building, leaving the roof off for access for the time being. Paint all over by spraying or using a brush, then glaze. Alternatively, cover it with brick paper cutting an X in the window openings and wrapping the paper around through the openings (this covers the edges). Assemble the building's elevations in turn working from the front first, then the back elevation to the main building, followed by the rear wall to the extension and finally the side extension walls, mitring external corners as required so that the building has its finished colour, then apply glazing and curtains. Now cut the roofs to shape, apply tile paper or paint, supporting the roofs along the party walls as necessary and glueing them in place. Finally cut out additional pieces of card to thicken the walls which show above the roofs. Paint or cover with brick paper and cap as necessary to form ridge tiles, etc. Finally add the chimney stacks, painted or brick paper-covered complete with rolled paper chimneys, the guttering and down pipes.

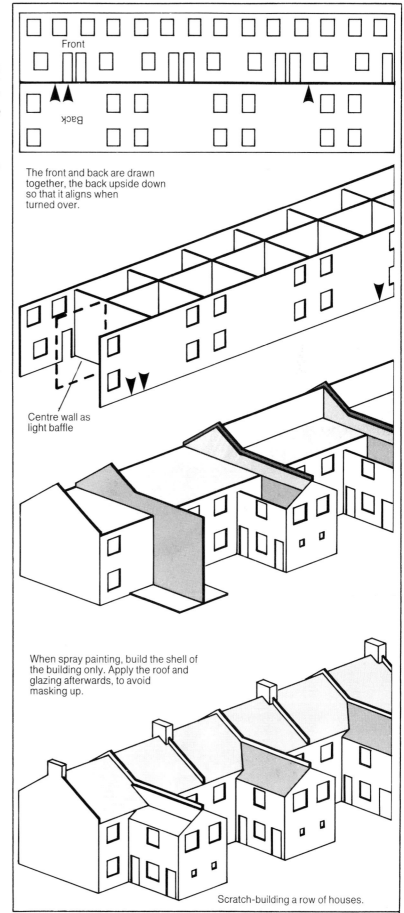

The front and back are drawn together, the back upside down so that it aligns when turned over.

Centre wall as light baffle

When spray painting, build the shell of the building only. Apply the roof and glazing afterwards, to avoid masking up.

Scratch-building a row of houses.

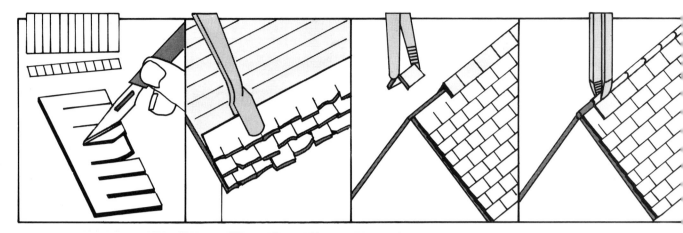

Above Slates applied to roofs in strips make construction easier. To add individuality to older roofs, recut the slates as shown and trim to random lengths before applying. Start from the bottom and work upwards, applying ridge tiles to suit.

Below Thatched roofs require a good structure to support the wool or horsehair. As it needs a lot of glue to hold it in place, this tends to warp thin structures.

Opposite page By photographing reality the different methods used or changes that occur can be studied, so that a street can be modelled with variations. Notice the way the narrow street has been discoloured by the builders doing the alterations, on both paving and road, also the half finished painting. Note also the garden clutter in the lower photograph.

SPECIAL WALLS AND ROOFS

Special walls can be made in a number of ways by using fire clay cement, 'Das' modelling clay, Plaster of Paris or Polyfilla, to name a few. Fire clay cement is obtainable in premixed tubs, and is ideal for spreading on wood or card surfaces, but not thin plastic since it falls off when the plastic is bent. This fact *can* be used to an advantage, Plaster of Paris likewise. Spread fire clay or a thin layer of plaster on to a thin sheet of plastic. Allow it to harden to a semi-solid state, and then scribe through the thickness into predetermined sizes. When it is completely set, remove by cracking off from the plastic. Depending upon their size, these chips can then be used for bricks, rough stone walls or paving slabs.

The Plaster of Paris left over when mixing up can also be broken up into small pieces as it sets, providing small rocks which can be sieved out to a selected size. In this state, whilst still reasonably soft, they can be embedded into a thin layer of newly cast Plaster of Paris, sprinkling the chosen material through a sieve, to spread it out evenly, and then pressing it down into the plaster, before allowing it to harden.

Peel the casting off the plastic sheet and examine it; if the texture is too coarse make up a runny mixture of Polyfilla and brush in to obtain the desired effect, then allow to set. Mark out, then cut to shape using a

saw. For the window openings drill through a required, file and sand to shape, then repeat for other walls. For a garden wall, both sides of which will be seen, stick two pieces together, file and make good the top and the corner joints. The effect thus provided is o random stone walling, ideal for old cottages.

STUCCO WALLS AND PEBBLE DASH

To make stucco and pebble dash walls, first cut the cardboard or balsa wood elevations to size, assem ble the walls of the building and brace them well then seal with an oilbound paint. When dry, sponge PVA woodworker's glue on to the elevations and sprinkle on Polyfilla, using a sieve. Tap off unwanted material and allow to dry, then brush off any furthe unwanted material and paint. This gives a pebble dash effect, which can be sanded down slightly for stucco effect.

ROOF SURFACES

Since there are many roof surfaces already com mercially made, in most cases it is not practical to make one's own, but in some instances there is no choice. The smaller the scale the more difficult becomes to model specialized tiles, as they are lai out very precisely and in a repetitive way.

To model tiles or roof slates, carefully mark out th roof both horizontally and vertically. Then embos card or score plastic sheet vertically, making th length longer than required, and cut it across int strips. Lay these strips starting from the bottom o

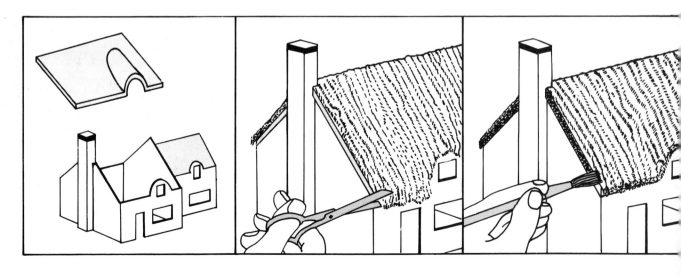

he roof, using the lines drawn as a guide. Lay the
next row on top but half overlapped so as to stagger
the tiling. Cut and trim the roof when finished or as
each length of tile is laid. Use as little solvent or glue
as possible to avoid warping the roof on a modern
building, but don't worry too much on a period
cottage as these are often heavily warped in reality,
and you may wish to create this effect deliberately!
Finish the roof with a capping strip to form the ridge
tiles on small-scale buildings or use individual ridge
tiles on larger-scale buildings. To add a decorative
ridge on small-scale buildings glue micro rod in
place; on the larger scales glue the rod in place first
then cover with the ridge tiles, crimping the tiles with
bent flat ended tweezers.

For older roofs, to add variety the prescored tiles
or slates can be further worked upon, by cutting the
material used through and recutting the ends to a
random length, with the odd long tile inserted or a
tile missing.

THATCHED ROOFS

Thatched roofs are a traditional style made of straw
or reeds, which give a house character. In model
form wool or horse hair is suitable, but you will need
a stout support for the material as a lot of glue is
used. Soak lengths of wool in water and detergent to
reduce their oil content then unwind the twists in the
strands so that they lay straighter and blot off excess
liquid in newspaper. Lay them on to the roof after
precoating it with PVA glue and then sparingly drip
thinned PVA glue on top of the wool so that it soaks
into it. Sprinkle on flock grassing material and
Polyfilla, then brush in the direction of the lay of the
roof, from top to bottom and allow to dry. Finally trim
with scissors or a sharp knife to shape and texture
the ends and paint in the chosen colour, new thatch
usually being yellow and fading to a dull greyish tone
with age. Make the thatch darker under the eaves.

CORRUGATED IRON ROOFS

Small-scale corrugated iron roofs can be easily
made from thin aluminium foil of the type that
builders use, scored with a rounded scriber (see
illustration elsewhere) on top of very soft card. The
second method is to make a jig by glueing a series
of round metal rods on to a strip of ply or chipboard,
then placing the foil on top, covering it with a strip of
soft card or pulp board and squashing it in a vice, the
pressure shaping the foil over the rods into
corrugations which can be repeated very quickly. By
precutting the foil to size you avoid damaging the
corrugated shape.

ASPHALT AND LEAD ROOFS

Asphalt and lead roofs can be quickly made laying
masking tape in strips. To show a rolled join glue
micro strip or thin string to the roof structure first,
then cover with the masking tape, pressing the tape
into the ridge shape of the raised lines formed by the
string. Paint to suit.

PLASTIC KIT BUILDINGS

The assembly of plastic kits is very much like that of
the cardboard kits, in the sense that everything is
pre-made, and in many cases pre-coloured, and a

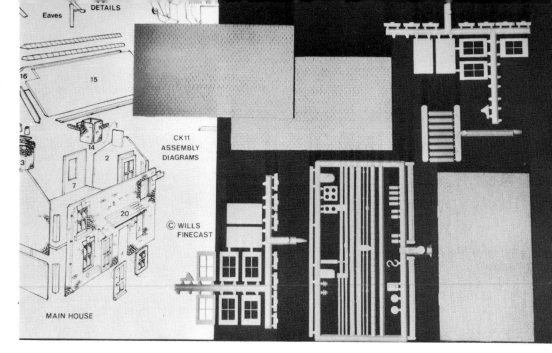

Right and opposite page The Wills Finecast Craftsman series prototype building uses their range of injection-moulded panels, plus some additional accessories. This type of kit is very different from the signal box kit also produced by Wills shown below, as in this case the components simply need careful assembly. The Wills Craftsman series require the modeller to undertake more of the cutting and shaping of the building, working from plans and elevations. Since this is the case, unlike conventional plastic kits, it leads to easier alterations or conversions—the first stage of scratch-building. To construct the kits, first mark out the elevations on to a sheet of tracing paper and then double-sided sticky tape on to the moulded surface, aligning with the brick courses and cut out to shape. (Complete details of this are in the kit, plus many hints and tips on modelling). Having completed this assemble the building like a plastic kit adding windows, doors, roof, etc. On the opposite page are examples of finished models from the Finecast series.

Centre The Wills signal box is a typical plastic kit in which all the components are premoulded to size. The elevations are beautifully moulded, requiring only the windows and glazing to finish them.

Right Carefully position the glazing bars and, using a paint brush, sparingly apply solvent to fix them in place.

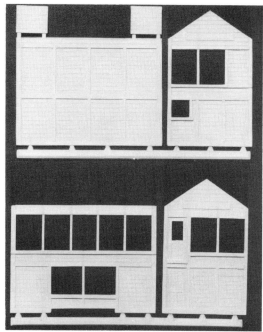

set of instructions can be followed. The real difference is the method of construction and finishing, since the plastic will accept various types of paint on its surface. The surfaces of plastic kits also contain moulded detail, which can be picked out when painting, so in this sense the plastic kit is very different to the cardboard variety, as the cardboard kit has its detail printed on its flat surface.

Plastic kits are manufactured by the injection-moulding technique, which uses a sprue to feed the molten plastic into the mould and into the components that make up the kit. These components are numbered, generally in order of assembly, so they should not be cut off the sprue until required.

The approach to building the kits varies, as some modellers prefer to make up the entire kit and spray it with a primer, then repaint all the detail by hand. Other modellers prefer to part assemble the bulk of the kit and paint it, painting the remaining parts whilst they are still on the sprue, and then continuing with the assembly of the kit. The latter method is suitable for difficult small pieces with fine detail.

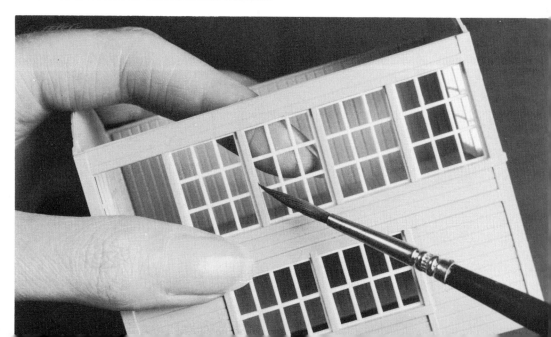

There are various glues and solvents available on the market. Tube glues are the most difficult to use, although they form a sounder join than do the liquid solvent types which only weld the plastic together where the two surfaces touch (ie, they do not have any gap filling qualities). Whilst a solvent is quicker and cleaner to use, it requires a good fitting join to work efficiently. To overcome this problem the building can be glued together using solvents and then the hidden joins (eg, corners inside the building) strengthened with glue from a tube which has gap-filling qualities.

The technique of building plastic kits is to carefully cut from the sprue each component as required. Clean by filing and scraping each component, so as to remove the 'flash' that is sometimes formed by the mould join and to reshape edges or round mouldings, etc. Use a very shape knife for this in a scraping action, so that the join of the moulding line is cleaned off. Round objects generally are the worst offenders, sometimes being moulded slightly out of alignment and needing to be re-shaped.

Begin assembly of a kit by first cutting the base and two adjoining walls from the sprue, glueing all three together in one go. This ensures that the two walls are upright. Next cut the remaining walls and assemble, so they form a basic box, adding detail to the elevations as supplied. The roof can be joined in the middle along the roof ridge line and allowed to dry, then removed for painting separately if required. The same applies with other components still left on the sprue.

The solvent or glue will attack all surfaces it comes into contact with, so care must be taken not to place fingers over a join whilst applying glue or solvent as fingers tend to smudge glue and attract solvent through capillary action, causing damage to the plastic's surface. This is particularly important when one is going to leave the kit in a natural plastic finish.

Plastic kits readily render themselves to converting or extending by adding, for example, two or three kits together. Engine sheds are a particularly good example as many manufacturers design their kits with this in mind. When several kits are joined together the pieces that are left over (eg, spare walls and windows) make ideal starters for the construction of part kit, part scratch-built buildings. As pre-moulded sheets of brickwork, windows and doors are available, the bits left over can be readily used in the making of a different building based upon the spare components but adapted to suit a particular situation.

COMMERCIAL BUILDING COMPONENTS

Various materials, ranging from brick papers to plastic moulded windows are all available separately in model shops, either in packets of, for example, windows of assorted sizes, or as a plastic strip that can be modelled into window frames.

Pre-moulded random stone walling is also available in vacuum-formed or embossed card sheets, although it is very easy to manufacture one's own by scoring card or plastic. Pebble dashing effect can

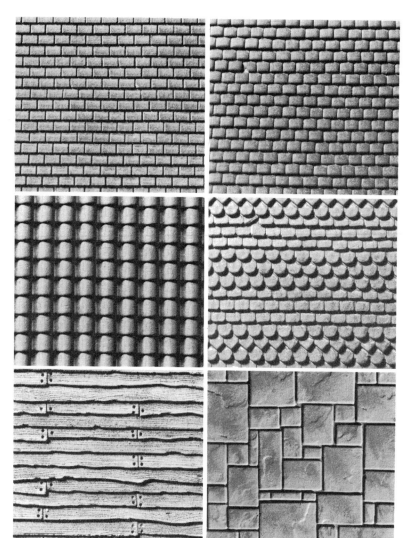

also be simply pre-produced by using sand paper o paper which has been pressed on to sandpape using a rubber roller. The latter method, althougl producing a softer texture, is easier to cut, as sandpaper very quickly blunts the edge of the knife The brick walls commercially manufactured either ir card or plastic sheet, although not producing quite the same effect as individual bricks, do produce a brick texture. Pre-printed brick papers are ther simply applied over the surface of the elevation anc the windows cut out. The best method for window opening is to cut an X, the cuts running from one corner to the opposite diagonal corner so that four flaps are formed. These are then glued through the opening of the window on to the back of the elevation, covering the edges of the window. Unfortunately this method cannot be used with plastic brick sheet as it is too rigid so in this case the plastic needs to be firmly fixed to its backing of thicker card or plastic and then cut out using either a very sharp knife (if cardboard backing is used) or a fretsaw if plastic sheet is used. The edges of the windows are filed square afterwards and gaps between the plastic and its backing filled (carpenter's brummer paste or car body filler being ideal for this) prior to painting in the brick detail in the recesses. The windows are fitted after the painting is completed, thus avoiding the task of masking them. Doors can be produced in much the same way by overlaying a series of oblong plastic or cardboard panels and painting them to suit. To add extra realism to the scene don't show all doors and windows in the closed position but pre-plan some to be open. In the case of doors a group of people can be arranged outside as if a neighbourly chat was in

Above Wills Finecast premoulded panels are probably the most realistic of all the premoulded textures. *Left top* Slate tiles, *middle* Pantiles, *bottom* Rough timber boarding; *Right top* Hand-made tiles, *middle* Fancy tiles, *bottom* Random paving.

Right The finished Wills Finecast signal box kit.

progress or somebody was entering or leaving the building (eg, the milkman calling).

Roofs can be modelled in much the same way using pre-printed card or moulded plastic. The slates can be very easily modelled by scoring a sheet of thin card or plastic. This is then cut into strips across the scored lines and applied, starting at the bottom of the roof and overlapping as described earlier. There are several methods of scoring and which is used depends upon the material: for example, to scribe on paper a blunt scriber is used similar to a dried-up ball point pen. The paper is laid over a sheet of card and the scriber pressed hard on the paper, guided by a steel rule to form a straight line. By carefully choosing a paper with a texture a terracotta tile effect can be obtained. The paper is then cut across the ridges to form strips of tiles and laid on the roof. The same method can be used on thin aluminium sheet cut into strips, but in both cases care must be taken not to flatten the ridges when cutting and glueing into position.

For cutting cardboard the knife blade should be sharpened on one side only so that the steel ruler keeps the wanted side of the cut flat. If you use a thick steel rule the edge of the blade can be held against it to keep the cut square and clean.

When scribing plastic a different technique is used as the back edge of the blade is used to remove a portion of plastic each time a cut is made. At the same time take care to avoid burning the edges of the cut. Ideally the scriber should be ground and sharpened to the shape shown, the idea being to groove the plastic with a clean V cut so that the plastic is weakened and then when a bending pressure is applied at the point it snaps cleanly in half along the scribed line. Alternatively the scriber is ground with a flat tip. This flat scriber is ideal for brick scribing or filling with paint as the width of the blade used forms the width of the scribe line. This always remains constant irrespective of the depth of cut (the flat-tipped scriber is only useful for groove scribing and not for breaking along its line). A 1/8 in (3 mm) chisel is also useful for scribing weather boarding on styrene sheet; simply remove the unwanted styrene with a scraping action along a steel rule.

SCRATCH-BUILT BUILDINGS IN PLASTIC

By referring to earlier chapters it can be seen that buildings consist of a series of walls and a roof, and the assembly of a plastic kit is similar to building a cardboard kit. Each component is numbered and assembled in sequence, cutting from the sprue or separating from the cardboard as required. The cardboard kits are pre-coloured and the plastic kits need painting, to remove the plastic appearance of the building which is always apparent despite the manufacturers' going to great lengths to disguise it. One of the problems of kit buildings is the repetitive way they assemble, each house being exactly identical to its neighbours in an unrealistic manner even if doors and windows, etc, are painted in different colours.

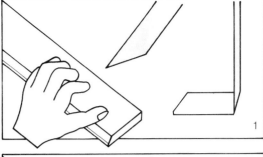

1 Cutting card using a blade which has been sharpened in a chisel-like way produces a square cut when used against a thick ruler.

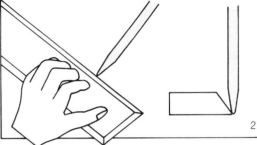

2 By using a rounded scriber, embossed lines can be formed. Similarly, using thin card or foil on a soft surface, raised lines can be made on the back when turned over.

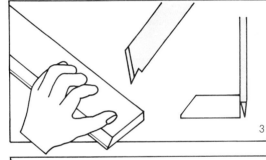

3 Grinding a knife point as shown makes it suitable for scribing plastic.

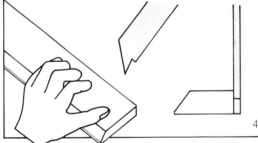

4 Grinding a knife blade with a flat tip makes it suitable for cutting grooves.

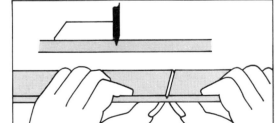

5 Scribing and cracking. By using the pointed ground blade and scribing the plastic several times you form a 'V' cut. Place your thumbs as shown and bend, causing the plastic to break away along the line.

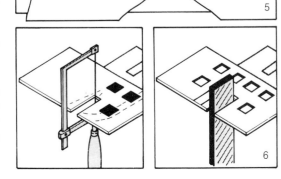

6 A fret table supports the work, both for sawing and filing.

Prepare a drawing to the required size and cover with perspex, oraglass or plexiglass (not clear styrene) sheet. Using a ruling pen and emulsion paint redraw the window glazing bars. When dry turn over, so the glazing bars are face down and re-cover with a second piece of perspex. Looking through the two layers and holding the cuting scriber vertical, scribe out around the outside of the window frames. Turn the two pieces over and place the scribed one on top, then break up the scribed perspex and lay the pieces required on top in their corect positions. When satisfied glue into place using a solvent and a brush. Sand the surface smooth and repeat for other elevations.

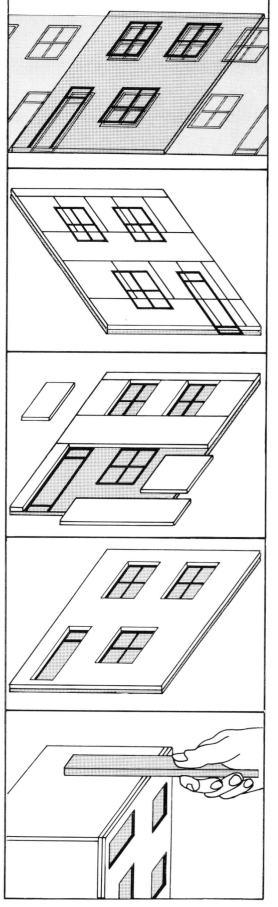

Right *A street of terraced houses reproduced at OO scale. The elevation uses Wills finecast brickwork plastic panels, doors and windows, while the window surrounds are made from Slaters 'micro strip'. The brickwork panel joins can be hidden behind drain-pipes as in the street scene photographs.*

Below *Reproduced at N scale to show size comparison and the amount of detail which can still be modelled, although considerably finer.*

To counteract this each house needs to be customized. That is to say, each house is made into an individual, even on a new estate for example. The houses, although basically identical, are made individual by varying the gardens and curtains. As houses become older, external repair work will have been carried out. Older houses in the same street can well have old dirty brickwork, pebble dash finish left in its natural colour, painted brickwork or painted pebble dash. The roofs will have been repaired or replaced with new slates or tiles, and finally the windows replaced so that in the end each house, although identical in its overall shape to its neighbour, becomes an individual dwelling through numerous detail changes.

Obviously it is impossible for the manufacturers to cope with this type of change in detail, as it is infinitely variable. Not only does it change throughout the length of a street, but from county to county and finally from country to country. At their best the manufacturing companies can only produce a typical house of a type. All railway modellers suffer from the same problem, and I have chosen a typical terraced house found in the UK to illustrate basic scratch-building techniques. The style of house and its detail can be varied to suit the requirements of your own layout.

CONSTRUCTION METHODS

Whatever method of construction is chosen, using either perspex or pre-formed plastic walling material, you will first need a drawing to work from showing all the elevations. This should preferably be drafted out to the correct scale, as the majority of construction mistakes occur through incorrect rescaling, and unlike a drawing a mistake in the modelling is often very difficult to rectify. The drawn

Below A row of terraced houses with ground floor shop fronts, easily modelled in front of the existing elevation.

Bottom A street of terraced houses with small gardens. The photographs on this page show how the same basic building can be made to look very different.

elevations can be overlaid with 1 mm clear perspex, oraglass, or plexiglass (not clear styrene) and ruled up on their faces with emulsion paint to represent the windows' glazing bars (see illustration). When the paint has dried, turn over the clear ruled perspex or plastic and overlay it with a second piece of clear perspex. Now, by aligning a steel rule or square, scribe the window pattern out by looking through the clear perspex layers carefully. This forms the overlay (see illustration). When completed crack out the unwanted window areas by applying pressure on the back of the 'V' scribe cut and as each piece breaks off place it back into position, this time on to the ruled side of the clear perspex (face) ready for glueing into position. By cracking the overlay in the horizontal direction first (see illustration) and then in the vertical direction the windows will remain horizontally in a straight line. This is important as the eye can see straight lines running horizontally very well, and will quickly spot a window that is higher than the rest. When you have completed cracking out of the overlay check its alignment with the window glazing lines and touch in any discrepancies in their ruling with a glazing bar colour to suit. Finally fix the overlay carefully in position (use liquid solvent applied with a fine tipped brush). Since the scribing for the overlay has been completed on the back of the sheet of perspex, the join should now be virtually invisible and require the minimum of filling. The elevation is now ready for masking.

There are a selection of masking materials available on the market and clear sticky tape is ideal, but you first need to check that it does not leave a sticky mess behind when it is unpeeled from the perspex and that is does not react with the paint that is used, by shrinking, etc. (Note: the paper tape

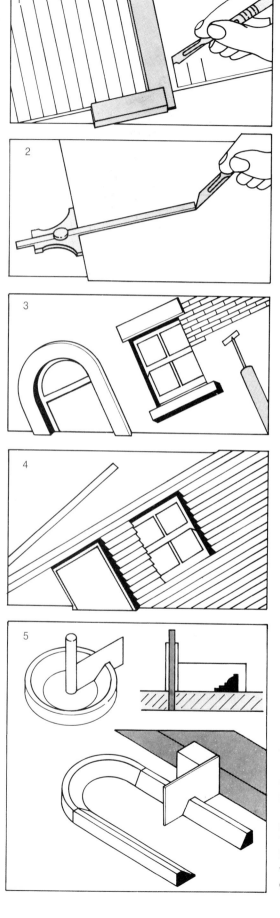

1 With a cutting scriber mark out plastic using a metal engineer's square. Align the cutter first, then bring the square into the required position.

2 For cutting long lengths of plastic, mark out using a depth gauge and align with a steel rule, scribing and breaking in the usual way.

3 Add additional detail as required, computer punching making ideal bricks, although slightly oversize. Position by using a needle on a piece of dowel.

4 Weatherboard is overlaid by starting at the bottom of the building and working upwards, cutting around doors and windows to suit. Pre-coat the paper with balsa cement, cut to size and place into position. Use a solvent such as dichloromethane to dissolve the balsa cement which sticks in place as it evaporates.

5 By cutting templates, car body filler or plaster can be shaped by wiping the mixture by applying several coats until the required shape is obtained. Use a spigot and tube, wiping in circles for round shapes and using a straight edge for parallel pieces; cut and join as necessary.

manufactured for general masking does not give the same crisp line as the clear tapes and is more difficult to use.) This completes the first elevation detail ready to be trimmed to size. Repeat this on the other elevations around the building as required.

An alternative method is to fretsaw out the overlay, especially in the case of plastic injection moulded brickwork or random stone walls (eg Slaters or Wills finecast materials). The method is to redraw the elevation's detail on to a sheet of tracing paper and fix the tracing paper in position with double-sided sticky tape (work from the front). Then drill a small hole in the middle of the window and fret out the openings for the windows and doorways. Trim the openings to size and square up with a sanding stick or flat file. On completion place the overlay on to the sheet of clear perspex and mark out around the openings with a pointed scriber so as to transfer the positions of the windows on to the clear perspex. Follow this by ruling the windows' glazing bars to fit these marks. Alternatively, use glazing bars from a commercial manufacturer. If this method is to be used check the fit of the pre-made windows into the openings and allow some tolerance around them for the thickness of the paint. Since plastic or metal etched windows are difficult to mask, they are applied afterwards. The clear perspex is masked up only, and on completion of the building and after spray painting, the window glazing and bars are finally applied.

The technique for ruling glazing bars is quite simple as a draughtsman's spring pen is used. This is filled with paint of a colour to suit, which should be sufficiently thinned to allow it to flow, but not run. The perspex should be pre-washed in washing-up liquid and thoroughly rinsed and dried on a kitchen paper towel, taking care not to scratch its surface, so that the clear perspex or plastic is free from grease. One simply rules the paint on to its surface using a steel rule or square to keep the lines straight.

Horizontal lines of brickwork can also be ruled in this way or scored into the plastic or card, or as the ultimate method single bricks or stones can be applied to an elevation one at a time. Computer punchings make ideal bricks which saves cutting up individual pieces of plastic or paper. If this detail is to be produced in mass quantities, then it could be practical to mould sections or pieces. The masters can be made by using any of the methods described for the construction of buildings, and this method saves considerable time. The place to invest time is in making the masters perfect, as any damage or flaws will repeat on every casting. For the same reason details such as damaged bricks or tiles should be added on the castings, not the master, to prevent each wall having identical characteristics.

One manufacturer who encourages a mixture of scratch-building and kit building in HO/OO is 'Linka', who produce component pieces which interlock. Linka market a series of moulds from which one casts one's own sections of brick, stone or windows. This is an ideal way of starting

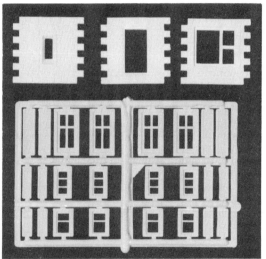

The 'Linka' system is one of the most flexible and inexpensive ways of producing 00/H0 scale buildings. The ready made moulds can be purchased separately or as part of a kit, containing all materials required. In addition to this 'Linka' also produce accessories, including window frames and drain pipes.

Top far left Part of an elevation produced using 'Linka'

Top left One of the moulds used.

Below left Castings and plastic windows.

Below 'Formcraft' also produce a method of making buildings using individual bricks or sections of brick walling and are moulded in plastic. This method is completely unrestricted, since any type of brick—work bond can be constructed, brick by brick if necessary.

scratch-building as more and more hand-built pieces can be added until the building becomes completely scratch-built.

CASTING AND MOULDING

Since roads and streets do tend to have a lot of repetitive buildings along their length, and because a large number of model buildings are required to make a town setting, some form of mass production system is needed to speed up their construction and reduce the time and effort involved.

The technique described is suitable for all scales though details vary. For example, on an outdoor layout the materials used need to be waterproof, so they do not deteriorate under the extremes of weather conditions, but buildings on a smaller indoor layout, being protected from the weather only have to be sufficiently strong to withstand general usage. Size also needs to be taken into consideration. Small N gauge buildings can be cast in one piece; HO and OO models can use elevations moulded in plaster, resin or plastic, but the O gauge outdoor layout requires resin and glass fibre or cast concrete, complete with wire reinforcement. The common factor is that in each case a mould is needed from which to produce the castings.

Since the buildings will have to be rigid, the moulds must be designed so as to enable the castings to be released easily. Although rigid moulds can be used for large glass fibre castings they will require release angles and release waxes and films. For all large-scale mouldings I recommend the use of the rubber and plaster backing method, as this allows more detail and undercuts to be made on the master. For smaller scales the solid rubber mould is best. Since the rubber is flexible it allows undercuts to release, unlike a rigid mould

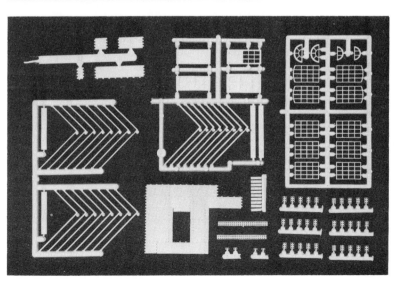

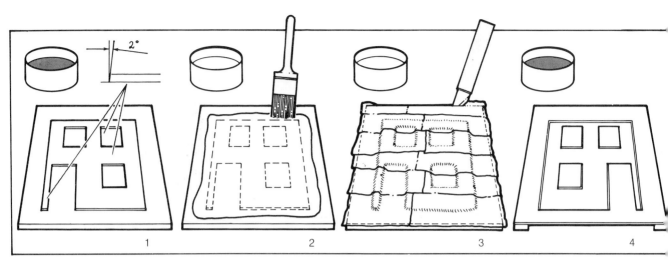

1   2   3   4

Above
1 Make a master using a suitable material, wax it, apply a PVA release film and then rewax.
2 Apply a gel coat; this is thicker than the resin and does not run off vertical surfaces.
3 Cut squares of thin matting and stipple well in the resin, avoiding trapping air pockets. When hardened apply a second layer using a coarser matting, trimming off the edges when half set with a sharp knife.
4 Remove the master when set, clean it up and repeat the procedure to make the moulding.

Centre right Plaster and rubber moulds. Make a box around the master and coat the mould with the latex or moulding rubber (Vinamould or Coldcure). When set pour in the plaster backing, remove master and replace the rubber carefully into position. Cast or lay out the mould to produce the moulding, and when set clean up as necessary.

Right Solid rubber moulds. Make a box around the master and pour in the heated Vinamould or Coldcure rubber, cover with plastic so as to produce a flat back and allow to harden. Dismantle the box and remove the master, washing it if necessary and drying it. Pour in the casting material, re-covering to produce a flat back to the casting. When set remove and clean up.

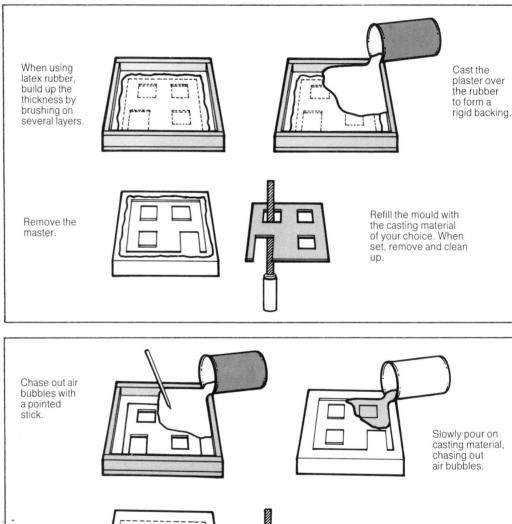

When using latex rubber, build up the thickness by brushing on several layers.

Cast the plaster over the rubber to form a rigid backing.

Remove the master.

Refill the mould with the casting material of your choice. When set, remove and clean up.

Chase out air bubbles with a pointed stick.

Slowly pour on casting material, chasing out air bubbles.

Cover with waxed plastic.

Refill the mould with the casting material of your choice. When set, remove and clean up.

which will lock an undercut firmly into place, making completely impossible to separate.

There are a variety of moulding materials available the market, air drying latex rubber being one. is is applied in a series of thin layers so as to build the required thickness and is one of the most onomical materials to use, as the rubber is backed th inexpensive plaster. It therefore requires very le of the latex rubber, compared with casting a lid mould using a cold cure casting rubber. This cond method, although more expensive, allows t moulds to be produced, which are very nvenient. The same applies to the hot re-usable sting rubbers. This time the disadvantages are at the master pattern must be heat-proof and that is type of moulding rubber does not give the same eness of quality in its reproduction as the cold re rubbers. On the other hand, since it is -usable you can save money, if you are prepared accept the slight loss of quality.

The master pattern is the most important compo-ent. For hot casting rubbers it can be made in card, sin or metal, as they are heat-proof, whilst for cold re rubbers, in addition, plastic or plaster can be sed. The air drying latex rubbers can be applied er all these materials, including Plasticene, odelling clay or wax masters. This provides a noice to suit the requirements of the job in hand, nd the individual.

The basic method with all casting rubbers is to w the rubber from one corner of the mould, lowing it to slowly spread over the surface of the aster, so that it does not trap air. Latex rubber has be brushed on in much the same way, again being areful to avoid trapping air in the mould. The same pplies when mixing cold cure two-part rubbers. on't beat the rubber into a foam when mixing, but ir the hardener slowly into the rubber, avoiding as uch as possible aerating the mixture. When

pouring from the mixing vessel, pour in a thin stream close to the mould's surface, again to avoid trapping further air in the mixture, as air bubbles are a mould's worst enemy. (Ideally the rubber should be degassed in a vacuum tank to remove all the bubbles.) To prevent the rubber escaping from the master, build a wall around it, using a suitable material compatible with the rubber, and fill to the top of the walls, then cover with a flat piece of plastic so as to produce a smooth back. This is necessary so that when the mould is turned over it remains flat, and the same applies when backing a latex mould with plaster. When the rubber is set remove the master by bending the rubber mould.

The material used for casting again is the modeller's choice. Fine casting plaster is easily available in hobby shops and in some ways is easier to use than the casting resins, although these are much stronger. However, some of the casting resins generate heat as they cure which can destroy the re-usable rubber moulds. A good casting mixture can be made from car body filler mixed with glass fibre resin, which is used to thin it so that it flows. The hardener from the car body filler pack will cure this mixture but requires careful mixing to avoid trapping air bubbles. The mixture should generally set hard without a sticky surface, but if this does occur, reduce the amount of hardener. If the casting resin becomes warm in the mould (through chemical reaction producing heat), the resin and rubber mould can be immersed in cold water to dissipate the heat generated (immerse when the moulding resin is just beginning to set). This method of underwater curing will also reduce the shrinkage of the casting. So as to obtain a flat back to the casting cover the liquid with a piece of release-waxed plastic. This applies when casting plaster as well (although of course it is not immersible) since it also requires a flat finished back. If, when using casting

Warning Do not use commercially-produced items as masters as this will infringe the manufacturer's copyright.

Left The 'Linka' system which can be purchased with ready-made rubber moulds and casting materials. This very large range of moulds allows endless variations of buildings to be made.

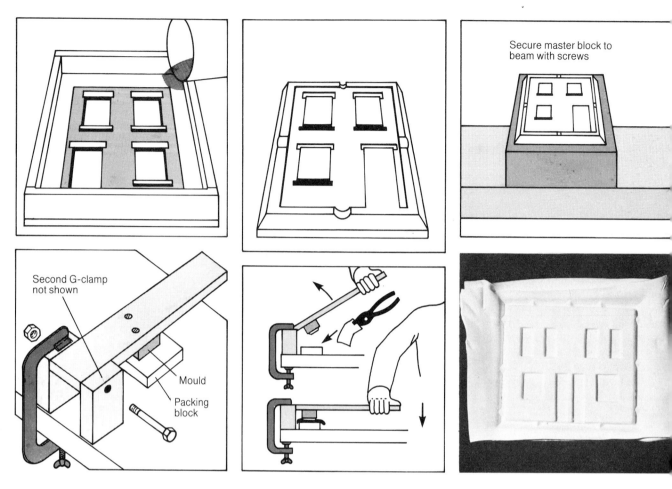

Secure master block to beam with screws

Second G-clamp not shown

Mould

Packing block

Make a box around the master and cast using car body filler mixed with resin thinned so that it flows. Remove and file slots and bevel the edges. The depth and width of the slots are critical as they allow a portion of the material being pressed to escape, and are obtained through trial and error. Mount the mould on to a piece of wood and fix on to the beam used for pressing. The other end of the beam is fixed via a bolt to two blocks of wood clamped in place on a bench. The heated material is placed underneath and squashed to shape. Allow to cool whilst still retaining pressure, then remove, cut and trim to size.

resins, a sticky surface accidentally appears on the moulded surface, it can be scrubbed off with a household abrasive powder of the type used for cleaning pots and pans (Pumice powder is ideal). It is a bit difficult to remove so a lot of scrubbing with a stiff nail brush will be required.

MASS PRODUCTION AND MOULDING

The biggest problem in mass production is finding a way in which components can be made quickly, accurately and with the minimum of finishing. Casting from rubber moulds in epoxy or polyester resins becomes a long process, especially if a lot of cleaning up is required. The plaster method is ideal from the cost point of view, but still requires a considerable amount of time. Also, after the castings are made they will require time to dry out before use. They are also brittle and easily damaged, again a problem.

By moulding in hot stamped polystyrene sheet many of these problems can be reduced, but this method again has its limitations. The technique is to make the master in the usual way (ie, in Plasticine, modelling wax, plastic and styrene, etc), taking care to bevel the sides of each vertical edge (master laid flat) so as to form a release angle. Then place the master in a box taped into position with double sided sticky and apply a coat of wax, then water soluble release agent and wax again. This time, instead of pouring in rubber pour in a mixture of car body filler

and glass fibre resin, mixed up approximately 50:5 so that it is like a cream. Carefully add hardene mixed in much the same way as casting into rubbe moulds, and fill to the top of the walls of the bo then cover with a piece of waxed plastic. Check o its setting time and when it sets to a cheese-lik hardness, immerse in cold water and leave until has finally hardened.

Dismantle the box and remove the master fro the mould then mount it on to the press as shown the illustration by glueing to a block of wood; scre into position as shown and the press is ready fc use.

The sheet styrene (not expanded ceiling tile typ of about 1/10 in (2.5 mm) thick is then cut to a sligh larger size than required and heated in an oven on flat piece of wood until it is soft. Using glove remove the wood and styrene from the oven, the take the heated styrene from the wood with plie and place into position under the press. App pressure onto the hot styrene sheet via the mou so as to emboss the shape of the mould into th sheet of styrene. Hold pressure until the styren sheet cools then remove from the mould. If th mould tends to stick brush a thin coat of ne washing-up liquid on the face of the mould. Th washes off the moulding in warm water. This metho of hot pressing considerably speeds up productio time although the moulds have a limited life o approximately twenty to fifty pressings. Howeve eir costs compared with rubber moulds are nsiderably cheaper.

Using the same technique good quality thin card n be moulded instead, this time using a hard bber to form a backing so as to emboss the card. nfortunately this method is only suited to small nounts of embossed detail as the card cannot be nched into a deep recess without tearing, but it es avoid using hot moulding methods and, being rd, the mouldings are easier to trim to size.

Vacuum moulding can be undertaken in much the me way by producing a master and mounting in a x to which the tube of a vacuum cleaner is ached. This technique is quite simple as thin rene is used. Begin by making an airtight box with opening the size of the vacuum cleaner tube, and e top of which has a series of small holes, covered th expanded metal and edged to locate the metal position and form a seal when the hot plastic eet is pressed on it. Then make a male master or male mould in the pre-described method for aking solid moulds and mount this on to the box. r a female mould drill small 1/32 in (0.5 mm) holes rough the master and into the box so that the air n be drawn through these and into the box. Seal other unwanted holes with masking tape.

The styrene is then drawing-pinned on to a piece of wood which has a hole cut into it larger than the mould size. The styrene is then heated up over a flame until it is soft. The vacuum cleaner is now switched on and the styrene, on its piece of wood, is pressed down over the mould, the wood acting as a backing to seal the edges. The vacuum from the cleaner sucks the plastic into the mould and shapes it. Allow to cool and switch off the vacuum cleaner, then remove the moulding from the mould and trim to size. Alternatively, shaped pieces of wood can be used and the styrene pressed over them. This time the hole in the piece of wood needs to be slightly larger than the shape being pressed, and with round edges so as not to tear the styrene.

When one has a good workshop many other quick, repetitive construction methods can be used. The use of a circular saw considerably increases the range of components produced quickly; for example, wooden roof supports can be constructed in such a way they end up being cut off like sliced bread. The method is to machine strips complete with angles on them and glue them together so that a long length of roof support section is produced. This is then sliced into thin sections using the circular saw. Boxed corrugated sections can be produced in much the same way, only this time you machine the grooves with a flat tipped saw.

Heating styrene 1 An oven will produce an even heat over the entire surface. 2 A flame will concentrate the heat in places, therefore keep the plastic moving to avoid burning. 3 An electric fire (note the open bar type) will produce an even heat; heat the plastic until it is soft and pliable.

Below A model made using the hot press method. The windows were made using a photographic method explained elsewhere in the book.

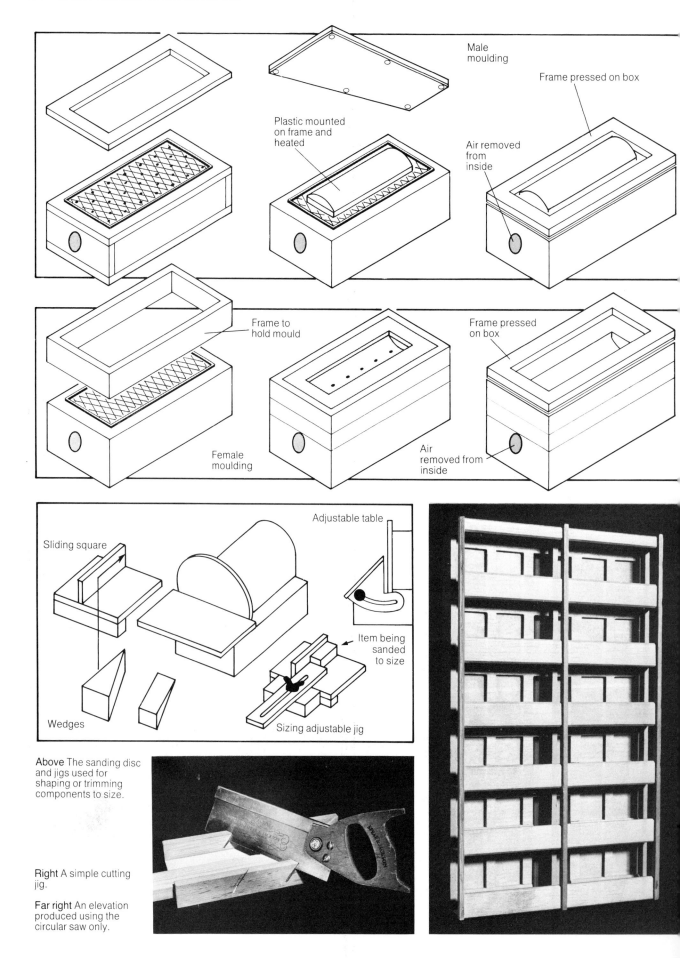

Male moulding

Frame pressed on box

Plastic mounted on frame and heated

Air removed from inside

Frame to hold mould

Frame pressed on box

Female moulding

Air removed from inside

Adjustable table

Sliding square

Item being sanded to size

Wedges

Sizing adjustable jig

Above The sanding disc and jigs used for shaping or trimming components to size.

Right A simple cutting jig.

Far right An elevation produced using the circular saw only.

N IMPORTANT WORD OF WARNING

ways follow the safety code of practice. This eans it is your own responsibility to take care at all mes of both yourself and of others and to take ecautions against fire when working with hot or flammable or other materials. Work in a well-ntilated place with any material that fumes. Never se or work with equipment that is beyond your kills or knowledge, or that is in an unsafe state or ndition, or in conditions or manners that are safe. Think always 'safety first'.

ASS CUTTING AND SANDING

ooden bridges and other structures generally quire hundreds of repetitive sized pieces. If oduced individually, it is very difficult to maintain exact consistency of size, and this then causes nstruction problems. This method is also very ne-consuming, compared with carefully setting up series of jigs which cut the piece exactly to a ngth or an angle.

Surprisingly, the method for setting up jigs for tting is very simple, only requiring scrap pieces of nber. These should be of a hard wood so that they e sufficiently durable, and one and a half times the ickness in height and width of the material being t. This extra thickness is required so as to start the dge of the saw in the grooves of the jig, so that the t is made in the right place. The wood that forms e guide is nailed into position on a scrap piece of ock or chipboard. Then the master groove is cut sing a steel square to guide the cut, so that it is true oth across and vertically. Use double-sided sticky

tape to hold it into position for trial cuts and when it is sized properly nail it into position, so that it is not accidentally moved. A gap is left between the end of the jig guides and the stop so that dust from the sawing can be removed easily and to prevent it from interfering with the jig's sizing. For the next size of cutting a second jig will be required, made in the same way, so that in the end a series of jigs are made which are kept until the model is complete. This method becomes especially convenient when it is difficult to calculate the exact number of same-length components required. When the number is known the jig's stop can be clamped in position. Jigs can also be used for assembly as they speed up construction time, each sub-assembled component aligning with the next. Covering the jig's surface with masking tape and waxing helps prevent the glue sticking to the jig.

Burgess produce a small sanding disk which is also very useful for sizing pieces. Again a jig can be made which is taped into position with double-sided sticky tape. This fits on the down side of the disk (don't use the up side or the work will fly in the air), and fitted on to this can be wedges of wood at set angles—a 45 degree wedge being ideal for mitring corners. So as to be able to produce continuous identical lengths of components make a further jig that controls the length, and which fits the front edge of the sanding disk's table, or use a depth gauge.

LOW RELIEF BUILDINGS

For the advanced scratch-builder the idea of just photographing a building and then using the

Far left above How the vacuum former works. The natural atmospheric pressure of around 14 lb per square inch presses on to objects on all sides. Reducing pressure on one side creates a force on the other side. The plastic is heated so that it is very soft and pliable. By placing it on the box and pressing down the edges, you seal the box so that it is airtight. By creating a partial vacuum within the box, reducing air pressure to, say, 10 lb per square inch, a 4 lb per square inch pressure is created on the outside. This presses the plastic into the shape of the mould.

Below Part of the 'Tuscah Rock' layout built by Lee Clark. This depicts a very finely detailed model of the narrow gauge 'Rio Grande Line' built to Hn03 scale, which is the American equivalent of H0 (3.5 mm to 1 foot).

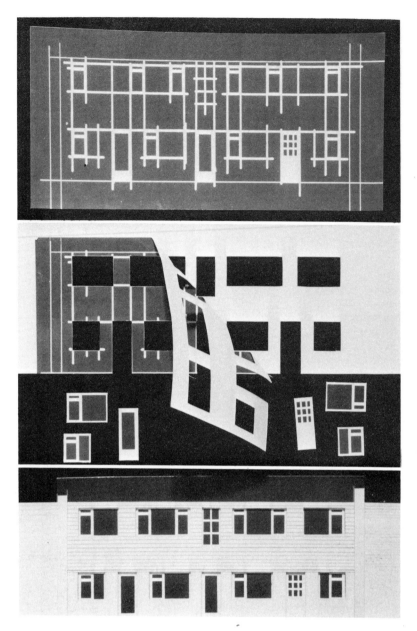

Photo Elevations To use this method successfully, the photograph's contents will require to be scaled to size and to have the verticals corrected. This can be achieved in the taking stage or altered in the printing (see chapter on photography). Use black and white photographic materials, then colour the prints using oil based paints; this provides the opportunity to use various colour schemes on the same photograph, thus avoiding repetition. NB Don't forget to use non resin coated photographic paper for prints that are going to be painted.

photographs to turn them into a model is not a dream, but a practical method of model construction which saves a considerable amount of time. It does have its limitations and for the best results you need a compromise of two methods.

The technique is to first photograph the elevations (described in the chapter on photography), ideally on a bright but cloudy day as this provides even, diffused lighting without shadow. The film to use is Ilford Pan F (black and white) and develop in Patterson's 'Acutol', mixing the chemicals at half strength (ie, 1-20 (normal 1-10)) and then develop for twice the normal time (ie, ten minutes instead of the normal five). This reduced chemistry mix and increased development time uses the 'Acutol' as a compensating developer. For the photographer the outstanding feature using this compensating development method is the developer's ability to produce a good full tonal scale together with maximum resolution, definition and sharpness, and

more importantly it provides increased exposu latitude between highlight and shadow, a proble with all outdoor photography.

Having photographed the buildings the film developed and printed to model size, correcti verticals either in camera or in the darkroom. T prints of the elevations are then glued on 'Featherlite' board. This is a foam-filled boa available in various thicknesses, covered on bc sides with paper, and which is remarkably stab primarily being used for mounting photographs. T board, being polyurethane foam-filled, is easy to c despite its thickness and easily glued with a wic range of adhesives. After glueing the elevations place you cut them out, by simply cutting throuc them with a sharp knife. The cut-out windows the can be partially pushed back into the board, leavin a recess around the window, and glued back place. The corners of the building are cut in a degree mitre or half wrapped and the elevations a then glued together, bracing as required. The ro and its detail is then added to finish constructio The building is now painted using oil-bound paints the desired colours. Add the finer detail (dov pipes, guttering, etc) to finish the building aft painting.

The compromise method when detail is missi or unobtainable is to use the scaled-to-size pho graph as a drafting guide by covering it with traci paper and then redrawing out using black ink (fu described in the photography chapter) so as produce a series of tone and line prints. These turn are then mounted on to 'Featherlite' board ar cut out as previously described or mounted on cardboard. The technique is to glue two comple sets of elevations on to cardboard, one being us as the backing, the second being cut out around th windows, doors, etc, and covered with brick pape coloured paper, texture, or sprayed to colour. The the cut-out elevation is glued to the backing, so th the photographically-printed glazing bars sho through in the window openings. The doors hav separate colours applied, either by painting th backing sheet's doors or by applying separate doc detailed out on coloured paper, cut and glued place.

Instead of using the printed line and tor elevation as a backing to provide the glazing bar these can be redrawn on clear plastic such perspex or oraglass with a ruling pen and emulsic paint using the photograph as a guide. This way th windows have clear glazing instead, and can fitted with plastic window frames, etc. Addition detail such as curtains can also be added behind th glazing. Constructing the elevation as a series overlays makes the work easier but it is the attentic to the finer detail that makes the elevation lo realistic.

BUILDINGS: THE SETTING

The previous pages in this chapter have described wide variety of ways to model buildings, as there no hard and fast rule. Each building is an individu

Above left Start by photographing the building, then print or have printed or project using 'slide' film, the photograph to the size of the model building.

Above Cover this with tracing paper and ink in the window and door frames.

Middle left Produce several prints using darkroom methods as described in the chapter on photography. Using spray mount lightly fix the prints onto card and cut out the door and window openings. (save these if the window glazing is to be flush mounted). Then remove the print from the card which was used as a template. Add detail to the elevation repeating as required, for a row of buildings, then paint. Finally adding the windows by replacing the ones cut out or using a second print mounted behind the elevation.

Left A finished building using a coloured photograph mounted onto card and cut out. Alternatively a black and white print could have been used and coloured.

Above *The highly realistic effect of the water is shown in this view of part of Base 4.*

Right *Aerial view of the town station on the ova base.*

Below *View across Bases 4, 5, 6 and 7.*

Above A typical street scene.

Below A draughtman's springbow ruling pen, which allows the use of any type of paint.

having its own modelling problems, so that each will require mixed modelling techniques. A wide variety of buildings will be found in even a small area of most towns, so you can choose which types to model to suit your inclination and skills. The beginner can thus choose simple block-like buildings, the expert complex ultra-detailed buildings which will stretch one's modelling skills. But it is the finer detail that will add not only the feeling of scale, but the feeling of reality. Street and road traffic signs, lamp posts and cars, etc, commonly known as 'street furniture', and finally the people themselves, all add life to the setting. It is quite surprising just how many cars and people are needed; for instance, a busy high street can be full of traffic and the pavements absolutely crowded with people going into and out of shops, crossing the road, etc. A road crossing forms a good focal point for people and by using the crossing to stop the traffic, some explanation is given to the eye as to why the traffic is stationary. Thus the scene in the end can become like a still photograph, fooling the eye into believing it is reality.

Model people generally look very static unless they are particularly well sculpted, and due to technical reasons in mass production figures can look rather lifeless. This impression can be overcome by arranging figures with static postures at the edges of roads as if waiting to cross, in queues at bus stops or in groups apparently talking to each other, generally positioned in the most awkward of places which cause pedestrian congestion!

Shops themselves will contain all sorts of advertising and signs adding colour to the scene. All the buildings will be in various states of repair, some

newly painted in fresh colours and of mode design, whilst others will look weathered, worn ar in need of repair, all again adding character to th street.

THE RULING PEN

A lot of fine line detail can be completed using draughtsman's spring bow ruling pen of th old-fashioned type. These pens have adjustab settings so that the lines they draw can be varied width. Also, since the pen's nib is made from meta it can be used with all types of paint without damag and easily cleaned with thinners or by scraping wi a knife. The secret of using this type of pen lies mixing the paint. If it is too thin or the nib over-filled then it blobs, if it is too thick it will n work at all. So it requires some trial and error wi each paint to get the mix right. Fill the pen using paint brush and take care not to paint the sides of th pen, so clean smudge-free lines can be drawn. T help prevent paint creeping under the ruler suppo the ruler on a strip of thick card taped into positic with double-sided sticky tape about 1/8 in (3 mn back from the edge or make a bridge rule supported on blocks at each end. This is ideal fc working over wet lines to speed things up. By rulin a tone over a colour, shadow can be formed on a fla surface. Shutters, for example, can be made ver quickly this way by ruling a series of lines. Th technique is first to paint the main shutter colou over a piece of card, then to rule in a series of darke tone lines horizontally using the same base colou but with black added to it. Draw these lines at th distance apart that the shutter slats would be, thu forming a shadow line, then directly underneat these draw black lines, representing the gaps in th shutter. Now vertically size the shutter by drawing thin dark lines followed on the outside with a line of the original shutter colour, then paint the surround using a brush. When dry cut out the shutter and paint the edges to match the original main shutter's colour, which finishes the job.

Doors can also be produced in the same way by ruling on a series of dark and light lines to represent the panels. The technique is to draw the top and one side of each panel in a dark line and the bottom and the opposite side in a lighter line. Always keeping the dark to the right and the light to the left (or vice versa) so that as a series of doors are made over a period of time they always match. Brickwork can also be ruled up in the same way but this is very time-consuming.

Small lettering on shop signs, etc, can be hand-written using this type of pen or by using dry transfers such as Letraset. The technique with these is to use a straight line as a guide. A strip of the backing paper is ideal, sticky-taped into position, as this also helps prevent unwanted letters detaching themselves from the main sheet. The letters are positioned and spaced by eye or with the end of the automatic spacing printed under the letters on the transfer sheet. Then rub the surface of the sheet with a blunt instrument (eg, the end of a paintbrush or a dried up ball point pen), taking care to rub only over the letter you want removed, then carefully lifting the sheet of letters to make sure it has properly detached itself. Since dry transfer is available in a very wide range of sizes and typefaces, virtually any lettering can be reproduced. Unfortunately the colours are restricted.

Repetitive signs can be made up photographically by photographing the original or by producing artwork to suit, using dry transfer or hand-written methods. These can be made considerably larger than required then photographed on line or litho film which 'sees' no tones, only black and white, then sized using the enlarger. The print is then dyed to suit, producing coloured lettering on a dark or black background or black lettering on a white or dyed colour background. The same artwork can be used a number of times without being too obvious. Alternatively, plastic or rubber letters of the 'John Bull' printing kit type can be used, although they will only produce signs in one typeface. However, the letters can be used over and over again so this method is far cheaper than using dry transfer sheets. Signs made this way can also be photo-graphically reduced or enlarged, of course, and coloured.

FITTING THE BUILDINGS

The correct siting of a building upon a baseboard is one of the most important points of a layout, as buildings which do not sit squarely and which lean at all angles look most unrealistic. The easiest method is to arrange the site of the building to be flat. Unfortunately this is not always possible. On a flat baseboard one simply models to ground level only, but on a contoured base this is not possible so the

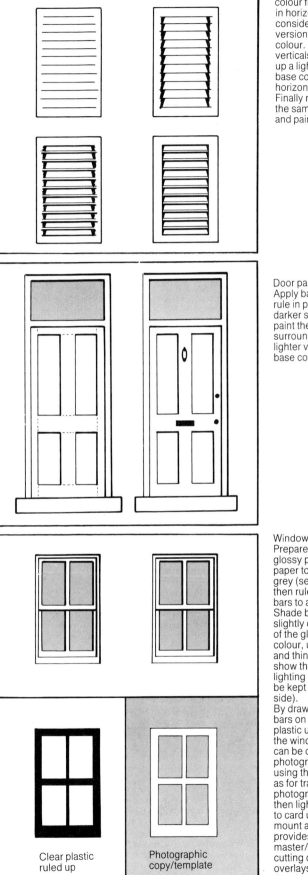

Shutters. Apply base colour first then rule in horizontals with a considerably darker version of the base colour. Now rule the verticals and shade. Mix up a lighter shade of the base colour and rule in horizontal highlights. Finally rule in verticals in the same lighter shade and paint surrounds.

Door panels. Apply base colour then rule in panels with a darker shade. Then paint the frame surround a slightly lighter version of the base colour.

Windows. Prepare a sheet of glossy photographic paper to a mid tone of grey (see Chapter 9), then rule in the glazing bars to a suitable colour. Shade by ruling in a slightly darker version of the glazing bar colour, using thicker and thinner lines to show the direction of lighting (which should be kept on the same side).
By drawing the glazing bars on a sheet of clear plastic using emulsion, the window glazing bars can be copied on to photographic paper using the same method as for tracing paper. The photographic copy is then lightly mounted on to card using spray mount and cut out. This provides an exact master/template for cutting out cardboard overlays, which fit over the clear plastic.

Clear plastic ruled up

Photographic copy/template

Note Black rub-down dry transfers can be used on tracing paper and copied using the photographic method previously described for windows.

buildings have to be made below ground level as well and placed on a flat platform inside a hole which is cut out to the shape and size of the building's base so that it fits without leaving gaps around it.

For a series of buildings going up a hill the ground can be twisted to suit the buildings by using the front and back garden and placing the buildings on the 'flat' formed by cutting and twisting the ground level. The differences are disguised by using walls which cover the change in levels. Alternatively, the buildings can be placed upon a raised level and the ground shaped to meet the road and surrounding area. Many houses are built in this way, to the extreme when at the rear of the building the garden level is well above the street level at the front, and the building may require retaining walls and steps

leading up to its level. But for the high street, or houses without front gardens, you have to make a hole in the baseboard which is packed up to a convenient height, and the building extended below ground level. Fortunately the rear of the building generally can be built on the flat, the change in levels being hidden by walls and the front of the building matched up with paving. Unfortunately there are times when the slope around the building is diagonally across the site and there are no walls to disguise the change in levels. This calls for careful cutting out of the base's overlay using a razor saw and carefully sanding to match the shape of the building, then packing up to suit the building's level. Paths and planting, etc, can then be added around to help disguise the join line.

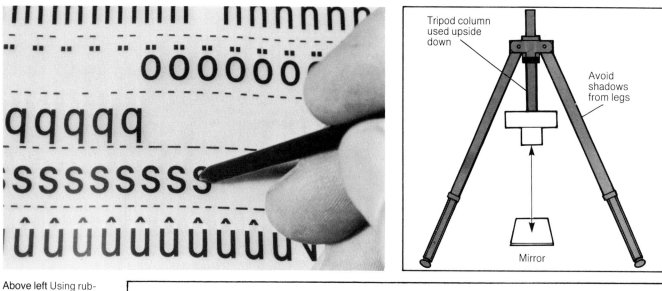

Above left Using rub-down dry transfers, using the rounded end of a paintbrush handle.

Above right By looking through the viewfinder of a camera and aligning the mirror to reflect back through the lens, the camera can be adjusted until it is vertical.

Tripod column used upside down

Avoid shadows from legs

Mirror

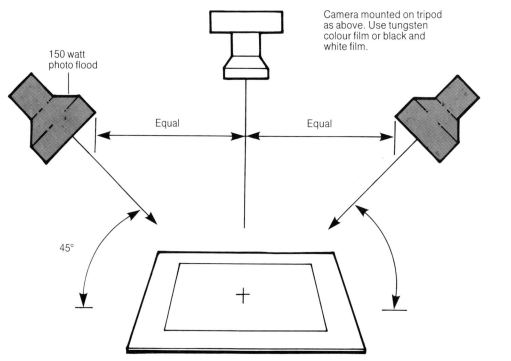

Right Lighting for flat copying. The lamps should be placed at 45 degrees as shown and equally spaced apart. Take a light reading from a mid grey piece of matt card and use the exposure given to 'set the camera'. Note—household 100 watt bulbs are only suitable for black and white film.

Camera mounted on tripod as above. Use tungsten colour film or black and white film.

150 watt photo flood

Equal   Equal

45°

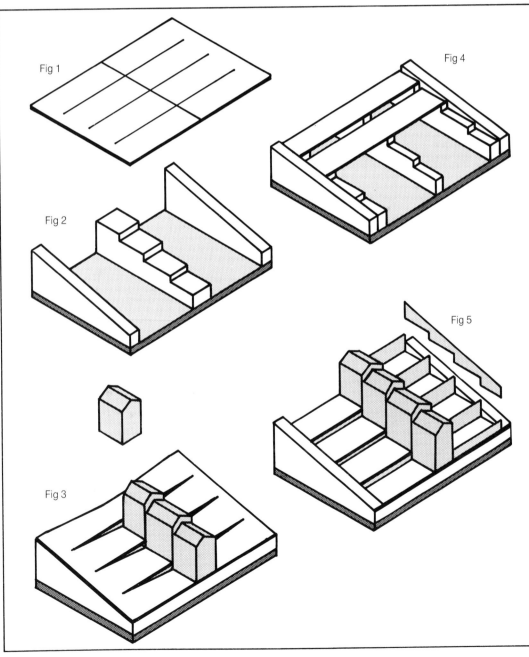

Above left Sinking a building into a prepared cut-out, down to foundation level. Note materials added to building to form a flat base.

Above Typical example of how to fit buildings on a slope using blocks.

Left By cutting hardboard and warping it to suit the contours of the ground, a series of concealed steps can be created, giving a flat base on which to stand buildings.

Fig 1 Hardboard or cardboard with slots cut

Fig 2 Blocks cut out to levels required and fixed to base with nails and glue

Fig 3 Hardboard or cardboard fixed to the blocks using nails and glue, warping the surface to provide flat areas for the buildings to sit on

Fig 4 Alternative method—strips of hardboard or cardboard fixed over blocks

Fig 5 Buildings fitted to strips and walls used to disguise changes in level

Fig 1

Fig 2

Fig 3

Fig 4

Fig 5

6. PAINTING AND WEATHERING

Previous page The well-weathered 'King George V' locomotive produced by Lima. The 'smoke' in the photograph has been added using darkroom trickery.

Below The return loop base 03 is shown with the covers removed. These allow access to the track. Paving is used to conceal the join on the road edges. To locate the removable panels there is a lip (covered in grass material) around the baseboard edges, which also help to prevent them falling out when the base is tilted sideways. All buildings, people, cars and trees, etc, should be firmly fixed to the bases for the same reason.

Painting and weathering complement landscaping in creating the overall impression which gives immediate impact to a layout, as the eye sees these first before going closer to inspect the detail of the model. It is well known that the painting will make or break the appearance of a model, and surprisingly a poor model well painted can look far better than a good model spoiled by poor painting.

COUNTRY SCENERY

Landscaping the country scenery on a baseboard is best started with the roads, by applying basic colours depending upon the road's surface. Tarmac, for example, is a very dark brown-black, roads surfaced with slate chips are a light grey whilst natural stone chips are a biscuit colour. I have found that the best type of paint to use is matt emulsion. On top of this base colour is added the weathering, caused by passing vehicles' tyres which tend to keep certain parts of the road clean, whilst depositing dirt and dust in other parts, especially the edges. This changes the road's colour in places and is particularly noticeable on single width country roads where the traffic is forced to use the centre part of the road only.

To represent this dirt colour mix up matt emulsion paint using white, brown and black plus the soil colour of the adjacent fields. Mix all the colours together in approximately equal amounts so that

they total about an egg cup full of colour. Then thin with about 65 per cent water and about five per cent white PVA glue so as to form a thin dirty wash of colour. Apply liberally to the road's pre-coloured surface then, using a soft camel or sable haired brush which has been partially dried on household kitchen roll, brush along the part of the road that the vehicles travel along, so as to dry it. Finally sprinkle on some very fine dirt and dust that has been sifted through a nylon stocking on to the remaining wet areas, so as to form a dirt texture deposit by the edges of the road. Use very little as the diluted glue/paint mixture has very limited glueing capabilities. Just enough is needed to form a dusting of texture. When dry, clean off any unglued texture with a vacuum cleaner and soft brush.

Now paint the edges of the road and surrounding fields, etc, with soil colour using emulsion paint. This again forms a base colour on which to work. Now repaint the edges of the road with soil colour, this time using an oil-bound matt paint, and texture on top of the wet paint with the fine dirt texture and allow to dry before cleaning off any unwanted texture. Finally repaint the remaining areas in soil colour again, using matt oil-bound paint as this stays stickier longer, making the larger areas easier to work on. Over this wet paint sprinkle a series of textures, starting with various shades of grass

coloured texture. Begin at the edges of the road as these tend to be a dirty colour compared with the grass a few feet away from the edge of the road. Constantly mix the grass colours by sprinkling on using your finger and thumb to give finer control over the amount of texture applied. Allow some bald patches of grass by sprinkling on soil texture, again sieved through a fine mesh, and finally on top of all this sprinkle through a sieve the main grass-coloured texture chosen and allow to dry.

Remove unwanted texture with a vacuum cleaner fitted with a tube, to which the toe part of a nylon stocking has been taped so as to form a small fine mesh bag in the tube. By using this method the unglued texture sprinkled on the baseboard can be carefully salvaged for re-use but any smaller dirt particles disappear into the vacuum cleaner itself so that the grass texture remains clean.

On top of the grass texture now glued in place add ground cover in the form of small bushes, etc, made as described in Chapter 4, and build up height to the sides of the road with foliage or hedging, fencing, etc, to denote changes in land use or ownership.

Grass changes colour according to its environment. When it is near water, inside dips and hollows or otherwise sheltered, it will be a rich green colour. When exposed to strong sunlight, on stony ground, it will be bleached, ie, browner and slightly dried out. Alongside footpaths, or in front gardens where the grass is well looked after, it will be a rich colour, but where it is a nuisance it should be straw coloured as if being treated with weed killer. Constantly change the grasses' colour and texture so as to represent well-kept short grass and rough unkempt long grass. Allow thin patches of grass to show the soil underneath. This is particularly important at gates and openings into grassed areas, so don't cover the baseboard with a single solid texture. Remember grass is a living plant of a constantly changing colour.

Above Paint the basic ground colour then, using thinned-down PVA glue, stipple with a sponge, painting the awkward bits with a brush. Whilst still wet sprinkle with an assortment of grass and ground colours, cleaning off when dry with a vacuum cleaner.

Below A very good example of scenery, made by John Piper Ltd. The trees have been made using metal etching for the foliage, the rocks carved from expanded polyurethane foam coated with car body filler and painted to suit. The ground cover was completed using the above method.

It is important to paint the ballast area a suitable colour before laying the track. Weather the track before applying ballast. Using plastic containers each containing ballast of a different colour makes the application and blending of the ballast easier. Use a container filled with thin PVA glue to fix the ballast in position. The same applies when applying grass texture—use several colours of a similar tone so that they form a blend of colours. Apply the largest texture first followed by the finer textures over wet paint or PVA glue.

BALLASTING THE TRACK

First paint the track's sleepers and rails so as to weather them, leaving three parts of each rail clean, both ends and a small stretch midway along the rail on the outside. These are for electrical contacts, which are soldered on at a later stage.

The track ballast can be applied to the baseboard using two different methods, each being suited to a particular situation. The first method is when laying a long uninterrupted length of track. The baseboard is first painted ballast colour over the area where the track is going to be laid, ie, over the cork noise reducer underlay, then each side of the track is landscaped up to the painted ballast edge. The track is then positioned and dressmarker's pins pushed in alongside the outside rails so as to show their location, as the track is now removed and PVA glue is applied to the area where the ballast is going to be applied. The track is then repositioned using the pins to locate it on top of the wet glue. Check it for alignment, then apply the ballast directly on top of the wet PVA glue and track and allow to dry.

When dry the ballast is vacuum cleaned off using the nylon stocking in the tube method, leaving the track and ballast firmly fixed in position. I have found that this method considerably speeds up track laying and ballasting on the easy lengths of track.

For the difficult parts of the track such as curves and points the track is laid and permanently pinned into position on the pre-painted cork underlay, and the landscape is completed each side of the ballast area. The ballast is then applied on top of the dry pre-coloured underlay very carefully, by brushing so that it is precisely in place. Glue watered down 50:50 is then applied to the ballast between the sleepers using an eye dropper or syringe, taking care not to touch the ballast but allowing the PVA glue to soak into it and hold it in position. The points or other moving parts of the track must be kept free of ballast and glue leaving just the pre-painted underlay showing. This should obviously match the colour of the ballast being used. Finally, when dry thoroughly vacuum off loose ballast from the track, as ballast is generally made from a grit which tends to get into the working components of the rolling stock, causing unnecessary wear. This factor also applies to all the textures used so after construction clean and remove all unfixed particles not required.

EMBANKMENTS AND ROCK FACES

The basic construction for rock faces, embankments and cliffs have been explained in Chapter 4 but it is the painting and texturing which creates the final effect. Unfortunately, like the basic construction it is also something of a messy procedure and thus needs to be finished first on any baseboard.

For painting and texturing this type of natural topographical formation I have found over the years that emulsion paint is again best suited as it has so many advantages. There is a good range of colours, can easily be mixed with acrylic or poster paints to change its tone or colour, it dries matt, it can be thinned and is waterproof when dry; the brushes are easily cleaned under the tap in running water, and it is reasonably cheap. Most important of all though is the fact that it can be used in the way one uses water colours, by applying washes, but it also successfully dry brushes and mixes with white PVA glue which is also water-based. This is a very useful point to remember as by increasing the glue percentage a matt paint can become a semi gloss, ideal for painting odds and ends that require a slight sheen when gloss paint is too shiny.

The technique for painting rock faces and embankments is first to apply two coats of paint to the plaster, cork, coal or whatever has been used for the foundation of the face. The first coat is a priming coat and is applied straight from the tin. This seals the surface and, because of the nature of the material it is being applied over, quickly dries. The second coat is a texturing coat in which a mixture of colours are applied 'wet'. Thin the paint on the surface of the rock face by flicking with water from a large household wallpapering brush. This causes the mixture of colours to run into each other and also down the surface of the rock face. Whilst the paint is still wet strong unthinned colours are applied as necessary to highlight points and are again allowed to mix on each side with the earlier coats. When the desired effect has been reached allow to partially dry so that the exposed protruding parts of the rock face are dry but the cracks between are still wet. At this point texture with a mixture of grass colours by literally throwing the texture at the surface of the rock face, so as to force it into the cracks. Allow to dry thoroughly, then clean up the baseboard using the vacuum cleaner method to regain unused and unglued grass texture. Use a soft paintbrush over the rock face surface so as to dislodge texture material that has not properly glued in place. Then dry-brush high points of the rocks so as to further highlight them. Add indications of bird droppings, etc, to give the impression of wild life existing on the rock face. The final effect is provided by planting small shrubs and flowers in some of the nooks and crannies of the surface. By using the wet paint and the glue method additional texture can be added as required without showing glue lines until the final overall effect is reached.

PAINTING NEW ROLLING STOCK

The way a model is painted can make or ruin it, so

from the start care must be taken. Each piece must be prepared for painting by careful cleaning. This is particularly important with metal kits, especially when soldering has been used during construction, as the flux is corrosive and will eat its way through both the paintwork and the metal. The second offender is grease, as this stops the paint bonding to the surface of the material.

Thoroughly wash all components of the kit that are to be painted in warm water and a mild detergent. Do not have the water too hot as even relatively low temperatures can weaken some adhesives. Scrub the components gently with a soft paintbrush. On

Loose stone and shale. Paint the surface with a selection of colours. Whilst still wet sprinkle on the larger stones, followed by the finer textures such as grass, and allow to dry. Vacuum off the materials that have not glued on to the surface with the aid of a soft dry paintbrush. If any areas still require further treatment, repeat the procedure, this time using thinned down PVA glue.

The following pages on painting and weathering should be read as an introduction to spraying as well as brush painting. The methods shown are suitable for finishing all types of model.

Right A well-used factory finish model suitable for re-spraying, brush painting, lining and lettering. Since this model dismantles into separate components, clean and degrease, removing windows if possible, and repair any damage. Degrease again before priming the surface. Spray the central band of colour first and mask before applying the main body colour. Mask and apply the roof colour, then the front as required, and brush paint the yellow visibility panel and the buffers by hand. Re-apply the logo using transfers.

Using a simple spray booth prevents unwanted paint colouring the surrounding areas, after masking the windows, etc. Start spraying by pointing the gun or airbrush away from the subject, then spray across, pointing up with even strokes. Now spray upwards and downwards starting from both ends. When you have finished spraying, point the gun away from the subject before switching off the air supply.

See p 136 for an illustration of the effect of air pressures on paint flow.

metal components use some pummice powder—domestic scouring powders contain this. It is very important to use this method when the component has been well handled or when the model has taken a long time to construct, as oxidation will have taken place on the surface of the metal. Then thoroughly rinse in clean water using the paintbrush to remove all traces of cleaning detergents. Dry the model using cotton wool buds (sold in baby care shops) or kitchen roll and then place in a warm (not hot) place to dry. Stubborn drops of water can generally be blown out with the aid of an air line.

AIR BRUSHING

All air brushes and spray guns require a supply of compressed air. This can be in the form of liquid propellant which is one of the most popular ways of powering an airbrush or small gun. The liquid propellant has a couple of disadvantages, however. First, it drops in pressure if used for a period of time. When this happens the can becomes cold and will have to be warmed by placing it in a bowl of lukewarm water to restore the pressure. Also, of course, cans of liquid propellant run out. Alternatively a car tyre that is in good condition can be used via an adapter and pressure regulator. This can be recharged by foot pump or at the local garage.

In the long term, however, the compressor is the cheapest and most efficient way of supplying air to both the spray gun and air brush. A compressor also supplies air at a higher pressure (between thirty and sixty pounds per square inch). Although this is not always needed it is handy to have when cleaning out a stubborn air brush or gun. Spray guns also need higher pressures than air brushes. An air regulator is used to control the pressure, as you only require sufficient pressure to atomize the paint into a mist, not the hurricane commonly blown by the inexperienced sprayer. Over-pressurized spraying pre-dries the paint and blows their particles on to wet areas to form blowback, which looks like sandpaper glued in

place. Much the same effect is formed if the pain too thick.

A problem to watch when using compressor water in the airline. Due to the air being compres it has a tendency to condense its water content o the cool surfaces of the pressure storage vessel air line walls. This results in water droplets com out of the spray gun or airbrush nozzle and on to surface being sprayed, with disastrous results. overcome this problem a moisture trap should fitted in the last piece of airline between the sp gun and the pressure storage vessel or compres outlet. Avoid fitting this too close to the compre or's outlet if there is no storage vessel as the air be warm at this point and pass through the trap

The pressure regulator and the water trap o compressor are generally combined, but on propellant can there is just a regulator valve, as gas does not generate water. The regulator va controls the volume of air allowed to pass thro and into the airline. This can cause back pressur build up in the air line between the valve airbrush, causing momentary high press spraying before the required low pressure reached. A diaphragm regulator valve overcol this problem, but will be more expensive purchase.

So as to contain the mess that can be made w spraying a cardboard box may be used with the f and top removed. For convenience the mo should be mounted on to a support for handling rotating base has advantages, as the subject ca easily moved into a new spraying position with fear of knocking it over.

Spraying should be carried out in a well ventila place, free from open fires or naked flame. Thi particularly important when using cellulose as it a low flash point and like all inflammable pa exudes heavy fumes which will burn readily.

Masking material is used to cover areas on

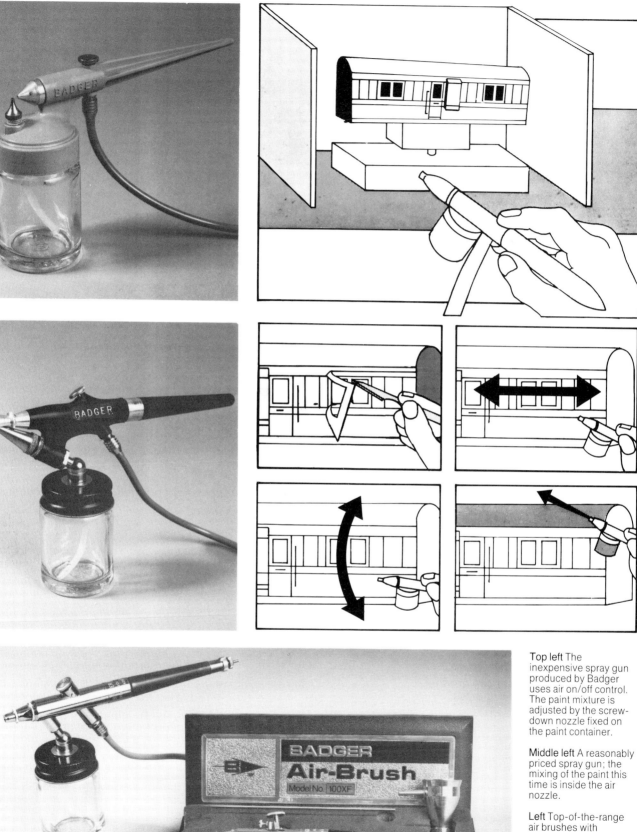

Top left The inexpensive spray gun produced by Badger uses air on/off control. The paint mixture is adjusted by the screwdown nozzle fixed on the paint container.

Middle left A reasonably priced spray gun; the mixing of the paint this time is inside the air nozzle.

Left Top-of-the-range air brushes with adjustable needle and air supply provide the user with complete control.

The equipment needed to undertake spray painting is expensive as good quality is required. The compressor must produce a strong flow of air, more than sufficient to meet the spray gun's needs so that the gun can work efficiently. The guns and airbrushes also need to be good quality as less expensive equipment does not work so well.

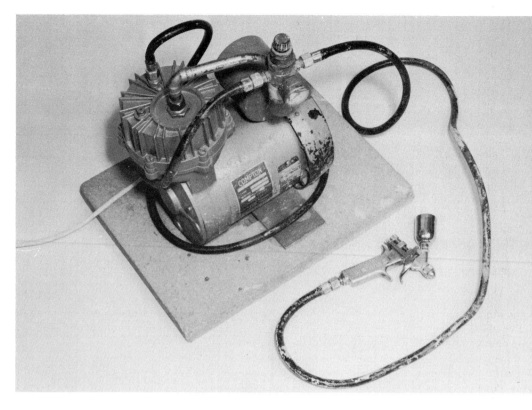

model, so that they are protected from unwanted paint. Two types are available. The first is in the form of a tape, the second is a fluid which when dry forms a protective layer that can be peeled off later. The first material is available in rolls of various widths, and of different types. Paper tape is the most commonly used for masking but does not provide a crisp edge, since the paint creeps under the paper folds. This is because the paint thickness that we use in modelling is considerably thinner than that used for industrial purposes. Clear sticky tape is better for our use, and is available in high or low tack. High tack is the sort of tape, such as Sellotape, most normally found in the stores. Low tack is for special purposes, such as artwork when high tack would stick to the paper too well and spoil its surface on removal. 'Frisk' film is a good example of low tack masking material.

Low tack tapes are used for masking polystyrene, in which the majority of kits are moulded, because it has low paint adhesion properties. Alternatively, normal tape can be used provided that its stickiness has been reduced by passing it between the fingers a few times. The secret of successful masking really comes down to using a sharp knife; using tape for flat areas and masking liquid, which is simply painted on for difficult bits; and taking one's time.

PAINTING AND WEATHERING ROLLING STOCK

The model should be masked for the first stage of colour, working preferably from the lightest colour. The reason for this is that darker colours have greater covering power. Pigments used in paint are also of different densities: yellow I have found to have the least covering power, so for this colour I

use a white undercoat. Red should be one of the la[st] colours to apply as it tends to bleed throug[h] especially if white is required and when cellulos[e] paints are being used. (Note: Never use cellulos[e] paints on polystyrene as they dissolve it.)

The paint thickness should be kept as thin a[s] practical, so as to retain as much detail as possibl[e]. The term 'a coat of paint' does not refer to a sing[le] layer aplied in one go, but to a series of very th[in] applications, sometimes up to fifty layers to build [up] the density of colour. It may at first seem stupid [to] have this many layers, but each is so fine and th[in] that it barely covers the surface, and since it is s[o] thin it dries very quickly. This prevents the pai[nt] running into thick streaks and forming tidal wave[s] associated with wet and heavy spraying or sprayin[g] too close. Spray cans are particularly prone to d[o] this as the pressure cannot be varied. Thus, when [a] small component needs to be painted and is he[ld] too close to the nozzle, the result is that it become[s] swamped with paint, which runs all over the place[.]

SPRAYING DISTANCE

The distance from the nozzle to the subject [is] important and will vary depending upon the equip[-] ment used. A recommended minimum distance w[ill] be found on spray cans, which also need to be we[ll] shaken. This is to mix the colour up and to mix th[e] propellant into the paint. The minimum spra[y] distance is to allow the propellant to dissipate in[to] the atmosphere, so that paint only reaches th[e] surface of the material. There is no such minimu[m] distance when using an airbrush or spray gun, s[o] the distance can be varied over a wider range. Th[e] spraying pressure and the thickness of paint ca[n] also be changed to suit the job in hand. Airbrushe[s]

used at a very close range, from around an inch
mm), and with much thinner paint than are spray
s. The size of the gun and its nozzle pattern
ermine the distance. When a large pressurized
 is used the paint is very thick and is forced out,
 spraying distance needing to be around
nteen inches (450 mm). With a small gravity-fed
 it is around six inches (150 mm). These
imum distances are for general spraying at
mal pressure, but can be increased or decreased
ng with the pressure and the thickness of the
nt. If you wish to achieve a speckled effect, for
mple, the pressure should be lower than normal
 spraying distance two to three times further than
minimum.

NT VISCOSITY

nts' thickness is completely variable and will
end upon type, make and use. Each particular
nt will have to be mixed to match the job in hand
 its viscosity established through trial and error to
ch the equipment being used.

RAYING TECHNIQUE

ving prepared for spraying have a good practice
scrap material first, preferably of the same shape
e sprayed and of the same type of material (an
 kit is ideal). Start by blowing the dust off the
ject with a dry gun and use a clean dry
tbrush to remove stubborn bits. For high gloss
shes overlap the spray area slightly. Start with the
ks and crannies, working each one in turn and
efully checking the surrounding area for wet paint
d-up. When this is completed continue with the
ier areas, finishing with the largest areas,
king through the primer coats and then the
shed colour coats. Allow the paint to completely
 before remasking other areas. On very small
as it will often be found more practical to mask
 paint by hand.

ING

 best method for lining is to use a draughtsman's
ng pen filled with paint using a paintbrush. Do not
over-fill the pen as this will cause it to blob. Support
the pen and hands well by using a jig as shown in
the illustration. Rule the straight lines first and fill the
radius corners in by using a fine-tipped paintbrush.
Wider lines can be achieved by ruling in two lines
and then filling in the gap between by brush painting.

WEATHERING

This is a very individual thing and is achieved in two
ways, the first by using the spray gun, the second by
brush. The first thing to do is use the airbrush in and
around areas on the rolling stock where rust
appears, caused by metal particles that come off the
track and wheels and then oxidize. Rust forms on
the lower part of the running gear, particularly
around wheels and the lower chassis. This is
sprayed in an upward direction, along the direction
of travel.

Dirt colour is then applied from the top in a
downward direction to give the impression that dirt
has settled on top of the subject. Individual pieces
are picked out and painted by brush using a very thin
wash of colour, particularly around areas where
steam emerges which are given a thin white coat
painted to form a run in a vertical direction. Whilst
the paint is still wet add a rust colour and allow this to
run down in the white paint so that the two
intermingle.

Areas that are well handled remain comparatively
clean so use a cotton bud to remove the dirt and rust
colours, or alternatively paint as if the original
paintwork has been worn away to expose bare
metal.

The choice of weathering colours should match
the location of use, as dirt can vary. A classic
example of this is when the rolling stock belongs to a
cement works, the cement powder colour dominat-
ing the natural dirt colour. However, the locomotive
collecting these wagons could be from a pool
service, used up and down the country, so that its
dirt colour will be completely different.

The paint's consistency
is extremely important,
as if it is too thick it will
obliterate detail and if it
is too thin it will not have
sufficient covering
power. Since each
manufacturer's paint is
different and paint in the
tin thickens with age, it
is impossible to state a
particular make that is
ideal—this will have to
be established through
trial and error. One
important comment I
will stress, do not mix
manufacturers' paints
with each other, as
peculiar things can
happen.

Below Fill a ruling pen
using a brush. Support
your hands well using a
bridge and ruler, the
brush touching both
surfaces to keep it
straight. For wider lines
rule two lines then
brush in the middle by
hand.

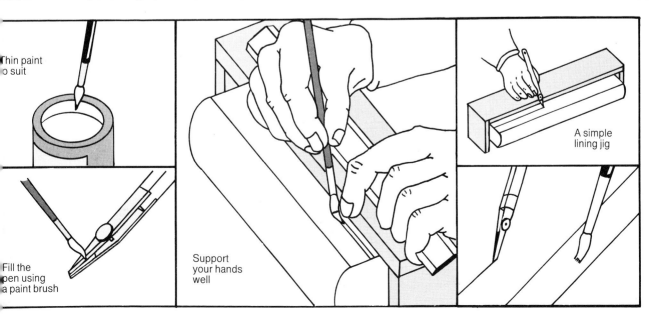

Thin paint
o suit

Fill the
pen using
a paint brush

Support
your hands
well

A simple
lining jig

Above and above right
The street of terraced houses represents a series of changes to the same building which has occurred through time. Houses number one and two remain unchanged, the third house's elevations detail changing by tiling the top part and a layer of stone cladding has been used on the lower part, finally all the windows being modernised. House four has its entire elevation clad with stone, the top windows remaining unchanged. The lower window and door having been changed in their position. House five has just had its windows modernised. House six, the brickwork has been painted, the windows changed and shutters added. The model making method used was the 'Linka' system, which by selecting various mouldings allowed easy planning of the elevation.

PAINTING AND WEATHERING BUILDINGS

Nothing made or grown retains its original appearance for long. Deciduous trees are an obvious example as through the seasons they grow leaves, being bright in colour, then become darker as the leaves mature during the summer months, then change colour again during autumn producing a wide range of colours. Finally, during winter they lose their leaves completely, so the tree has changed its appearance throughout the year.

Paintwork does exactly the same, it changes in its appearance. Once exposed to the elements it soon becomes dirty unless regularly cleaned and polished. A car is a good example, requiring regular cleaning to maintain its high glossy finish. In many cases this is not always possible. On a railway bridge or building, for example, the shiny gloss-painted surface soon becomes dull, because of dirt and grime (which have a matt finish) sticking to its surface. For this reason it is wrong to use a gloss finish on most painted surfaces exposed to the elements which would not be cleaned regularly.

Time is a key word and a simple example and justification for a glossy finish is a man painting a fence, the job being half completed. In front of him will be the old discoloured, dirty and weathered paintwork on the fence, but behind him, the newly painted fence which now looks entirely different. It is a point in time, and by applying this point in time on the model it can be made to look more interesting.

Take for example five adjoining buildings, each with different owners. Because of circumstances

and time, the owner of each of the buildings have carried out work on their faces, changing t[?] appearance, but due to time they will then h[?] changed again, because they have been expose[?] the elements. Weather builds up dirt and grime the surface of the building, rain and damp erode surface, the heat of the sun fades and discolour[?] and through time the building deteriorates v[?] flaking paintwork, rotting woodwork and dirty w[?] dows. The building will thus look very different fr[?] when it was new. The owner of the building n[?] door meanwhile, could well have repainted woodwork of the building and cleaned his windo[?] so that these look brighter. The third owner co[?] well have had the front of his building repaired a[?] cleaned, and also repainted and changed his sh[?] front recently so that it now looks very different fr[?] the first two owners' buildings, as it is clean[?] comparison. The fourth owner may have done t[?] several years ago so the elements have weathe[?] it, but he keeps some of the building clean on[?] outside, by washing his windows and keeping shop front in good condition. The last and f[?] building owner has just acquired his build[?] through a property developer, who has stripped building and then remodelled it, putting on a n[?] roof, new windows, new shop front, etc, cleaned a[?] plastered over the brickwork of the building and th[?] repainted it in a modern colour, so that the build[?] looks new. Five originally identical buildings, through time having changed their appearance.

From the modeller's point of view, five ident[?]

s can be purchased, each being changed slightly, volving very little work, but being painted different- to its adjoining neighbour. This is a process that n be expanded along an entire block of differently vned buildings so that each individual building aking up the block becomes different in appear- ce, although it is the same basic structure.

AKING PLASTER

create the impression of flaking plaster, first wax clean plastic or styrene sheet using furniture polish release wax, then prime with cellulose car spray int. Continue by brushing on six coats of matt nulsion paint. When dry a layer of brittle paint will ve been made, as the wax on the plastic allows e paint layer to be peeled off. This thin layer of int is then laid on a piece of card which is pported on a soft surface. By applying pressure th a finger or blunt instrument it can then be oken up into pieces, but kept in order. This is portant as each piece is glued to the front of the ilding as it is broken up. By leaving some areas ear the brickwork remains exposed, creating the fect that some of the plaster has fallen off. This can further enhanced by painting.

LD DECAYED BUILDINGS

d ruined or derelict buildings can be made by sing thin expanded polystyrene sheet of the ceiling e/wall covering type, cut to the size of the building d assembled, including window openings. This is en covered with a thin layer of plaster which is lowed to harden. The building can then be electively broken up as if parts of it have fallen to

Expanded polystyrene core

Expanded polystyrene dissolved with thinners

Stones

Left The 'Linka' system allows easy construction of ruined buildings, since the material used can easily be cut and carved to the shape of a broken wall. Alternatively featherlight board can be used, as this material is constructed by using an expanded foam core covered on each side with thin card. By removing some of the centre core and then refilling this with small stones glued in place, the top of a broken random stone wall can be made. The rough stone walls effect for the sides can be obtained by sprinkling household 'Pollyfiller' or 'Linka' powder on top of wet PVA glue (see above houses 3 and 4). The final finish is added by lightly sanding the sprinkled material when dry and scribing joint lines in as required, then painting to suit.

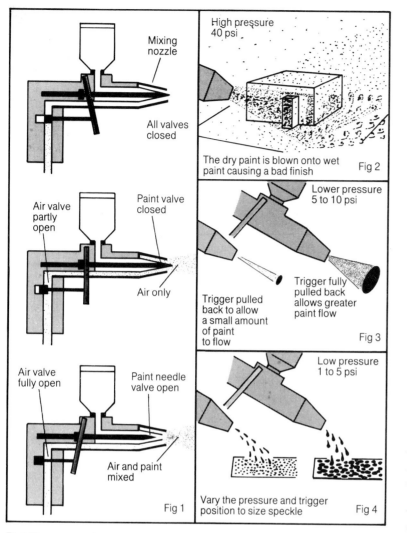

Mixing nozzle

All valves closed

Air valve partly open

Paint valve closed

Air only

Air valve fully open

Paint needle valve open

Air and paint mixed

Fig 1

High pressure 40 psi

The dry paint is blown onto wet paint causing a bad finish   Fig 2

Lower pressure 5 to 10 psi

Trigger pulled back to allow a small amount of paint to flow

Trigger fully pulled back allows greater paint flow

Fig 3

Low pressure 1 to 5 psi

Vary the pressure and trigger position to size speckle   Fig 4

Fig 1 The spray gun's mixing nozzle vaporizes the paint into droplets. If it is correctly set up, the air should come through first as the trigger is pulled back, followed by the paint as the trigger movement continues to the full on position. By varying the trigger position, control over paint flow is possible at all air pressures.

Fig 2 Spraying at high pressure pre-dries the paint and causes blowback of particles, creating an uneven finish.

Fig 3 Left. The trigger partially pulled back allows a small amount of paint to flow. Right. The trigger fully pulled back allows the paint to flood through the gun.

Fig 4 Too low a pressure causes the paint to splatter which is useful for speckle finishes.

the ground. To disguise the exposed expanded styrene, melt it back 1/8 in (3 mm) by using liquid plastic cement, leaving the plaster higher than the expanded polystyrene on its edges. Now fill the groove made between the plaster sides with white glue and sprinkle in small stones and allow to dry. Finally paint as required. This forms a plaster-covered random stone wall effect where the building has collapsed, exposing its structure.

PAINTING BUILDINGS

Buildings require a series of different painting techniques ranging from paintbrush to spray gun use. Each method produces a slightly different finish. For example, dry brushing gives a different finish to spray painting on dirt and grime, the paintbrush being used to apply colour in solid form or as a wash rather than dusting paint on as with a spray gun.

The first stage in painting buildings is to apply a primer coat of paint suitable for the material it is being applied over. Sheet styrene is noted for its dislike of cellulose paint, as mentioned earlier, so its surface is best primed with an oil-bound paint. This forms a key for further applications of paint. The

primer coat should be sufficiently dense to make building appear 'solid'. This is very important wh using clear perspex as it is a material that tends glow if insufficient paint is applied, since be transparent it allows light to pass through it.

Cardboard is best first sprayed with cellulo primer or brush-painted with oil-bound paint to s the surface, before using water-based paints wh would otherwise tend to warp it. Castings will ag require priming, cellulose being ideal in the majo of situations, but if in doubt test a small piece fi Plastic kits *can* be sprayed using cellulose paint a car body repair spray cans are ideal for this as paint mixture in the can is extremely thin and quic dries when applied, so it has little time to attack plastic surface. By virtue of being thin it does hide detail under a thick layer of paint either.

On top of the priming coat apply the final colour colours using a brush. Emulsion applied in seve thin coats produces a far superior finish than c thick coat. The hobby oil-bound paints available te to be slightly thicker than required so they should thinned down as required, using the matchi thinner to the make of paint being used. If you u ordinary white spirit or turpentine as thinners there a tendency for the paint to harden in the tin separate out if stored for a period of time. Wh spirit is, however, perfectly suitable for cleani brushes when changing colours or as a pre-wa prior to finally cleaning the brush with soapy water the end of a painting session. On the last water rir of the brush always use hot water and flick the bru so that the hairs form a point, then store it away.

The use of a spray gun produces a very differe type of finish as a series of colours can be appli over each other by using a low pressure and speckled technique. The paint is applied in a ser of small blobs, rather than as a fine mist as o normally associates with spraying. The size of t blobs can be varied by increasing or decreasing t airline pressure and by controlling the trigg movement. By using this speckled techniq several colours can be applied over each other so to form a texture of colour rather than a solid colo This is ideal for representing brickwork, etc.

The technique is to first spray on the basic br colour, then to speckle it with a lighter colour a then a darker colour, finally repeating with the ba colour. Repeating this process until an ev speckled effect has been obtained, increasing decreasing pressure as required to vary the size the speckles.

BRUSH PAINTING

Painting buildings using a brush the technique very much like an artist painting a picture. A sing colour is never applied to represent the brickwork roof, etc, but a series of colours are used, all simil in their tone, so as to form a texture. A brick wall, f example, contains several tones, as each brick is individual with its own but similar colour.

When brush painting, the building should b constructed in such a way as to make it easier

Above A mixture of brush painting and airbrushing
[us]ed to weather the locomotive. An airbrush
[pr]oduces a finer spray than a spray gun.

Below The left-hand elevation was brush painted
using the same colours as the right-hand side
elevation which was speckled using a spray gun.
This was considerably quicker than painting by
hand.

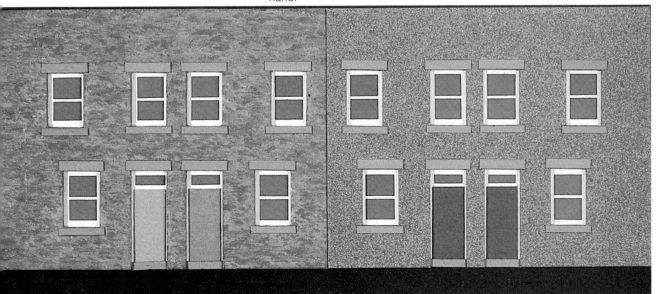

paint. For example, doors and the windows' glazin
should be left off, as the plastic pre-moulde
window bars are much easier to paint without th
clear glazing in place. When the ruled line windo
method has been used, the complete window ca
be masked, as the windows' surfaces are flat. Th
applied window glazing bar method is alway
difficult, requiring utmost care when painting, as th
method relies on the glazing to hold the glazing ba
in position. Alternatively this can be made easier b
pre-painting the glazing strips used and touching
as required.

The choice of brushes is very important, fine sab
haired or tapered nylon bristle brushes being idea
The technique that I use is first to prime the surfac
using a can of spray primer or household oil-base
undercoat, thinned down 50:50. When dry I ad
further colour, using oil-bound or household emu
sion paints and forming several toned colours b
adding black or white to the basic colour. App
several thin coats to build up the colour rather tha
one thick coat. By adding texture to the paint (e
fine pummice powder or sand) further effects can b
obtained. Unfortunately this type of mixture in th
paint quickly destroys sable haired brushes, so us
the nylon types.

It is very important to buy good brushes, as th
coarse-haired cheap types really do prevent fir
workmanship. I have found through practice that it
very worthwhile to invest in a selection of goo
quality fine-haired artist's brushes of the sable ar
the 'Daler Dalon' nylon type, which properly looke
after return their investment. These types of brus
have a very long life when using oil-bound paint, b
their working life is considerably reduced whe
using emulsions, so always clean brushes proper
after use and store so as to protect their points.

The choice of bristle length is also important, a
short-haired brushes carry very little paint. Th

onger-haired brushes still come to a point but carry much more paint, and I find them easier to use as one is not constantly recharging the brush with paint. This is particularly important when painting edges and straight lines. Chisel-pointed brushes are also useful as these allow you to paint up to an edge, by using an upwards stroke into the edge or recess rather than trying to paint along it.

The buildings' construction is also important as this influences the type of paint that can be used. Card buildings as noted earlier absorb moisture so they need to be primed with oil or cellulose paint before using water-based paints. Oil paint at times does have an advantage over water-based paints, in that since they do not warp card, and because they stay wet longer, textures can be sprinkled on to the paint's wet surface rather than mixing textures with the paint. Use fine sand or pumice powder filtered through a nylon stocking stretched over a wire frame to form a sieve, or a tea strainer. Carefully tap the sieve or tea strainer so as to apply very little texturing material, removing excessive material when the paint is dry. After applying the texture repaint with a suitable colour and again allow to dry to secure the texture into position.

The examples show two typical houses, the first a brick building and the second a painted stone building, each being first painted in their basic colours. The brick building then has individual bricks picked out in various tones, some lighter and some darker, by mixing the base colour with white or black. On top of this a wash of cement colour is then added, one elevation at a time. When doing this lay the building horizontal so as to form a flat surface and retain the paint in the cracks. The wash colour is made up using water and emulsion paint, mixed to the right colour, and applied with a large sable-haired brush and allowed to dry. On top of this then is added a series of very thin dirt and grime coloured washes, by mixing up brown, black and white emulsions to form the required colour. (I use the plastic film pots in which 35 mm film is purchased for this, as they can be resealed for future use.) Some of the dirt colour is then considerably thinned down (95 per cent water) in a second pot, which is then applied to the building, now placed in its normal upright position so that the wash runs down the building. Again use a large sable brush, and as the wash colour runs down the building brush undiluted colour under the window sills and other places where dirt collects. Wash down the thinned paint as it is applied; this darkens selected areas and excess wash is then removed with a drier brush. Keep cleaning areas with clean water until the desired effect is obtained. When dry the detail of some of the building can be picked out with fresh paint to represent newly painted areas.

The reason for laying the elevations either flat or vertical is to control the wash's flow; when they are laid flat it stays in cracks or score lines, when they are turned vertical the wash runs out and down-wards.

Final detail is now added, such as glazing, curtains and doors, some window glazing being given a dirty wash to make it look unclean, the centres of the windows then being dry rubbed clean with a cotton bud or piece of cotton wool on a cocktail stick to give the appearance of careless window cleaning.

CHOICE OF COLOUR

You have to be very careful in choosing colours and textures so that they remain in scale and harmonize together. Using colour photographs as a guide, although they are adequate in their colour rendering, can at times be very misleading due to the constantly changing way the film sees colours. The reasons for this are colour temperature, saturation, filters in front of the lens and processing. To the photographer this means that the film on an overcast day will produce dull coloured photographs, whilst on a bright sunny day the colours will be enhanced and the use of a polarizing filter, fitted in front of the lens, exaggerates the colours. (See top left photograph; the colours are strong, the sky is not its natural colour but a deep blue and the foliage is a

Above A dirt-coloured paint wash is applied with a large sable-haired brush and allowed to run down the building.

Opposite page, top Basic painting of solid colour. The plastic has been primed with white oil-bound matt household undercoat. The colour paint is household emulsion, thinned down and applied with a sable-haired brush.

Opposite page, bottom By applying several washes, varying shades of dirt can be built up. Re-paint selected bits to represent new or only slightly weathered paintwork.

Above *The village of Polperro, Cornwall, photographed with the sun at an angle to emphasize the textures of the walls. A typical photograph found in a visitors' guide to the area.*

Below *An aerial view of the oval base which loo[ks] like a small town. To obtain this effect careful layo[ut] planning is required.*

By obtaining visitors' guidebooks for an area of interest, picturesque locations can be studied and easily adapted to suit the layout. The best books are those that contain aerial views. To save travelling, a visit to your local library can be made, or books can be obtained from the tourist information centre of the place concerned on receipt of a stamped addressed envelope and the necessary payment. Crown Books (Colour Library Books Ltd, Guildford, Surrey) produce a series of books called 'Beautiful Britain', and these are inexpensive and excellent for use by the modeller.

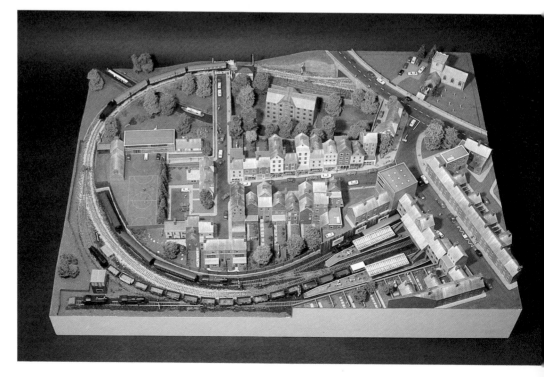

Researching for ideas I found an old photograph in my files taken whilst on holiday many years ago. The place is just outside the port of Dun Laoghaire looking towards Bray, Ireland. It shows a winding railway track running along the coast. Its track level is some 25 to 35 ft above sea level. The ground level slopes upwards at about 35 degrees. A road and wall wind their way upwards, and in the distance the bay sweeps around. This scene was the inspiration of the rock face base 7, being modified to meet the layout's requirements.

very dark green.) Finally, if a photograph is taken in the early morning or evening on a bright sunny day it warms up the colours.

Exposure affects the colour density of the finished photograph, irrespective of the light available. An underexposed slide film is dark and dull, whilst an overexposed one will have its colours burnt out. The same applies with colour negative film, but the filtration used in printing can well cast its own colour change as well.

The choice of how colours are finally picked is very much up to the individual. Colour is used to enhance or create atmosphere within a layout. In the age of steam, colours very quickly became drab due to smoke and grime in built-up town and city situations, whilst the country stations remained considerably cleaner with the aid of the local station master who took pride in his station. This still applies today, but to a lesser extent.

A cutting which has brick walls built up on each side and has a heavy flow of rolling stock passing through quickly weathers (the term given to natural discolouration). Grime is deposited from exhausts or by steel particles which settle on the walls and then rust, causing a dark brown discolouration. Much the same applies to the ballast of the track, as oil and grime settles upon it so that viewed from a distance it becomes a rusty brown colour intermingled with

new cleaner ballast at the points where the track has been relaid or adjusted. The same applies to the embankment where the grass has been cut or sprayed with weed killer, causing brown dead grass along the sides of the track intermingled with the fresh green of the newly cut grass, or grass that is regrowing.

The time of year also plays an important part as it influences colour too. Spring brings new fresh plant growth which is lighter in colour. In mid-summer the leaves are a rich mature colour and the autumn brings forth a rainbow of colours as the leaves go through their final change and prepare to fall from the trees. This is the most colourful time of all.

Grass also changes colour from rich green to straw colour, depending upon the amount of moisture in the ground, so that within a very short distance the grass will vary from yellowy-brown to a rich green. This especially applies along waterways where moisture will have soaked into the soil along the edge of the water, but the top of the embankment will have remained dry, causing the grass to discolour. This constant change in colour, when properly used on the layout, creates a natural feeling to the scenery which is much better than using one colour for the grass, one colour for the ballast and so on, which is most unrealistic.

7. LAYING AND WIRING THE TRACK

The importance of taking care in laying and wiring the track cannot be stressed too much as without this functioning properly the layout will never be successful and a joy to operate. This means that the track must be firmly fixed on to a smooth surface, and that curves must be progressive bends starting with a large radius, reducing into a smaller radius, and ending with the required radius, so that sudden direction changes are avoided.

The illustration shows how two large radii are linked up to a small radius to make a 90 degree bend. The radius of the track is marked out using a beam compass. For larger or progressive bends a bow is made from piano wire, which can be adjusted by sliding the toggle. This has an advantage over the beam compass as the ends remain straighter compared with the middle, which bends more, and is easily positioned into existing radii. Alternatively a

The small oval layout with its construction almost finished is ready for the track to be laid.

hin piece of piano wire can be used, held in place by weights. For fixed radii a track setter can be used; his is a piece of metal cut to a set radius.

The joins in the track should be as smooth as possible and the alignment of the track at the baseboard's edge should be parallel, so that both wheels of the rolling stock encounter the join at the same time.

The mechanical working components which help the tracks' use should also be easily accessible, just in case of a malfunction. Finally all wiring should be tagged and carefully secured to help prevent accidental damage. Glueing a wiring diagram to the underside of the layout helps in the location of faults. Remember, if it is easily accessible it is easier to repair.

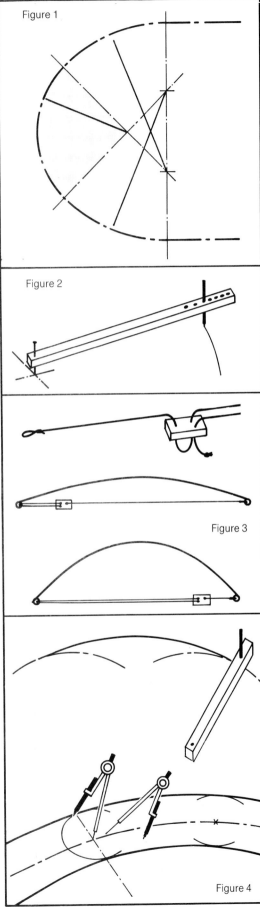

Figure 1

Figure 2

Figure 3

Figure 4

Fig 1 The illustration shows how the two different radii overlap to form a progressive bend.

Fig 2 A simple beam compass made from a strip of wood uses a nail and a pencil.

Fig 3 The bow is made from piano wire and is adjusted by moving the toggle back and forth.

Fig 4 Two radii drawn by the bow linked together by the beam compass to produce a combination of radii. The compass is a very useful tool for marking out repetitive dimensions, such as marking out track width working from a centre line.

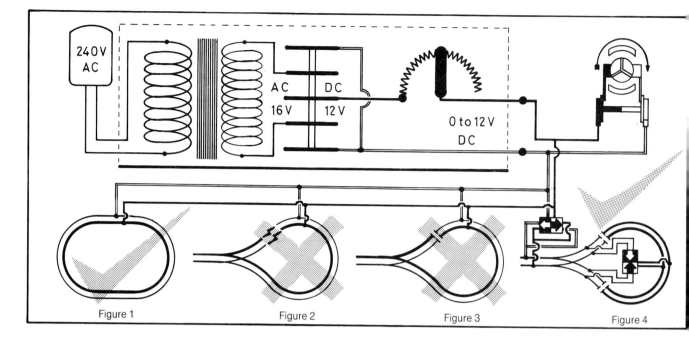

240 V
AC

AC   DC
16 V   12 V

0 to 12 V
DC

Figure 1   Figure 2   Figure 3   Figure 4

Above A section
through a controller
fitted with a transformer.
The latter reduces the
mains voltage of 240
volts to sixteen volts
AC. The rectifier further
reduces this to twelve
volts DC. The variable
resistor settings then
select the power to the
track, providing control
over the model's speed.
This also shows a
selection of good and
bad wiring
arrangements. **Fig 1**
Simple oval electrical
feed. **Fig 2** A return loop
without an insulated
section of track short-
circuits. **Fig 3** A return
loop with one insulated
section does not work in
practice as the
locomotive short-
circuits the gap. **Fig 4**
Correctly wired with two
sets of double pole
switches and two
insulated sections of
track.

HOW THE MODEL WORKS

Since the majority of model locomotives used on
indoor layouts are very small, they use electric
motors to provide the driving force, working
generally from twelve volts direct current (DC), the
same type of voltage provided by batteries. Unfortunately, due to the amperage drawn by the electric
motor batteries are soon exhausted of their power.
To overcome this problem a transformer is used.
This works from the mains 240/110 alternating
current (AC) and reduces the high voltage mains
supply to a safe low voltage. *On no account should
the track be wired directly to the mains.* The
transformer converts the mains voltage into sixteen
volts AC and then by using a rectifier finally into
twelve volts DC. This provides two sources of
power, sixteen volts AC for point motors and twelve
volts DC for the locomotive's electric motor.

In order to control the locomotive's speed the
voltage/amperage is increased or decreased making the electric motor run faster or slower. This is
done in one of two ways, either electronically by
using variable pulses of full power, which provides
greater pulling power at low speeds, or by using a
wire wound resistor. The latter method relies on
special wire that resists the electricity so that the
further the electricity travels down it the less power it
has. In practical terms the wire is wound around a

former either in a straight line or in a half circle, and a
wiper presses on to this. The positive side of the
electricity is supplied into the resistance wire and
taken out at the point of the wiper contact. This is
then wired to one of the rails. The second wire is
joined to the other rail, so that each pair of rails has
either a positive (live) or negative (return) electrical
status.

By using the wheels of the locomotive to pick up
the power from the rails, electrical continuity is
maintained. Each axle for each set of wheel is
insulated to prevent an electrical short circuit and so
as to provide a good running characteristic several
wheels are used. In some cases both the locomotive
and tender are used, the locomotive chassis picking
up the positive, the tender chassis picking up the
negative. This overcomes the problem of using
wiper pickups against the wheels which continues
the electrical circuit. From these pickups a pair of
wires go to the motor's brushes which are
spring-loaded against the motor's commutator. This
is a rotary switch, and as it rotates the segments
switch on or off the electromagnets which make up
the motor's armature.

The principle is a static magnetic field produced
by the permanent magnet. When an electromagnet
contained in the armature is switched on it is
attracted to the magnetic pole of the fixed magnet.

Right A locomotive
which uses a live
chassis. The engine and
the tender are both
electrical contacts
linked through a 'live'
coupling. The electric
motor is mounted
across the chassis and
uses gears to provide
the necessary reduction
ratio. Due to its size the
motor is mounted in the
tender.

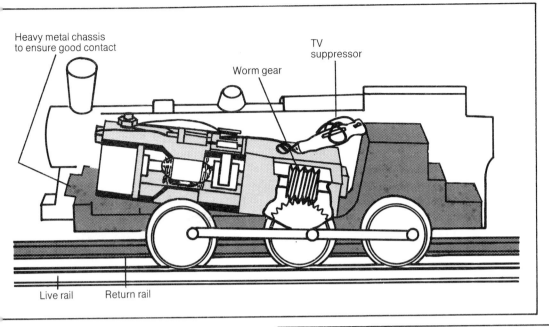

Heavy metal chassis
to ensure good contact

TV
suppressor

Worm gear

Live rail   Return rail

Left A section through a
typical locomotive
which has its electric
motor mounted
'longways'. To transfer
the drive through ninety
degrees it uses a worm
gear and picks up the
power through the
wheels from the track.

Below This
arrangement uses a
switch built into the
locomotive to take
power either from the
track or from the
overhead gantry, and
uses one rail as a
common return.

Since the electromagnet is on a drive shaft it rotates
towards the pole of the fixed magnet, then it is
switched off by the commutator. As this also rotates
on the drive shaft the next electromagnet is
switched on and is in turn attracted and the shaft
continues to rotate, the procedure repeating itself
whilst electricity is supplied. So as to make the
motor more efficient, several electromagnets are
used on the armature, five pole motors being more
powerful and smoother running than three (the
poles' being the number of electromagnets contained in the armature).

To increase the power output of the drive shaft of
the motor a gear ratio of around 30:1 is used. This
means that the motor's shaft rotates thirty times to
one revolution of the axle on which the locomotive's
wheels are fitted. In theory the axle is thus thirty
times more powerful than the motor's drive shaft.
Some power is lost, however, but nevertheless it is
still a considerable increase. The gearing also makes
the locomotive smoother running.

Two types of gears are used. One is a series of
gear wheels which provide the reduction necessary.
These are generally used on motors which are
mounted across the chassis. The second type is
known as a worm drive, used on motors mounted
along the chassis which require the drive to be
turned through ninety degrees.

Since electricity is supplied to the track, only a
single locomotive can be run when the track is wired
in a single one-piece circuit (ie, an oval passing loop
with a siding), but by breaking the track electrically
into sections several locomotives can be run, as
each can have the power separately switched to the
section of the track that it occupies. This is the basic
principle of wiring a layout: each length or several
lengths of track is linked via switches and becomes
a section independently controlled from the rest. By
then switching on adjoining sections the locomotive

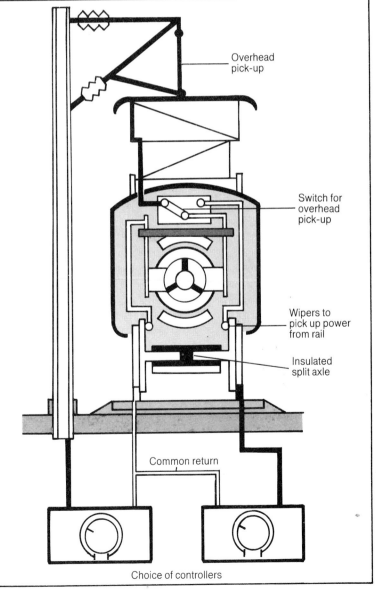

Overhead
pick-up

Switch for
overhead
pick-up

Wipers to
pick up power
from rail

Insulated
split axle

Common return

Choice of controllers

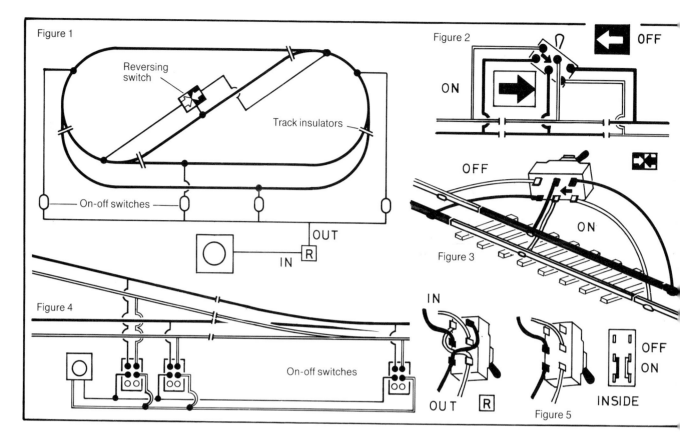

Figure 1

Reversing switch

Track insulators

On-off switches

OUT

IN R

Figure 2

OFF

ON

ON

OFF

ON

Figure 3

Figure 4

On-off switches

IN

OUT R

OFF
ON

INSIDE

Figure 5

Fig 1 An oval design which has a diagonal and a passing loop. The wiring shows a circuit reversing switch from the controller (only necessary on controllers without reverse), a series of on or off switches and one track-fed reversing switch.

Fig 2 This explains the wiring to the double pole reversing switch, using the power from each outside track length to power the inside length of track on which the locomotive has to stop whilst the switch is reset before continuing. (Use the same method for wiring two controllers into one switch).

Fig 3 The wiring of the inline reversing switch.

Fig 4 Wiring points using double pole on/ off switches, used to control each section.

Fig 5 Wiring a double pole on/off switch.

can be made to travel from one section to the next, being handed over from controller to controller if necessary. A problem arises on a single track return loop since a reverse wiring switch is required and that is why the oval layout shown at the front of the book does not work electrically. By simply returning the track back upon itself the polarity of the rails become electrically crossed, causing a short circuit.

THE TRACK

The track performs two functions: it guides the rolling stock and it supplies electrical power to the driving motor. This means the track must be wired up to a safe power source. This unit is called the transformer and is frequently built into the controller.

For a simple single-track oval layout, running one train only, this is very easy, as it just requires two wires leading from the controller's terminals, one to each of the rails. It is not even necessary to align the polarity of the power, as this is reversible via the controller. To run two trains on a single line oval, however, it will need to be divided up into three separate electrical sections, each independently switched on or off from the one controller, so that power can be selectively supplied to any section of track at any time or leaving sections without power.

On layouts using 'Zero One' or any of the two-wire microchip systems the sectioning of track does not apply, as the system supplies coded signals to every part of the track, the locomotives on the track responding to their own code via a built-in microchip circuit. This system is without a doubt the easiest to wire, but is at present only available for HO, OO and larger scales.

Dividing the track into sections is for conventional rolling stock built without microchips or coding devices.

Refer to the illustration showing the sectioned oval. The first locomotive (1) on section (A) of the track is stationary, whilst the second locomotive (2) moves from section (B) on to section (C) where it is stopped. This clears the (B) section of track, and the power to the (C) section on which the locomotive now rests is switched off. The power is now switched on to the (A) section of track, for the first locomotive (1) that has remained stationary. This can now be moved forward on to the cleared section of track (B) and it is stopped on this section of track. This then clears the section ahead for the second locomotive and the procedure is repeated over and over again.

To enable this to happen the track has to be electrically broken into three sections. The rails of each section are joined with nylon rail joiners, which unlike metal joiners do not conduct electricity. Thus the rail is mechanically but not electrically joined. Since there is no longer a continuous electrical link, each section of track will have to be wired, back to the controller via an on or off switch, and this is the basic procedure for the conventional type of wiring.

The passing loop layout with sidings is a good example of the use of two controllers, which allow independent control over all sections of track. The rolling stock is passed from the first to the second controller, when necessary, allowing two people to operate the layout.

The track arrangement of the oval base shown in

An earlier chapter provides wide scope for various running schedules which could be built on a flat baseboard, ignoring the lower canal levels (see the track plans for the one piece oval layout). The layout is capable of handling four locomotives plus goods and passenger rolling stock. The track has a continuous loop and by sharing part of the line with the rolling stock travelling in the opposite direction, a logical reason for having rolling stock waiting stationary is suggested. The track layout consists of a basic oval with two passing loops, one waiting loop and two sidings. It is serviced by seven sets of turn-outs (points), and for the beginner I would suggest that these are initially installed in manually-operated form (easily converted to power-operated points). This is to reduce the wiring of the layout, as it can be operated from one controller plus a number of switches to switch on or off individual sections of the track.

RECOMMENDATIONS FOR THE BEGINNER

For beginners wishing to build their very first layout, I suggest starting with a flat baseboard, the oval shown right being suitable. The roadway crossing the track by level crossings, and buildings, station and trees are placed to suit.

The material for this type of base can easily be purchased pre-cut from a local DIY shop as it uses ½ in (12 mm) plywood sheet supported on 2 in × 1 in (50 mm × 25 mm) timber battens. Since the base will be carrying very little weight the battens laid on edge will provide sufficient stiffening, as not only are the battens glued and screwed into position around the underside edge, but across the underside of the board as well (see construction of base 01 in Chapter 3).

The more experienced handyman can built the oval layout with contours which will make it more visually interesting (also described in Chapter 3). The track's level is raised above the basic baseboard level and kept at a constant height then the height of the ground either side of the track is varied. Fixing the cork and track is completed during the construction of the base, when the raised track supporting structure is finished.

LAYING THE CORK UNDERLAY

Having assembled the base and planned precisely the position of the track, mark out the track's ballast outline by drawing directly on to the top of the baseboard, using the track's exact position. Two methods can be used: the first is to trace this out using tracing paper and re-mark out on to the cork to be used as an underlay (this helps reduce running noise). The second is to cut the cork in long straight strips half the ballast width, with one beveled edge and one square cut. The square cut edge is made to follow the centre line of the track along the straights and curves by bending the cork as necessary. The reason for cutting out the cork with a beveled edge is so that it looks like ballast raised above ground level.

The cork is glued on to the base's plywood top with one of the contact types of adhesive (eg, Evo Stick or Thixofix), coated on both surfaces and allow

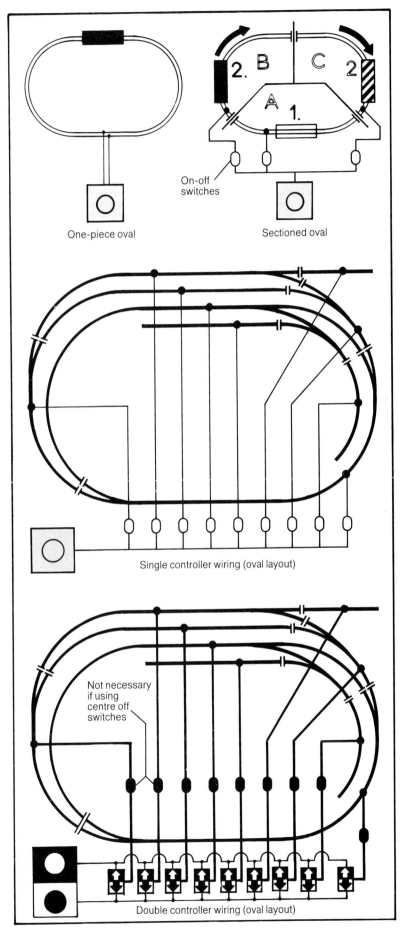

On-off switches

One-piece oval

Sectioned oval

Single controller wiring (oval layout)

Not necessary if using centre off switches

Double controller wiring (oval layout)

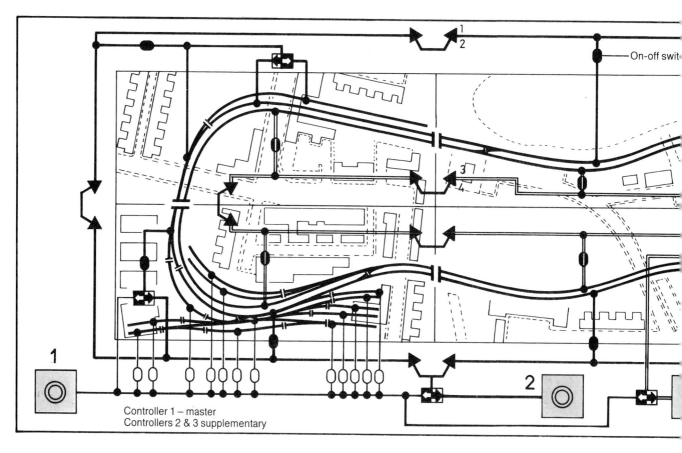

On-off swit

1

2

3
4

1

2

Controller 1 – master
Controllers 2 & 3 supplementary

The wiring to the interchangeable bases uses leads fitted with plugs at both ends which fit into the sockets built into the bases. To provide independent control to a section of track, on or off switches are also fitted into the base. By switching on all the sections, the layout can be controlled by one person or additional operators can help switching on or off sections, providing multi rolling stock use of the track, as described on the simple three-section oval.

Note By not plugging sections together, but by inserting power controllers instead, each section of the layout can be independently controlled.

to dry. (Contact adhesive is used as it does not wet the cork and expand the materials, as would water-based adhesives.) Place over the dry contact adhesive a sheet of greaseproof paper and position the cork, slowly removing the paper and pressing the cork into position (see illustration).

Assemble the track in position, taking care not to kink it or have sudden changes of direction. Cut off the unwanted lengths of rail with a small saw, file and make good the rail end and fit the rail joiners (fishplate or insulated). Pin the track into its final position as required, taking care not to split the sleepers as the track is laid. Wire in electrically separated sections. When it is working satisfactorily, continue the remaining structure of the landscape.

Ballast the track by putting the material in a container, preferably a small plastic bottle fitted with a fine nozzle. Carefully sprinkle the ballast into position and brush off unwanted ballast with a paintbrush. Finally dilute white woodworker's PVA glue with 75 per cent water and apply using an eye dropper for delicate places and a small plastic bottle for large areas (see page 128 for detailed information).

WIRING BASES 01, 02 AND 03

These are treated in the same way as the single oval layout, only this time they have to be linked together using plug-in leads. By connecting the leads in various combinations, different controlling methods can be used. One of the simplest ways to arrange this is through what is called 'zone control'.

Since the interchangeable bases are constructed as individual electrically insulated sections, each

section having to be plugged into the next, it is a very easy procedure to treat each base as a 'zone'. The plug-in leads which connect each of the bases is replaced by leads fitted with slave controllers and switches, the power to which is fed directly from the master controller.

By setting the master controller on full power and then using a slave controller, control is transferred to the slave controller, with some degree of master override, and full control over direction. Alternatively separate transformer controllers of the 'Gaugemaster' type with power input control can be used for smoother 'zone' change over, set on simulated load, as this reduces the change-over 'power step' difference on handing over from controller to controller. The slight difference in setting between the units is taken care of by simulated coasting or gradual build-up of power, unlike other units which immediately show this difference.

The track performs one major function, which is to steer the rolling stock and divert its path at times by using points. To do this effectively it must be properly laid on a smooth surface. This is easily obtainable on a one-piece flat board layout, but becomes progressively more difficult as gradients and changes of level are encountered. The worst situation is transferring rolling stock from one base to another, as a major join is encountered. To work efficiently the rails must align within fractions of an inch of each other, so the rolling stock can pass over the join without derailment.

If a layout is built for one's own use and does not

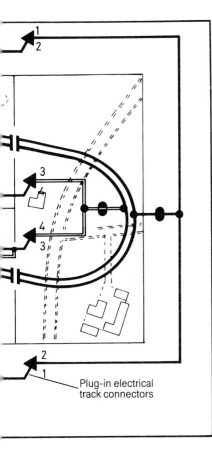

Plug-in electrical
track connectors

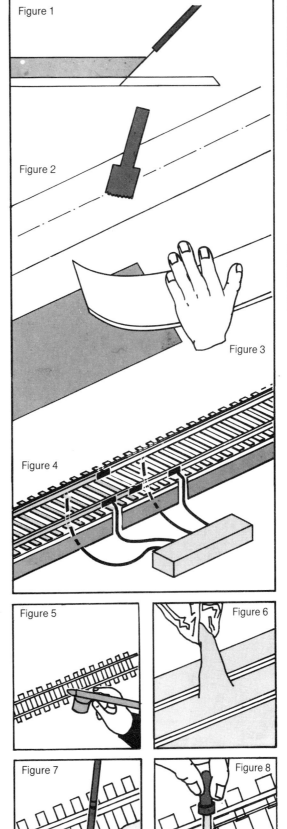

Fig 1 Cut the cork at an angle using a beveled edge straight edge (for tight radii it may be necessary to cut the strip in half with a straight cut).

Fig 2 Apply a contact adhesive to both the track support level and the back of the cork and allow to dry completely.

Fig 3 Cover with greaseproof paper and position, then carefully slide out the paper and press the cork into position.

Fig 4 Fix the track into position using track pins and wire up to a terminal block.

Fig 5 The track can be painted in situ or prepared beforehand. If pre-painted leave clean unpainted parts for the electrical contact of fishplates or wiring.

Fig 6 Sprinkle on the ballast.

Fig 7 Spread the ballast between the sleepers as required.

Fig 8 Using a plastic bottle or eye dropper, carefully apply the watered-down PVA glue.

have to align with other people's layouts the task is simpler. It also has straight track at the join, and making this type of join is relatively easy, as the two baseboards can be aligned and then bolted together, locating pegs also being fitted to the bases, to aid the alignment. The track is then laid over the join and fixed into position. On both edges of the baseboards' joints, brass screws are fixed into the base, on the outside edge of each of the rails, and then soldered to the rails so they are firmly fixed into position. (Alternatively, printed circuit board can be used. The centre part of the copper coating is filed away, and the rails are then soldered to this.) Either way, the rails are then cut through with a razor saw along the join line to separate them on to each baseboard. The bolts are dismantled, allowing the two bases to be parted. On re-assembly the locating pegs align the bases into the correct position, and the bolts secure the baseboards together.

Greater difficulties arise when the track runs diagonally to the join, and increase further still when it has to align with someone else's layout, or when building a layout that is interchangeable with itself. It is now virtually impossible to use the above method of fixing the track to obtain the critical track alignment, and it is necessary to devise some means of adjusting the track. This needs to be built-in at an early stage of the layout's construction if it is to be successful. (See Chapter 2—track adjusters.) The track adjusters should permit slight sideways movement to both tracks, *not* individual rails, so as to re-align the baseboards' track joints.

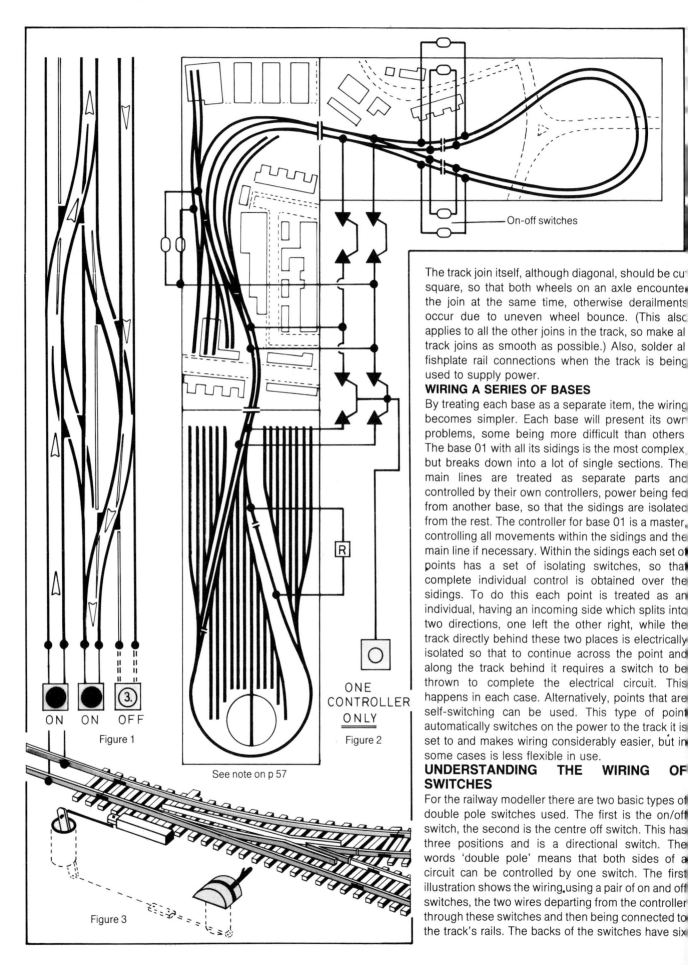

On-off switches

ON   ON   OFF

Figure 1

Figure 3

R

○

ONE
CONTROLLER
ONLY

Figure 2

See note on p 57

The track join itself, although diagonal, should be cut square, so that both wheels on an axle encounter the join at the same time, otherwise derailments occur due to uneven wheel bounce. (This also applies to all the other joins in the track, so make all track joins as smooth as possible.) Also, solder all fishplate rail connections when the track is being used to supply power.

WIRING A SERIES OF BASES

By treating each base as a separate item, the wiring becomes simpler. Each base will present its own problems, some being more difficult than others. The base 01 with all its sidings is the most complex, but breaks down into a lot of single sections. The main lines are treated as separate parts and controlled by their own controllers, power being fed from another base, so that the sidings are isolated from the rest. The controller for base 01 is a master, controlling all movements within the sidings and the main line if necessary. Within the sidings each set of points has a set of isolating switches, so that complete individual control is obtained over the sidings. To do this each point is treated as an individual, having an incoming side which splits into two directions, one left the other right, while the track directly behind these two places is electrically isolated so that to continue across the point and along the track behind it requires a switch to be thrown to complete the electrical circuit. This happens in each case. Alternatively, points that are self-switching can be used. This type of point automatically switches on the power to the track it is set to and makes wiring considerably easier, but in some cases is less flexible in use.

UNDERSTANDING THE WIRING OF SWITCHES

For the railway modeller there are two basic types of double pole switches used. The first is the on/off switch, the second is the centre off switch. This has three positions and is a directional switch. The words 'double pole' means that both sides of a circuit can be controlled by one switch. The first illustration shows the wiring using a pair of on and off switches, the two wires departing from the controller through these switches and then being connected to the track's rails. The backs of the switches have six

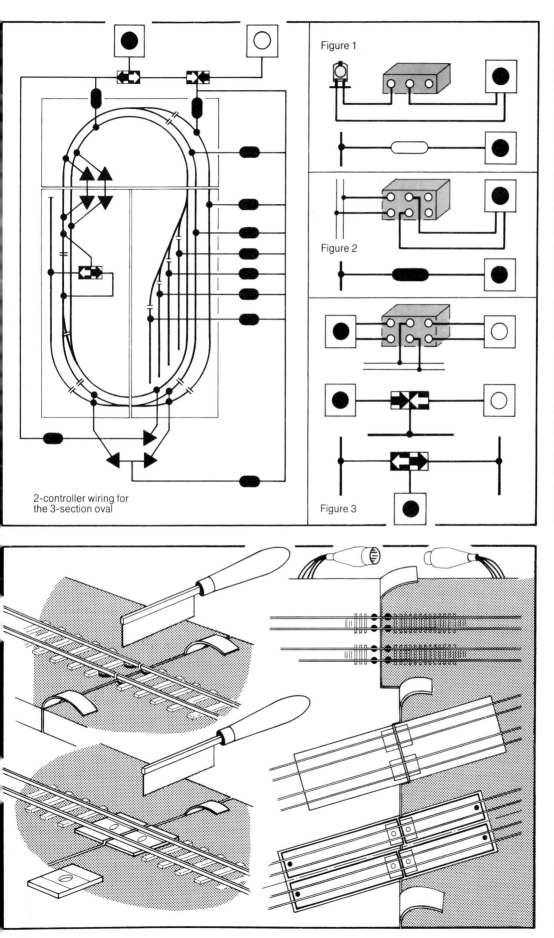

Figure 1

Figure 2

Figure 3

2-controller wiring for the 3-section oval

Opposite page. Fig 1 Shows the way the electricity flows around a track when insulators are not used, which can create all sorts of electrical problems unless controlled.

Fig 2 Shows the base 01 fitted up as a small 'L' shape layout providing an extremely wide range of running operations due to the large fiddle yard. The return loop, being a double track, does not require reversing switches.

Fig 3 Shows the Graham Farish cable method of point changing.

Left, Fig 1 The single pole on–off switch has three terminals of which only two are used.

Fig 2 The double pole on–off switch has six terminals of which only four are used.

Fig 3 The centre off double pole switch uses all terminals. The power can be fed from both sides but only one will link up to the track; alternatively, the power can be fed from the centre to one of the tracks, depending upon the setting.

Left Inserting card between the bases when laying the track allows for the thickness of saw cut on re-assembly.

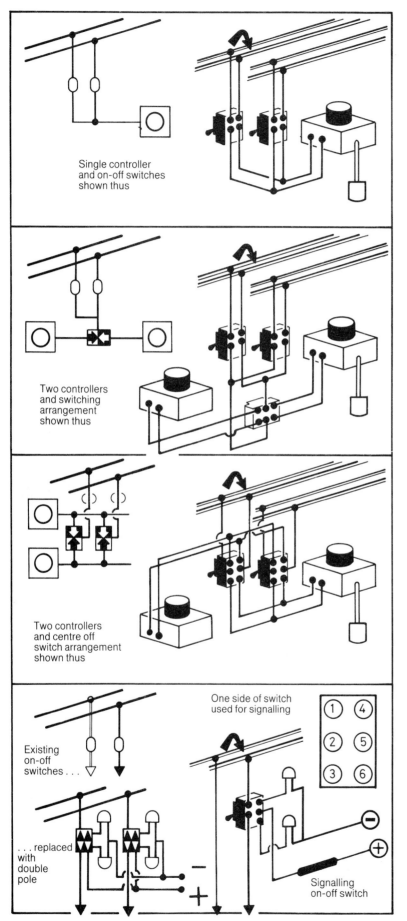

Single controller
and on-off switches
shown thus

Two controllers
and switching
arrangement
shown thus

Two controllers
and centre off
switch arrangement
shown thus

One side of switch
used for signalling

1	4
2	5
3	6

Existing
on-off
switches . . .

. . . replaced
with
double
pole

−   +

Signalling
on-off switch

connections and are split into two sides, the terminals reading one, two and three for one electrical side of the switch, called a 'pole' and four, five and six for the second side. To wire the on/off switch, terminals one and two are used for one side of the wiring and four and five are used for the other side. Terminals three and six are not used.

The second illustration shows the use of a changeover switch, for use with two controllers. This is inserted between the controllers and on/off switches and provides the choice, one at a time, of the controller to be used. This time the on/off switch uses all six terminals, terminals three and six connecting to the first controller, terminals one and four connecting to the second controller's terminals. Terminals two and five are connected to the second on/off switches' middle terminals.

Look at illustration 'A' on top of page 153, which shows double pole on/off switches. In practice this means the 'positive' side of the electrical circuit is marked with a cross or plus sign and departs out of controller 'B' and into terminal D3, through the switch and out of terminal D2 into S5, out of S4 then into the track. It then passes through the locomotive's electric motor. Having done this the electricity is now on its return journey, and is marked with a 'minus' sign to denote it is on the 'negative' side of the circuit. It continues back into terminal S1, coming out through S2, then into D5 and departing out of terminal D6, so that it finally returns back to the 'B' controller. This electrical circuit provides the choice of controller 'A' or 'B' and whether a particular track is switched on or off, the electricity making a 'positive' journey outwards, and a 'negative' return, these being the two 'sides' of direct current electricity.

The third illustration shows the use of two controllers, using double pole centre off switches. This provides the choice of either controller and also whether the power is on or off to each track. The wiring to these is much simpler, because it does away with the second switch and its wiring. This time the power departs from the controller into terminal three and out at two, into the track, through the loco's motor and back into the track, into terminal five, and out of six, back to the controller.

This method uses the centre terminals of the switch to go to the track, the two outside terminals in each case going to the controller. Since the switch has three positions, it provides an on and off setting to controller 'A' or 'B', which is designated by the switch's 'toggle' setting.

The fourth illustration shows the wiring of an on/off double pole switch, that uses diodes as an indicator to its settings. This system splits the electrics of the switch into two. The first half is used for the track and the second half for signalling. To make this possible requires a permanently connected wire from the controller to the track. The second wire has part of the switch inserted between the controller and the rail. Since the track is built in electrically-separated sections this is a perfectly cceptable procedure. The electrical power to the ack uses terminals one and two, the power to the ED's uses four, five and six. The positive side goes terminal five and departs out of either four or six, epending upon the switch's setting, then through e LED's and back to the negative terminal. A esistance is used within the circuit to reduce urrent and prevent the LED's being damaged or urnt out. By wiring in this manner the LED's can be ired back to the control panel and to signalling ghts. This, of course, provides an instant visual on e control panel as well as looking realistic on the yout.

The lower illustration shows how a manually-perated turn-out, using a push-pull cable within a be, can also be connected up through a pair of n/off switches. This time the track's circuit is kept ompletely separate from the LEDs' circuit, used for e indicator lamps. The switches in practice are ounted on a board and linked by a push-pull bar so at both switches are operated at once via a lever. his gives a very positive feel to the lever when it is perated, as the switches' springs position it and it lso locks the points into position at the same time.)n the indicator board the section of track lights up nd the signals change automatically.

IRING TURN-OUTS (POINTS)

Viring the turn-outs will vary as it all depends upon e type and make that are used. Two of the biggest pace-savers are shown at the top of the page; iese are the double slip, which is a diamond rossing and four turn-outs all in one, and the three vay turn-out.

The modeller has the choice of live or dead rn-outs. The important point about the live turn-out that it includes built-in internal wiring. These are uch simpler to install and provide trouble-free unning. Dead turn-outs will require the modeller to stall all the wiring. One of the most commonplace ositions for a pair of turn-outs is to allow the ansfer of rolling stock from one track to another, vhen both tracks are running parallel to each other. has already been established how the electricity ows around the track (see the illustration on page

150); to control this, electrically, all turn-outs need to be separated. It is thus vitally important to install insulated track joiners on each rail in this situation. If they are not insulated a cross-feed of power will occur from one track to another. Also, if two controllers are used simultaneously it would short-circuit the layout, because if one track (the 'up' line) is supplied with positive plus negative, and the adjacent track (the 'down' line) with the negative plus positive, a short circuit will occur.

If the layout is in use and suddenly stops working, and still short circuits after you have removed all the

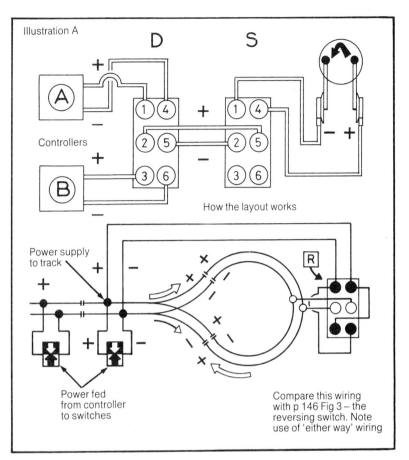

Illustration A

How the layout works

Power supply to track

Power fed from controller to switches

Compare this wiring with p 146 Fig 3 – the reversing switch. Note use of 'either way' wiring

Above The wiring of a single track return loop on which the rolling stock must stop whilst the setting of switches is changed.

Below Two switch wiring for track and signal operated via a lever and push-pull device.

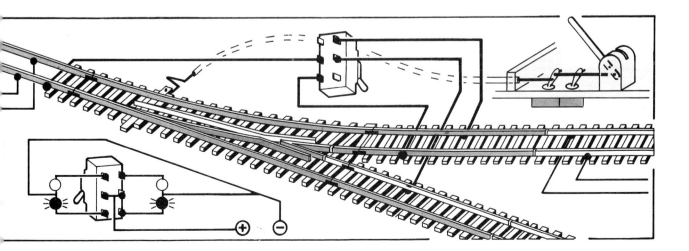

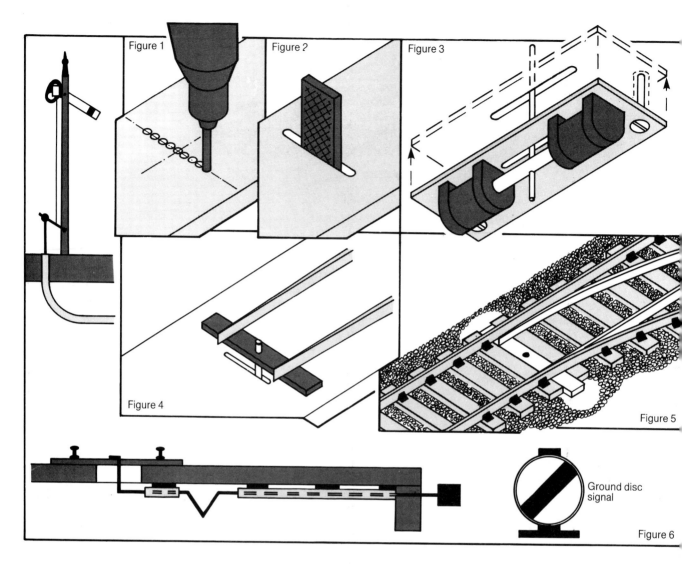

Figure 1

Figure 2

Figure 3

Figure 4

Figure 5

Ground disc signal

Figure 6

Fig 1 Mark out the position of the turnout then drill a row of holes.

Fig 2 File the row of holes into a slot.

Fig 3 Mount the turnout motor beneath the baseboard, centring the motor's turnout pin to line up with the centre line of the track.

Fig 4 Fit the moving sleeper over the pin, and check for smooth movement of the turnout motor.

Fig 5 Fit the turnout in place and ballast, leaving an area clear as indicated and keeping the ballast away from the moving rails.

Fig 6 Using push/pull rods for points and signals.

Right Working signals by Ratio.

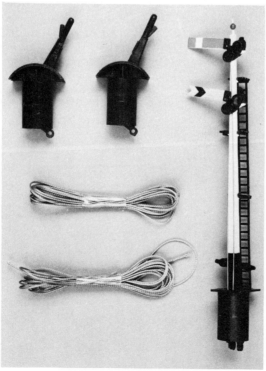

rolling stock, check out this type of situation, as it wi probably be due to a metal object bridging th insulating gap (see page 160 on fault finding). S check this out first, before looking for other source of trouble.

TURNOUT CONTROL

The turn-outs of the layout can be operated either b hand or by a mechanical device. In the first instance the operator of the layout reaches over the track and switches the turn-out into the desired setting. Fo the beginner building a first layout this is ideal as saves the problem of wiring and cutting holes in the baseboard to accommodate turn-out motors, etc. I many cases, though, hand changing is inconvenien so a remote control device is required. Again the power to operate the turn-out can be supplied b hand, by using a push/pull cable, either fitted in tube or via string, eyelets and pulleys. The latte method requires very careful setting up and by it very nature can be a source of trouble, unless fitte with adjusters. If properly constructed, however, can be a joy to operate as levers can be used on th control panel built into the layout.

SOLDERING WIRES

Soldering wires to both terminals and to the track i

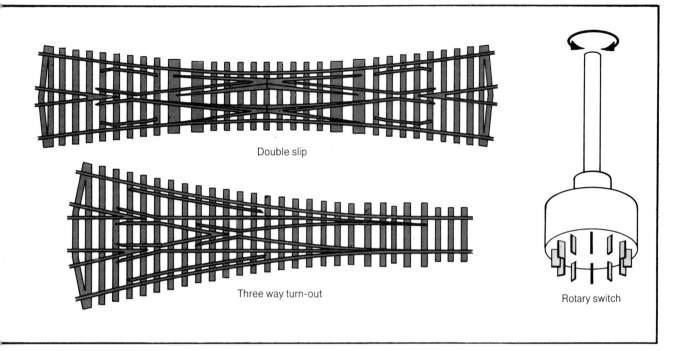

Double slip

Three way turn-out

Rotary switch

ne of the most important tasks to undertake; if this oes not work properly the layout will be doomed to constant stream of electrical failures. The secret of uccessful electrical soldering is to use a hot iron, lean the job well and apply the solder to the job and ot the iron.

The purchase of a good pair of wire strippers is a aust, as these remove the casing to expose the vire without, when set up properly, damaging it. This s very important since reducing the number of wires ffects the carrying capacity of the cable. A single mall strand of wire can in many cases act as a esistor in the circuit, because it alone cannot carry he amperage required. The same problem arises vhen using single-strand bell wire, the resistance of vhich absorbs the electrical energy, so that over a ong length it shows a voltage drop sufficiently to be ery noticeable. To avoid this use multi-strand electrical cable—the type sold for car speakers is ideal as it is available in fine strand wire which is easier to twist, tin and cut, carries amperage well and is available as four core (the number of individually electrically separated cables).

AUTOMATIC SIGNALS AND POWER-OPERATED TURN-OUTS

There is no end to the amount of automation that can be incorporated in a layout. It is not compulsory, of course, as a layout can be wired to provide the bare minimum of functions. Building-in some automatic features does ease the operation of the layout, however.

There are two basic types of turn-out motors, one fitted with switches, the other without. The electric turn-out motor itself is a very simple electro-mechanical device, fitted with two solenoids on each end of a bar. These are electro-magnetic coils,

Above The double slip and three way turn-outs, both space savers on a layout. Rotary switches are far more suitable when combination switching is required as they are available in one pole twelve way, two pole six way, three pole four way and four pole three way. These are used instead of a lot of switches to perform a sequence.

Below Soldering cables and tag boards.

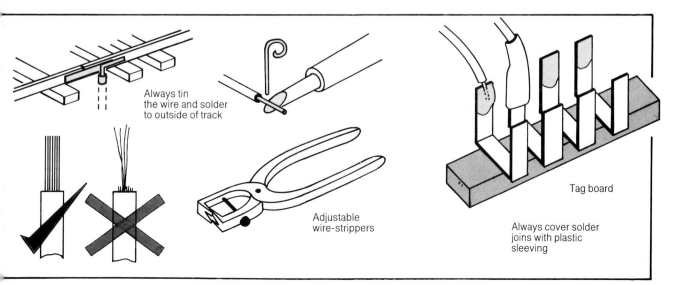

Always tin the wire and solder to outside of track

Adjustable wire-strippers

Tag board

Always cover solder joins with plastic sleeving

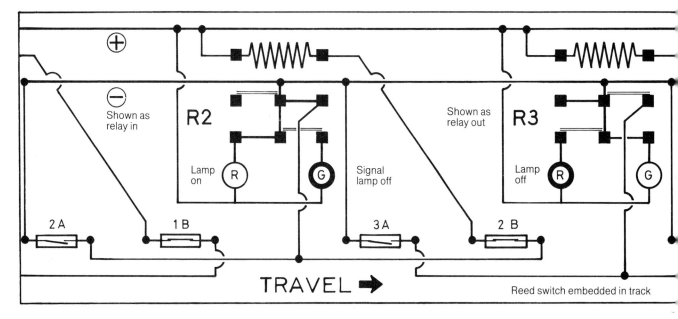

R2 — Shown as relay in

Lamp on

Signal lamp off

R3 — Shown as relay out

Lamp off

2 A   1 B   3 A   2 B

TRAVEL ➡

Reed switch embedded in track

Above Reed signal changing requires each length of rolling stock to have one unit fitted with a magnet (generally under the tender). This activates the reed switch, relays then being activated or disengaged as the circuit is made or broken, similar to a photo-electric cell system shown below.

Right The uncoupler is a simple electro-magnet which is fitted under the track and 'pops up' to disengage the coupling, wired to a simple press button switch.

powered by either DC (direct current) or AC (alternating current). The principle of the turn-out motor is that one coil is briefly charged with electricity, which attracts the iron bar into the coil's centre; when the power is switched off the iron bar remains there; when the second coil at the other end of the bar is switched on, it attracts the bar into itself, changing the position. Thus the bar shuttles backwards and forwards in a manner which can be controlled and mechanically linked to the turn-out.

Wiring turn-out motors is very simple as only four wires are used. The middle two link up to form a common return while the other two are linked up to a probe, push button or passing contact switch and then to the power source, so that a short burst of power is applied to the chosen side of the turn-out motor, setting its direction. The advantage in using a

motor fitted with additional contacts is that it als automatically sets the signals.

The various types of signalling combinations ar extremely complex as different arrangements ar used throughout the world, so some research will b needed. In Britain two types have been common The first is the semaphore signal which is mechanical indicator and the second is the ligh signal which uses a series of coded 'on' lights t indicate 'track clear' (green), 'sections ahea restricted' (yellow and double yellow) and 'stor (red). The simplest of signals to arrange to wor automatically is the red or green indicator ligh since the Seep turn-out motor manufacturir company produce a completely water-resistar variable power unit, fitted with or without switchges and a capacitor discharge unit, which boosts th

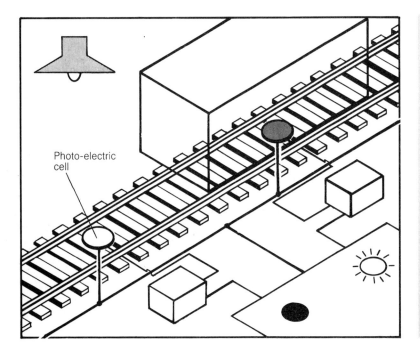

Photo-electric cell

motor's power and acts as a failsafe by cutting off the electricity (see illustration).

Semaphore signals will each require an independent motor to drive their arms, which increases their cost, whilst the indicator light method uses pea bulbs or light emitting diodes. These require more than simply wiring into the appropriate terminal, as much will depend upon the type used. Pea bulbs, for example, vary in their voltage requirements from 1.5 to 12 volts. Light emitting diodes (LEDs) require 1.5 to 3 volts and draw very little amperage. This reduction in amperage considerably extends the working life of the switch contacts and the LEDs have a prolonged working life, far greater than a bulb, but they do not burn as brilliantly.

Automatic signalling can also be designed to work by using the rolling stock's position on the track. This information is then fed back to the control panel. Two systems can be used: one relies on electrical contact across the track, but unfortunately it cannot sense non-electrical-contact rolling stock. The second system can, as it uses a series of sensors which monitor the passing of the rolling stock. Two methods are used. The first is a photo-electric cell (see illustration) which registers a change through being blacked out. This is then interpreted through a silicon chip into a visual signal change, and as the rolling stock passes over a second photo-electric cell this causes a second signal change. By arranging a series of photo-electric cells along a length of track, therefore, various signal formations can be arranged to suit the layout.

The alternative system uses overlapping reed switches (see illustration) fitted along the track. A magnet is fitted under one item of rolling stock, closing the 'A' or opening the 'B' switches. Then a series of relays shown as 'R' hold themselves in by being triggered by 'A' until released by the 'B' reed switches.

THE CONTROL PANEL'S USE AND DESIGN

The choice of the control panel's design is very much up to the individual, as so many factors govern any decision about its requirements. In many cases the transformer and controller unit is kept separate, as it is difficult to build into the facia of the panel without dismantling it. Another problem occurs when the layout is for home use most of the time, but needs to be portable. After considering these and any other problems which may arise when designing the wiring for the layout, you may decide that there are many advantages in treating each base as a self-contained unit, but capable of being connected both electrically and physically with other bases. In the end each baseboard will then have its own control panel, also designed to interlock, so that they can be changed around as well.

Below left The Seep point motors with or without switches, and the capacitor discharge unit are an excellent combination for both indoor and outdoor use. The point motor has a progressive power throw built in so that it protects small turn-outs, only utilizing its full power for large turn-outs.

Below The wiring for an electric pencil and self-switching turn-out motor used for signalling.

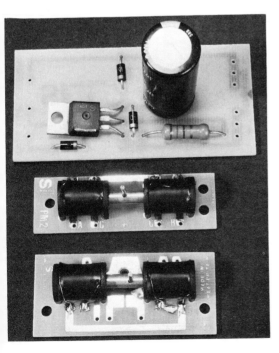

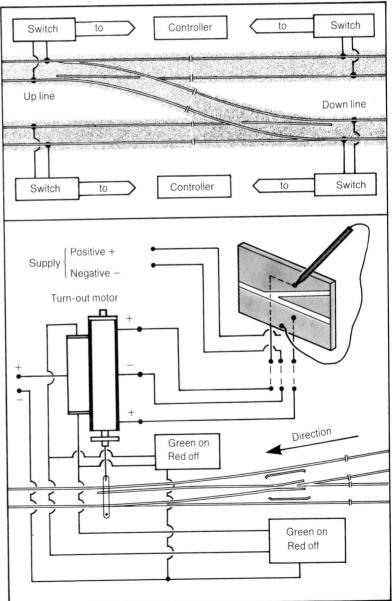

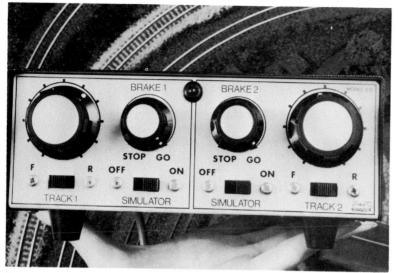

Top left Gaugemaster produce a transformer and variable selected power outlet controller, providing the choice of immediate response or simulated effect. The immediate response uses a direct output from the control setting for precise inching movements, the type used when shunting and positioning rolling stock very accurately. The simulated effect sets the output controller with a delay, so that it slowly builds up the power to match the setting, or reduces the rolling stock's speed very gently, to match the settings. This method of control produces a very realistic effect, as breaking can be applied to slow down the rolling stock if necessary.

Top right The hand held version of the controller.

The self-contained layout suffers from none of these problems. The control panel is built to suit the baseboard it is to operate and if the turn-outs are to be changed manually, a control panel is not even needed since the track isolating section switches can be built into the layout's baseboard and wired back to the controller. This method can also be used for interchangeable bases (see illustration lower right). The factory area is not built upon, but used instead for installing the turn-out's levers and section switches.)

This provides a choice: is the control panel to be a separate unit or built in? The fundamental point governing this is how the turn-outs are to operate. If they are mechanically linked the logical choice for reliability is to build them into the baseboard and avoid all the problems of disconnecting and reconnecting linkages each time the layout is moved. If the turn-outs are electrically-operated the connection problem is much simpler, as a suitable plug-in system can be built. This then allows all of the switch gear to be installed on the control panel and connected via the plugs to the layout, keeping

the landscape clear of switches.

Controllers are another personal choice. I prefer to use one that allows the rolling stock to slow down naturally, rather than skidding to a standstill when the power is turned off. 'Gaugemaster' produce a range of controllers which permit simulated control over the locomotive. When full power is applied very quickly the loco does not depart like a rocket, but slowly builds up speed to reach its maximum and vice versa, the operator applying the braking as necessary to stop the momentum of the train.

The simulator can also be switched off to allow fine shunting manoeuvres. This gives the operator another problem, however, which is observing these delicate movements closely. To overcome this a hand-held controller can be used, which enables the operator to move around the layout. Another problem with small slow manoeuvres is electrical contact, as the rails become dirty with time and use, and this prevents continuous electrical flow to the locomotive's motor which in turn causes intermittent stopping and starting so that it will often not restart until pushed by hand to a fresh piece of track.

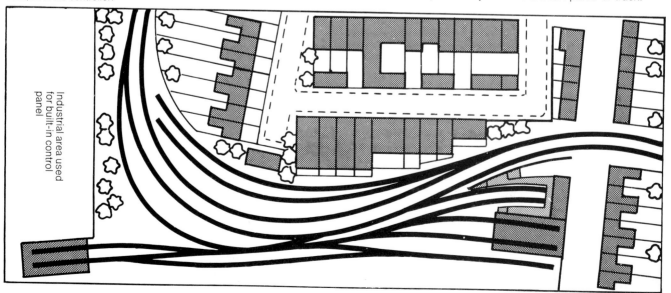

Industrial area used for built-in control panel

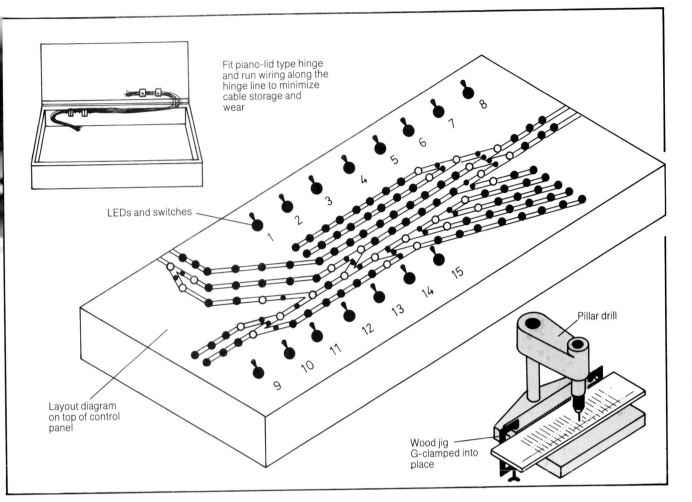

Fit piano-lid type hinge and run wiring along the hinge line to minimize cable storage and wear

LEDs and switches

Layout diagram on top of control panel

Pillar drill

Wood jig G-clamped into place

Above The control panel can be as simple or complex as one wishes. By using a pillar drill and a wooden jig, the control panel can be drilled accurately.

Left Fitting an HM Relco track cleaner in the system does help overcome the problem of intermittent running.

Far left Base 01 using the industrial area for a control panel and mechanical turn-out switching.

Right A typical electric direct current motor. Since it has a permanent magnet it is easily reversible by changing over the electrical polarity unlike the old alternating current motors which were a bit hit and miss on their starting direction.

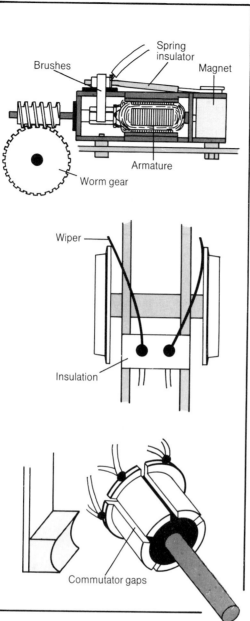

Spring insulator

Brushes

Magnet

Armature

Worm gear

Wiper

Insulation

Commutator gaps

Right The wipers rub against the rim of the wheels which pick up the electricity from the track. In the event of a locomotive not working, check for fluff pushing the wiper away from the wheel.

Right The commutator of the electric motor is split into segments. Check for particles bridging these gaps and also for badly worn brushes.

Below A typical portable work bench.

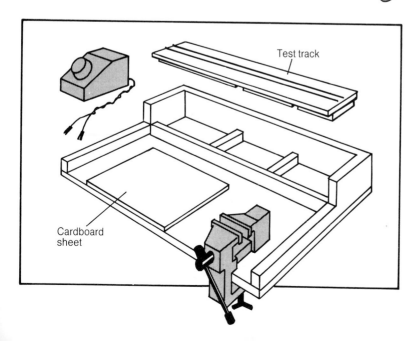

Test track

Cardboard sheet

To help overcome the problem of bad electrical contact Hornby Railways produce a unit called the 'HM Relco' unit. This operates on the sixteen volt outlet and the track's twelve volt outlet combined, producing an electrical high frequency generated at a safe power level which ionizes the air gap of a poor electrical contact. Since this unit is designed to work with the controller it is vitally important that these units are compatible—when using the 'HM Relco' and the 'Gaugemaster' they are.

The use of plastics for the facia of the control panel makes their construction easier, as plastic can be drilled and cut with hand tools, and LEDs can be glued in position using PVA glue (making them removeable in case of failure). Plastic can also be masked and sprayed complete with the layout diagram so that it looks smart and impressive. The use of miniature switches also helps considerably to reduce the panel's size. Alternatively the turn-out motors can be operated by an electric pencil, and the track and signalling diagrams can also be made to light up.

FAULT FINDING

When the layout is in full working order and suddenly stops, what is the cause? The symptoms generally fall into two categories—loss of electrical power, which is a track fault, or a loco ceases to work. The first thing to do is make a quick visual check to ensure the power is still on and then check the rails to see if an obstruction has fallen across them, after first removing all rolling stock. This splits the search for finding the fault into two areas.

If a locomotive stops working, first make a visual check to see if anything has fallen off. If no problem can be seen place it on a section of track known to be working. One of two things will happen when power is applied. Either the overload will kick out or it will still not move. Keep a visual check on the engine whilst doing this for a thin column of blue smoke which will indicate that something very serious is occurring. If nothing happens take a reading across the track with a multi-meter just to confirm power supply to the rails. Whether this is all right or not, switch off the power supply and set the controller to zero then take a resistance reading using the meter's own power source to establish whether an open or short circuit has occurred. If either is the case dismantle the loco and inspect for a broken connection, paying special attention to the pick-up wipers which rub onto the wheels as these do tend to wear out or pick up fluff, making them ineffective. Do this both visually and by taking a resistance reading by placing probes in appropriate places. An easy check is to replace the locomotive on to the track, position the probes on each rail and take a reading. If no resistance is found then place one probe on the rail and the second on each of the motor's brushes in turn. This should produce two direct readings from the four taken. If an open circuit to one is indicated repair as necessary, if more than two check the insulation for a short circuit.

If there is still a problem and both rail to brush

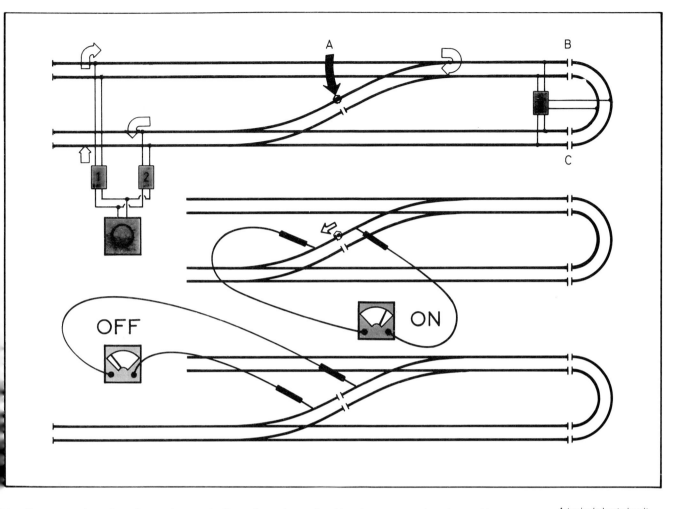

circuits are good, replace the probes on to the rails and rotate the motor's armature by hand whilst taking a reading. If an intermittent reading is found the problem lies within the brushes and commutator or a winding of the motor's armature. If both the brushes and commutator are clean and in good condition and only one section of the armature does not work a coil is broken or burnt out. This is a replacement job as the rewinding of a single coil is extremely difficult.

Unfortunately, dismantling an electric motor disturbs its magnetic field so that on re-assembly it is never the same unless re-magnetized. This loss can be ignored for general purpose work but will show itself if the motor is required to work hard, as it simply will not work as well as it used to. In general terms it is usually quicker and cheaper to replace the entire motor in the event of a coil burning out.

If all the coils are good clean out the motor's commutator gaps, its surface and replace the brushes if necessary. New brushes, like a new engine, need running in until they take up the commutator's shape, as before they do this they are working inefficiently.

If the track, with all the rolling stock removed and switches set at off, still shorts out, check each section between the controller and switches. If this does not reveal the fault, switch on one section at a time, checking for power using the multi-meter set to voltage in both forward and reverse modes. If all is well then switch on adjoining sections in pairs. The illustration shows a typical problem—the circuit works in one direction but when a reverse switch is used a short circuit occurs (at the insulated point A). To establish the location of this fault switch off all the power and then set the controller at zero. Use the multi-meter set on resistance so the meter supplies its own power and check the insulated joins to the sections. Both should read nil or off to indicate the insulated section joiners are in fact clear. The middle illustration shows a reading occurring and the meter is on. Clean out the join until the reading is zero or off (lower illustration), indicating no further electrical continuity. Remove probes, switch the power back on and recheck out. If it still does not work continue by repeating this procedure until the fault is clear. The turn-outs are particularly good at finding bits to short circuit them so these should be checked both visually and electrically very carefully. When using the multi-meter on resistance, so that it uses its own power, set the controller at zero, since a misleading reading can sometimes occur as it reads the controller's settings. One of the easiest loss of power faults is accidentally tripping over a wire which pulls off a connection, the loose end then finding a place to cause a short circuit.

A typical short circuit problem. By building the track in electrical sections the problem can be quickly traced to an area. This reduces the search. Start by visually looking, then with the aid of an instrument to check the electrics. If the fault is an intermittent one check the wiring for a broken or bad join. Quite often it can be traced to a cable which has been pulled, breaking the wiring within the plastic covering, but not the outside of the cable's covering.

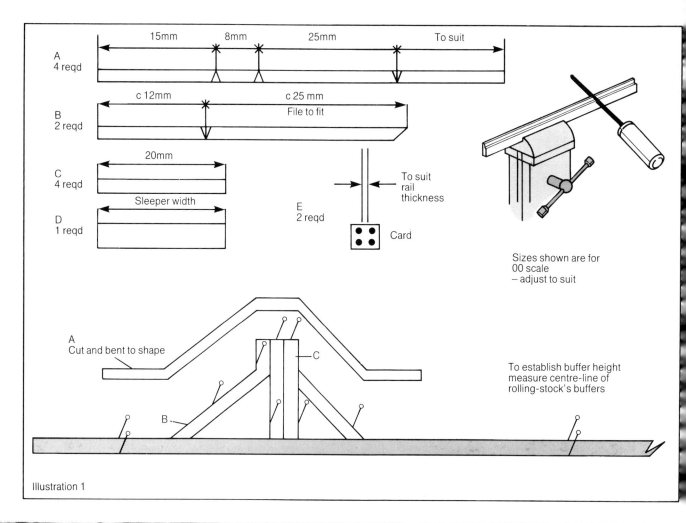

A
4 reqd

15mm   8mm   25mm   To suit

B
2 reqd

c 12mm   c 25 mm
File to fit

C
4 reqd

20mm

D
1 reqd

Sleeper width

E
2 reqd

To suit
rail
thickness

Card

Sizes shown are for
00 scale
– adjust to suit

A
Cut and bent to shape

C

B

To establish buffer height
measure centre-line of
rolling-stock's buffers

Illustration 1

END STOP (BUFFER) CONSTRUCTION

Illustration one contains details of the components
sizes and to start with we cut four equal lengths of
rail. Mark out and notch as detailed using a Swiss
file. Use the first one as a master by cramping in a
vice alongside the other rails, filing them one at a
time to match the master rail. Do the same with the
second shorter length of notched rail and bevel it to
suit the track. Then cut four more lengths of rail and
a length of wood (don't use metal or it will short
circuit the track), and finally cut out and drill the two
end plates. This supplies us with all the components.

Thoroughly clean all the metal rails and pin in
position on a piece of wood as shown. Bend one of
the four notched rails and lay it in place on top. When
you are satisfied with the alignment solder together
by pre-fluxing the join, then apply heat from the iron
to the rail. Apply solder to the rail (not the iron)
using as little solder as possible—this saves a lot of
cleaning up! Keep applying heat from the iron so as
to allow the solder to run properly and form a good
sound join. Repeat this on the other joins and when
they are cool remove the rail and turn it over, clean
and re-pin in position. Now lay the second notched
and bent rail in position, align carefully and solder in
place. Repeat the sequence for the second side to
make a pair.

Slide the longest length of rail back into position
on the sleepers, taking care not to miss one. Do this
until they touch the rail soldered to the track. Repeat
with the second rail. Cut off any unwanted length of
sleeper. Do exactly the same on the short length of
rail behind the buffer. Finally fit a short length of
sleeper between the bent rails, by cutting away the
web on the chairs (see illustration three). Square the
track and uprights by pinning the wooden strip into
position using the plastic plates. The track and buffer
can now be pinned down in place as required on the
baseboard, joining additional track via insulated
fishplates, and carefully wiring back to the isolator
switch on the buffer side of the track. Paint the track
to represent weathering and add ballast, emergency
sand, stop lights, etc, for effect. Repeat procedure
as required.

HINTS AND TIPS ON SOLDERING

Always use a medium fifty watt iron for track work
and for safety's sake use a cradle and point the hot
tip of the iron away from you. Clean and re-tin the
iron regularly and wipe off excess solder with a
damp rag. Clean metal and plenty of heat is the
secret of successful soldering.

Warning *Baker's fluid is poisonous and should be
kept out of the reach of children. It is also corrosive,
so avoid breathing the neat steam gas when
soldering, and keep away from tools and skin. If they
get splashed, wash off with lots of soap and water
and dry thoroughly. If your eyes get splashed, seek
medical attention immediately.*

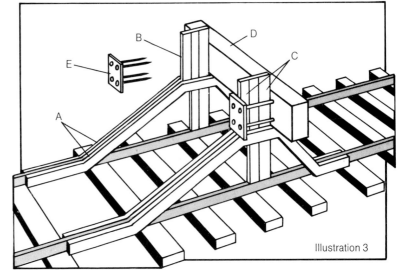

Illustration 3

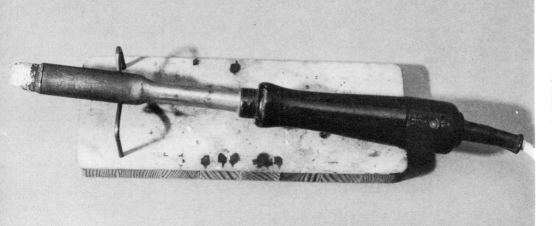

Opposite page, top The
components required to
make an end stop.

Bottom A commercially
produced end stop
manufactured in plastic
by Peco.

This page, above
Assembly of the end
stop.

Left Acid fluxes are only
used on items that can
be thoroughly washed
afterwards, or corrosion
will occur in time. Use
multicore solder and
electrician's flux on all
other work and wiring.
Solders have different
melting points. Low
melting solders (the
temperature of boiling
water) are ideal for
metal kits.

Above far left To clean a
soldering iron file until
bare copper shows,
then tin with cored
solder.

Above left The clean
and tinned tip of a
soldering iron.

Left Make a soldering
iron cradle from wire,
shaped as an M and
fixed into a piece of
wood.

8. ROLLING STOCK

Opposite page Peco produce an excellent range of small books each covering a particular subject. They also produce alternative bodies to fit some of the Graham Farish chassis.

Below The various scales use common track gauges (Peco Ltd).

Bottom The BR 'Britannia' and the GWR tank locomotives shown to give a size comparison.

READY-TO-RUN ROLLING STOCK

One of the great things about ready-to-run rolling stock is the selection available from both the main manufacturing concerns and the specialized kit building services, which have kits made up by professional modelmakers and which extend the range of rolling stock further still. A good example of one of these companies is the West Coast Kit Centre situated in Bristol (England), which offers a very large choice in the way different kits are built by them. This starts with their standard range for basic kits and progresses through to super detailing, complete with choice of chassis, of motor and of wheels, over a wide range of scales. This type of specialized service allows the individual (provided the kit is available) to obtain a rare item of rolling stock finished in a unusual livery, all of which is hand-painted and lined, for one's collection.

Collecting locomotives which are displayed in show cases is also part of railway modelling, as the model, instead of being shown on a shelf, can be displayed in a small diorama, so that it looks at home in a setting. This caters for the person who enjoys landscaping rather than building rolling stock, but wants an unusual prototype immaculately finished. This type of service is impractical for the mass market manufacturer.

RESEARCH INTO AVAILABLE ROLLING STOCK

The easiest way to gather information on rolling stock is to visit the local dealer, or preferably

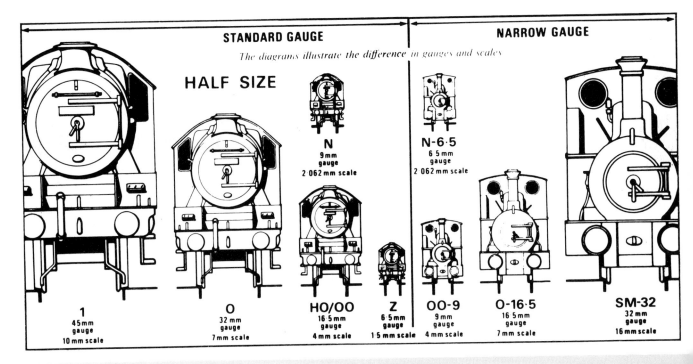

STANDARD GAUGE   **NARROW GAUGE**

The diagrams illustrate the difference in gauges and scales

HALF SIZE

1	O	HO/OO	Z	N	N-6·5	OO-9	O-16·5	SM-32
45mm gauge 10mm scale	32mm gauge 7mm scale	16·5mm gauge 4mm scale	6·5mm gauge 1·5mm scale	9mm gauge 2·062mm scale	6·5mm gauge 2·062mm scale	9mm gauge 4mm scale	16·5mm gauge 7mm scale	32mm gauge 16mm scale

several, and obtain a series of catalogues on various manufacturers' products. The reason for visiting several dealers is because there is a tendency for a particular shop to specialize in a small number of manufacturers' products. Because the range is so vast, it is impossible to stock everything.

By consulting the catalogues at a very early stage whilst designing the layout, a number of things can be taken into consideration, such as the availability of rolling stock, the types and the countries of origin. Are cars, people and buildings available to suit the type of rolling stock and are there any other accessories made to add interest to the layout?

Peco, for example, produce a comprehensive range of track work in several gauges to suit the different scales. They also back up this range with turn-out motors and switch gear, lineside accessories such as tunnel portals, stations, huts and buildings. They also produce kits and ready-to-run rolling stock, including both standard and narrow gauge prototypes all of which can be used to add character to the layout. To further back this up and to help the modeller Peco also produce booklets which cover track plans, both large and small, using both setrack and flexible track, and most important of all they provide information sheets printed to modelling size on their Streamline turn-outs and crossings to aid the planning of a layout.

Just as the range of different rolling stock available is enormous, so is the range of scales, giving the modeller a very wide choice. The most popular scales are HO/OO, probably due to the fact that they established themselves so many years ago. Also becoming popular is N gauge, the possible reason for this being its small size which either allows more countryside to be included on the layout, so that it looks more realistic, or permits a smaller physical size of layout, which is convenient for storage. All the remaining gauges vary in their popularity from country to country.

The terms scale and gauge can lead to misunderstandings as the same gauge can be used for various scales. The gauge of the track means the distance that the running rails of the track are spaced

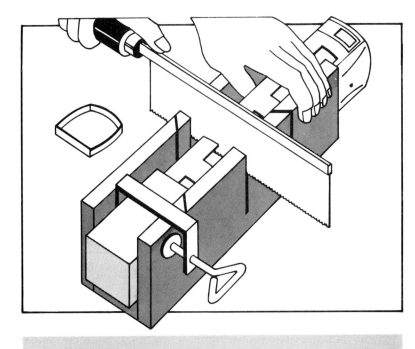

apart. The term scale is the ratio of the model size to the full size prototype. For example, if the model is 76 times smaller than the real prototype the scale is expressed as 1:76. This is modelled at 4 mm to a foot, which is not quite correct but a close equivalent used for convenience since 76 mm multiplied by four (to give 4 mm to a foot) equals 304 mm total. One foot converts into metric at very close to 305 mm, giving an error of 1 mm over 76 'scale' feet (equivalent to an error of three inches on each 76 feet measured full size). This error is so small that it is ignored and is a factor common to all the scale modelling size ratios.

The previous page shows an extract from the Peco catalogue illustrating how the track gauges can remain the same. Compare the narrow gauge 009 modelled at 4 mm to one foot running on standard N gauge track.

PLASTIC KITS

Several manufacturers of rolling stock produce plastic kits, providing a wide choice of subjects for the modeller. Slaters is one such company and probably best known for its plastic sheet, sold under the name of 'Plastikard', which is available in a selection of thicknesses. The company goes back a good number of years and during this time has developed a wide range of accessories and services which include chemical milling (etching), a very useful service to know about as your skills develop and your modelling becomes more adventurous.

The 7 mm O gauge kit shown uses plastic for the basic components and metal for the coupling, buffers, wheels and bearings, since they have to

nction. The smaller 4 mm OO scale kit uses all astic components, the wheels being purchased parately due to the choice of gauges OO, EM and available, as described in an earlier chapter. ere are the manufacturers' gauge sizes and the tra-scale modeller's track gauge sizes.

Since plastic is a reasonably weatherproof mate- l it is suitable for outdoor use. Nickel silver rails d plastic sleepers also cope with the elements ry well. Of course, when a layout is built in the rden the surroundings remain at a full size 'scale' espective of the rolling stock's scale. The LGB nge of rolling stock is designed for the garden and iilt in a chunky 1:22.5 scale, with Pola making a nge of buildings to suit. The ultra-scale modeller ll probably frown upon this but it really depends on w the individual enjoys modelling and many a od layout is that big it 'needs' the garden, the ain terminal usually being in a shed protected from nd and rain.

The kit shown from the many available is a very od example of a 7 mm O scale wagon, built tween 1905 and 1910. Its construction starts by eaning the injection-moulded sprue from the ouldings using a sharp knife and then filing them that all components fit. Since the kit includes rned buffers the hole into which they fit will require reful redrilling. This is best done with a pin chuck, hich holds the drill whilst it is rotated in the fingers d allows the drill to be 'felt' as it enlarges the hole. is is better than using a very large twist drill which n easily drill off centre and at an angle. Having ne this, assemble the floor to the chassis frame, d continue as per instructions within the kit.

For glueing components together, Slaters market solvent called 'Mek-Pak'. The chemical used in rand glass brush cleaner is also suitable, and in e trade we use a solvent called dichloromethane. ing a solvent it does not have a gap filling property

so joins must be well fitting, and since this is the case all kits should be inspected as assembly takes place, to make sure the components fit snugly.

Since plastic is a very easily workable material, it lends itself to adaptation, which is useful as a number of commercially produced ready-to-run models are scale-wise too short. This is especially true of coaches. By cutting two coaches at a suitable point they can be joined to form a corrected length of coach. The jig shown can be made from wood, the saw fitting into the gap so that its blade is guided to produce a good clean straight cut.

Plastic can be laminated in layers to form thicker pieces by using liquid cement or solvent, and then shaped, being either carved with a sharp knife or filed. Double-sided sticky tape can be used to temporarily fix small pieces, which would be difficult to hold, on to a larger piece of plastic, to form a handle.

Filling gaps when components do not fit very well is always a problem. Car body filler is a good general purpose material but it does have its limitations. It sets very hard, making it difficult to rub down or clean off in difficult places. I have found through practice that epoxy putty can be superior as this can be modelled to shape whilst it is still soft and requires no further work. For finer gaps I have found that a filler called Brummer Stopper (as used in woodworking) is ideal. Since this filler is water-based, it can be cleaned off with a damp rag, unlike other fillers which require filing or sanding, produc-ing the risks of damaging the component's surface. Dents, unfortunately, will require keying by scraping and drilling so that the filler can grip the plastic. Alternatively, a mixture of liquid glue which has had scrap plastic dissolved in it can be used, built up in a series of layers. This method works very well when the component has no fine detail, which could be difficult to remodel.

Above An outdoor layout built by the Rev Peter Denny, called the 'Trepolpen Valley Light Railway'. For further details see 'Your Model Railway' magazine September 1986.

Opposite page top Modifying a plastic carriage using a cutting jig.

Opposite page bottom The Slaters cattle wagon is only one of the many kits produced by this company. The larger kits are complete and the OO/HO scale kits are supplied less wheels, due to the various track gauges at OO scale.

Above Built by Ron Cadman, a fine example of the GWR 1028 'County of Warwick' locomotive.

METAL KITS AND MASTERS

The method of manufacturing white metal components has been developed to a fine art in recent years. The masters for these are produced in metal by hand. This is necessary since the most common method of making the moulds requires the use of heat and pressure. Two uncured rubber discs are used, the master being embedded into these to form the mould's shape by being squashed between them under pressure. To cure the moulding rubber so that it retains its shape, heat is then applied whilst the material is still under pressure. When this process is finished the moulds are separated and the master is removed. Next the moulds are placed in a centrifugal casting machine. The void created by the master is filled with molten white metal, which is removed from the mould when it has cooled.

Since this procedure is a simple one, skillful modellers can make their own masters and have them cast. This service and others is offered by a number of companies which advertise regularly in modelling magazines and specialize in metal casting and chemical milling procedures.

MAKING MASTERS

The technique for producing the master is to shape the components from brass and solder additional pieces in place, hollow components being cast in two pieces due to the difficulty of making a suitable core plug (examine a kit closely). The components have to be produced fractionally larger than required, due to shrinkage of the hot metal in the mould. Since this is a constant the easiest way of allowing for it is to photographically enlarge the drawing by approximately two per cent and work to the new slightly enlarged photocopy. The percentage by which the drawing will need to be enlarged will depend upon the specialist company that is used, as various casting metals have slightly different shrinkage rates. The method of mould production also influences this, as a cold cured rubber mould expands with heat, thus almost neutralizing the shrinkage rate of the metal.

Cold cure rubber is a new product and expensive so it is not used by all the casting companies. This means that in the end the modeller will have to do some research to establish from the company which is to undertake the casting what their shrinkage rate is. The master can then be made proportionally larger as necessary, and any other points can be discussed at the same time.

The advantage from the modeller's point of view of cold cure rubber is that masters can be made from suitable plastics, but as with all masters, the final result can only be as good as the planning, the fitting of the components and the standard of workmanship involved.

The commercially available metal kits are produced using two methods, either by casting or by chemical milling (known as etching). The latter technique is used to produce the fine brass components and again is a method that the advanced modeller can use, after producing their own artwork for the components required.

CHEMICAL MILLING (ETCHING)

For this an accurate drawing is required, produced at least twice size so that it can be photographically reduced. This enhances the artwork of the components and helps to minimize the size of any drafting errors. The drawing can be produced on artboard made by 'Letraset' or on drafting film; the advantage of using film rather than tracing paper is that it is unaffected by humidity and stays the same size. By using special inks and rubbers, the drawing can be altered without destroying the surface of the film, unlike tracing paper which damages easily. Another advantage of using film rather than artboard is that a provisional drawing in pencil can be produced first and the components then moved around to make maximum use of the area which will constitute the fret (the term given to the etching on its surround).

LOST WAX CASTING

Another method commercially available is the lost

Left The GWR 850 Class 060 saddle tank locomotive. Both locomotives are modelled at 4 mm to 1 ft (OO scale) and are from the range of over thirty premier kits manufactured by Ron Cadman (also available ready-to-run to order).

Below The GWR 850 kit laid out showing the basic components. The wheels, gears and electric motor are purchased separately, allowing a choice of drive.

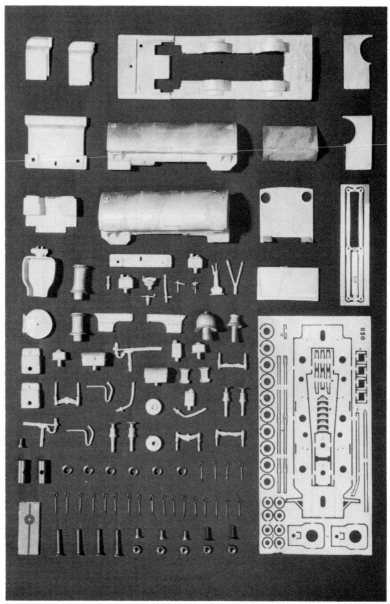

ax process. This is used to make the round brass omponents of a kit when strength is required on mall pieces, or for those kits made entirely from rass. This time the master can be made from any uitable modelling material, as a cold cure rubber ould is made from the master first, this then being sed to produce a wax copy casting. The wax copy embedded into a solid block by immersing it in a pecial fine cream-like mixture of plaster. The wax opy can either be dipped in the plaster or the laster can be poured over it. Note that a wax 'sprue' ust be left between the wax casting in the centre of e plaster and the open air. Once the plaster has et, the wax copy will be solidly encased apart from e tip of the 'sprue'. The plaster is then gently eated to both dry the mould and melt the wax, hich is poured out through the hole which ontained the 'sprue'. The shape of the wax casting thus left in the block. Using a centrifugal casting achine, molten brass is then injected into the aster mould. Once it is cool the plaster is broken way to reveal the brass casting.

HASSIS ASSEMBLY, WHITE METAL OR RASS

ssembly of the kit always starts with the chassis, so at wheel clearances, axle alignment and the riding eight can be checked. The axle alignment is done sing push fit, long straight metal rods through the xle bearings, the distances between them being easured and aligned for squareness. The axles nd wheels are now fitted as per the manufacturer's structions and checked so that they are smooth nd free-running, complete with spacing washers nd crank pins. A point to remember when fitting heels on locomotives with more than four driving heels is that the fractionally smaller ones fit in the iddle. This is to prevent the chassis rocking up and own on the middle two sets of wheels (easily hecked on a sheet of glass) and to restrict deways movement on the 'outside', as per the llowing example: front set no sideways play,

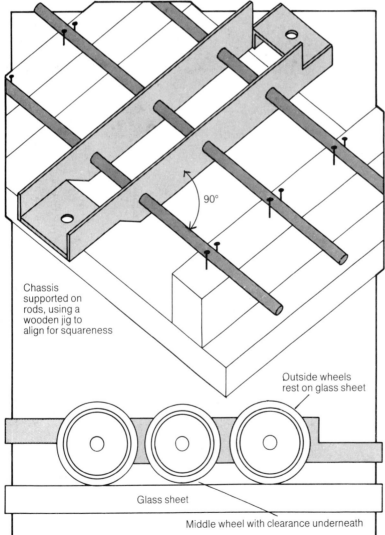

Chassis supported on rods, using a wooden jig to align for squareness

90°

Outside wheels rest on glass sheet

Glass sheet

Middle wheel with clearance underneath

middle set sideways movement, rear set no pla
(0-6-0 wheel configuration). This no-play situatio
also applies to the axle on which the gearing
situated. The middle wheels side play will b
governed by the minimum radius used, so this w
need to be checked on the track; at the same tim
look for places where the wheels may foul on th
bodywork or any part of the driving mechanism
When satisfied, and after the body has bee
checked for its fit with the motor temporarily in plac
dismantle as necessary and paint the chassi
before reassembling to continue.

Fitting the motor comes next. The alignment of th
gears must be carefully checked and shimmed wi
thin brass sheet until just the finest of play is felt i
the gearing. When satisfied that the motor's outp
shaft, gearing and wheels run freely, by rotating th
armature by hand, lubricate the gears and ax
bushes, then apply a thirty-second burst of ha
power, reducing this until it is zero, whilst careful
listening for a continuous and even tone, to deno
that there is not a mechanical tight spot. Whe
satisfied that all is well, run in the assembly at abo
half speed for around fifteen minutes in eac
direction, whilst constantly checking that it is n
over-heating. Make adjustments as necessary. Th
very careful alignment and running-in should pro
duce a sweet-running chassis which will be a soun
basis for the rest of the model.

FIXING METAL COMPONENTS TOGETHE

The components can be joined together in variou
ways, but by far the best method is soldering. O
white metal kits the use of special low-melt solde
and fluxes is strongly recommended, followed b
epoxy two-part glue and super glue (cyanoacrylate
The advantage of soldering is that it does not brea
down with age, but is a procedure that ma

modellers still avoid, probably due to fear of melting the white metal components. This is easily overcome by using a variable low heat soldering iron, operated on twelve volts from the controller's transformer.

The ideal soldering iron is the Oryx, twelve volt, five watt model. Mains soldering irons are not recommended for white metal, as their working temperatures are far too hot, exceeding the melting temperature of the metal used to produce the components. (This is not a problem with brass and a mains soldering iron can be used.) The low-melt solders start from around the boiling point of water upwards (100 degrees centigrade), and are available in various grades of melting points. The technique is to start with the high ones and work down through the grades, as this allows nearby joins to be made without melting the neighbouring, previously-assembled join. (This also applies to brass kits.) A second way around this problem is to use wet cotton wool draped over the adjacent joins to keep them cool (wet cotton buds are also useful).

The soldering iron's bit will have to be tinned and cleaned regularly, and at times reshaped to suit the

Bottom left The Micro Flame torch is a very useful tool for applying extremely hot heat to a small area.

Bottom right The use of blocks whilst components are assembled makes construction easier and more accurate.

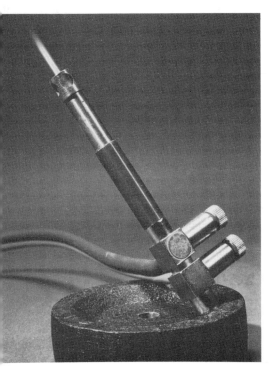

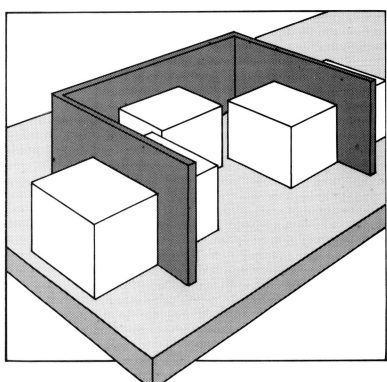

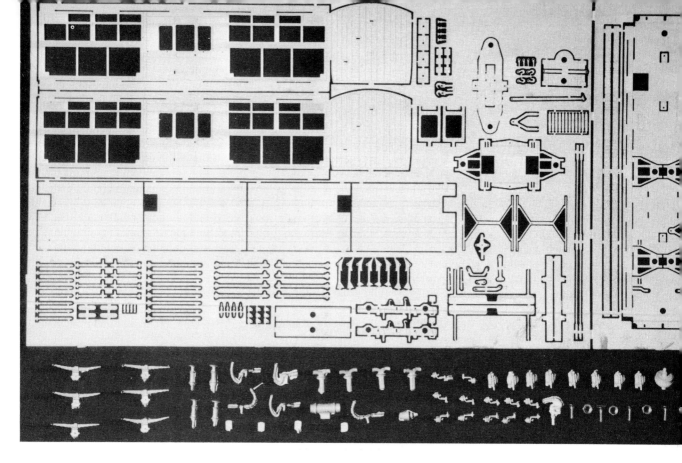

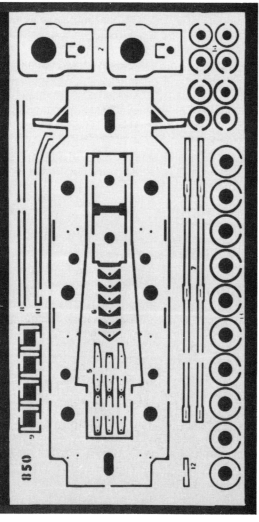

Above Brass kits are produced using chemical milling. By partially etching the surface some depth can be added, but since this is very limited the bulkier components ie: axle boxed are cast in white metal. The kit shown is produced by 'Micro Rail' and is of a C R Horsebox. The original was built at St Rollox from July 1907 to 1908.

Right The chemically milled fret, for the GWR 850 locomotive from which the chassis is made. Like the majority of 00 gauge kits wheels are purchased separately.

particular job in hand. A building board will also be found useful as the components can be pinned into position, or held square by using wooden blocks taped into position with double-sided sticky tape. For brass kits I prefer to use a 'Microflame' gas torch, as by tinning the components and fluxing, heat is applied very quickly to a localized area, which minimizes heat travel. On completing assembly of all the components, thoroughly wash them to remove all traces of flux.

(Note: For the beginner there is a soldering exercise on pages 162/163, which shows how to make an end stop (buffer). This has been designed to use left-over pieces of track. I strongly recommend that this is successfully completed before attempting to solder a metal kit together.)

CLEANING

Before soldering or gluing, all of the kit's components will have to be cleaned in batches as packed to remove the manufacturer's machining or release compounds. My favourite method is to use a kitchen pan cleaner, ie, Vim and an old toothbrush or wire wool and some liquid detergent. Work in an old bowl, cleaning the pieces until they shine, then rinse them in a sieve under running water, keeping the plug in the sink at all times just in case a piece escapes. (Count the pieces before and after washing.) The components are then dried using paper kitchen towel and restored in self-seal plastic bags.

Assembly of the components can now start, each piece being individually checked for fitting, and reshaped as necessary until you are satisfied. The components are then washed a second time to remove any oils deposited by the fingers; stubborn irt is removed by scraping or sanding, so that the in area is absolutely clean prior to soldering or uing. This is very important as white metal oxidizes ery quickly and dirt will affect the way solder flows hen heated or the bonds' strength when glued.

ADVICE FOR THE BEGINNER

 you are building your first metal kit, start with the ender's bodywork after assembling the chassis. Make sure it aligns with the loco's running plate eight by temporarily assembling the tender using Blue Tack, sticky tape and elastic bands to hold it ogether, so that the assembly sequence is understood. Fortunately a tender can have a separate nderframe which eases adjustment of the riding eight. When you are thoroughly familiar with the vay and in which order the components go together, ssemble the tender using glue or solder. Just tack he joints to begin with, so that as assembly continues adjustments can be made. When satisfied llet the corners and across the joins with glue or solder on the inside.

Each kit will require its own special construction methods and since there are so many kits of different prototypes, the variations in assembly echniques are endless, although the basic techniques of soldering and gluing remain the same.

Other principles also apply to all kits. Always ry-assemble components and check the fit over unning components for clearance, as it is easier to make adjustments when the kit's components are in separate pieces. The kits all have explicit instructions and as your skills and confidence increase, more complex kits can be built. As always start with a simple kit which needs the minimum amount of vork, as it is far more satisfying to complete a kit han be defeated by it.

Having finished the assembly of the kit, filled in any holes and dents and made good the joints, horoughly clean the model in lukewarm soapy vater, scrubbing the stubborn dirty bits clean with an old toothbrush, and then rinse everything well. Finally dry the model in a warm dust-free place so hat it is ready for painting.

PAINTING

The first paint on bare metal is always a priming coat,

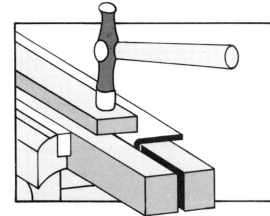

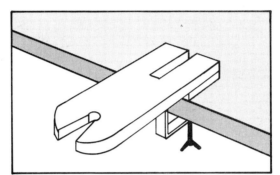

Left Most metal kits will require some form of light metalworking facilities. The vice should have a minimum two inch jaw width and a reasonable opening and depth. Cover the serrations of the jaws with hard wood blocks, held in position with double-sided sticky tape. These protect the materials being worked upon. Keep a hammer specially for bending the metal so that it retains its smooth head. A piercing saw of the jeweller's type and a fret table are also very useful for cutting and filing small components.

preferably of the two-part self-etch type. This provides a good key on the bare metal's surface, on top of which all the finished colours are applied. This first self-etch coat will have to be left for at least 24 hours to dry before you apply the first coat of colour. Having done this, the first rubbing-down can commence. Start by using 1,000 or 1,200 grade wet and dry sanding paper, gently smoothing off any bits that feel like tiny pieces of grit in the paint's surface but taking care not to go through the paint's surface. Dust off and apply the second coat, then again carefully and lightly sand down, repeating until an even, smooth coat is obtained. The thickness of each coat should be kept as thin as possible, to avoid too great a paint build-up, which would obscure detail.

Further painting instructions will be found in the chapter on painting and weathering.

Below A finished LNWR inspection coach used by F. W. Webb, built and painted by Ron Cadman, from a 'Premier' kit. The locomotive is the Cornwall which was used exclusively with this coach for many years.

MOVING OUT INTO THE WORLD OF MODELLING

To the beginner it may seem very daunting to move out into the world of modelling, but bear in mind that there are hundreds of other people who have exactly the same problem and would like to go ahead with railway modelling, but really do not know just how or where to start. Books and magazines may contain a tremendous amount of information but on average this is aimed at the reader who already has some modelling experience (although to be fair regular articles written for the beginner are published). For the complete beginner who really does need to gain the basic knowledge, modelling clubs play a crucial role, as they provide the chance to meet various people all at different stages of experience. Because of their combined knowledge they will be able to help solve many of the fundamental early problems. Doing this should help prevent repeating common mistakes.

The first stage in locating a club is to attend one of the exhibitions, details of which are generally well published in magazines and local newspapers. Having done this of course, one can wander around the exhibition and have a chat with the various exhibitors who will be running their layouts. Knowing modellers as I do, I have found that the vast majority will be only too willing to help the newcomer to the hobby. At the same time an exhibition will provide a chance to look at the different scales, so that an assessment can be made on the size of area that will be required for a layout. You can also visit the manufacturers' and retailers' stands, and obtain catalogues, etc. At the end of the day an overall gathering of information is accomplished and some new friends are made.

Top The Beckenham and West Wickham Model Railway Club running their exhibition 0 gauge layout which requires some 40 ft by 20 ft of space. The sign board welcomes new members.

Above Dave Lowery (editor of *Your Model Railway*) showing interested visitors his layout at the Cannon Street Exhibition.

Right The Isle of Wight Model Railway Club running one of the many live steam locomotives. The larger 5¼ inch gauge is always popular with the younger visitors, since it allows them to have rides.

Above The 1986
Cannon Street
Exhibition proved to be
very popular since
models and the real
prototype could be
viewed. BR staff
explained to visitors the
drivers' cabs and one of
the modern signal
boxes.

As a hobby railway modelling is undertaken by people in all walks of life but it is surprising just how many people do not discuss it for fear of ridicule. Many years ago I was loading my car with bits of dolls, and amongst great giggles a group of young women accused me of playing with dolls. Then I showed them the engineering drawings, the prototype model and the complicated mechanism required to make the eyes work. Suddenly a change in attitude became apparent, it became a fascinating job to do for a living.

The attitude of many people towards model making has changed and the hobby has gained a great deal of respect, probably partly due to *Star Wars* and other science-fiction films which use a considerable number of models to produce the special effects. TV and films are great consumers of these since in many cases the reality does not exist and creating the illusion that it does becomes a job for the model maker. This recognition over the years had led to full time courses at higher Day Tech level and is a supportive subject to many other subjects— architecture being a prime example, the model being easier and quicker to understand than a handful of drawings.

The approach to professional model making is very different to making models for a hobby, as unfortunately money determines the amount of detail shown and time spent. For the hobbyist the time costs nothing, so that the amount of detail shown is very much up to the individual. A visit to the Model Engineering Exhibition in London will confirm just how much can be made with so little in the way of tools, and even professionals stop to admire the workmanship.

My advice to the beginner is start in a small way, begin with simple kits, both for buildings and rolling stock, experiment with less expensive kits (a goods van is a useful starting point as if it does not work properly, you can always remove its wheels and use it as a makeshift lineside hut). Make a second one and avoid the mistakes made on the first one. If that one does not work you have two makeshift huts and can have a third go! The same applies to bits left over—since they are scrap in the first place, nothing is lost if the construction tried does not work, but you will have learned what not to do! I don't think I have met a modelmaker yet, who has not made a disaster which has landed in the dustbin with a thump. Don't be put off, skill and knowledge take time to learn and years of work are needed to produce an exhibition winner.

9. PHOTOGRAPHY

Below A selection of cameras. Three are 35 mm format and one is 6 cm by 6 cm. The camera on the tripod is the interchangeable lens 35 mm single lens reflex, Canon A1, which can be used in the fully automatic mode or as a priority camera and as a manual camera (the term 'priority' referring to aperture or shutter). The photographer sets this half of the exposure and the camera's micro computer works out the other half of the exposure. The camera to the right is a 35 mm SLR Pentax Spotmatic F. A manually-operated camera, it can also have its lenses changed. Continued on 179

There is a vast selection of different types of camera available on the market, ranging from the manual to the completely automatic type. Each has advantages or disadvantages: the automatic camera sets its controls by itself, whilst the manual camera requires the photographer to set them. It is extremely easy to use a camera for recording information in a snapshot way, but to use one in a creative way or for model photography requires a complete understanding of the camera's controls or 'functions', to give them their proper name, and its limitations.

Basically any camera is just another tool which needs learning to use, but it does not stop there. The exposed film will have to be processed before it can be viewed. This itself depends upon the type of film that is used. With colour slide (or transparency) film the finished photograph after processing is exactly what the camera 'saw', so if you need to incorporate any special effects this has to be done when you take the picture. Negative (or print) film requires two-stage processing to turn the negative into a positive; first the film is developed, then the negative image is printed on to paper. It is at the printing stage that further darkroom effects can be added. The quality of the final picture in either case, however, relies upon the sharpness of the image captured on the film. A bad image on a negative film, no matter how well printed, will always produce a poor result.

A camera has a series of easily explained functions, but they are so interlocked and reliant upon each other that, unless each function is properly understood, a series of poor results can occur. For the newcomer to photography the single lens reflex camera's body is simply a device for securing and advancing the film in such a way that no light reaches the film surface until required. As each photograph is taken, the film is advanced

forward a given amount so that fresh unexposed film is ready for use. The light reaching the film is decided by the shutter, also fitted in the body. This controls the amount of light reaching the film's surface by regulating the amount of time the shutter is open. To make the shutter more useful it will be capable of various speeds from ¼, ½ or 1 second at the slower end of the scale up to ¹⁄₅₀₀ or even ¹⁄₁,₀₀₀ of a second at its fastest speed range. The important point to note from these shutter speeds is the fact that each shutter speed is approximately twice the speed of the one in front of it, so that in effect the shutter lets in half the amount of light due to the fact that it is open for half the amount of time. It can thus be seen that the shutter controls the amount of light which reaches the film's surface and this forms one half of the two-part requirement for film exposure.

The second half of the exposure is controlled by the aperture, which is a metal iris similar to that in the human eye. This opens and closes and by doing so controls the amount of light passing through it. The iris, or to give it its correct name 'aperture', is generally fitted between the camera's lenses so as to provide maximum optical performance. Again, it will be marked up in such a way that each time it closes down one 'stop' it lets in half the amount of light. The term 'stop' is derived from the fact that each 'f' number controls the amount of light emerging from the lens and on to the film's surface by a known amount and effectively 'stops' the rest of the unwanted excess light.

The 'f' number of the lens is the focal length of the lens divided by its diameter. Thus a lens which focuses at the skyline (infinity) and does this at 100 mm from the film's surface is said to have a focal length of 100 mm. If the diameter of the lens was 25 mm, this divides into the focal length equally by four, providing the 'f' number of 4 which is expressed as f4. It can easily be seen that the numbers f4, f8 and f16 divide equally, whilst f5.6, f11 or f22 do not and are fraction numbers. However, it is the *area* of their opening that mathematically shows twice the amount of light to pass through. f4 and f8 allows four times the amount of light through, because the area of the aperture has been increased by 4. This is why the fractions are used. f5.6 is twice the *area* of f4 and allows twice the amount of light through, and this is why the aperture is marked up f4, f5.6, f8, f11, etc.

When judging exposure these two elements, shutter speed and aperture, both have to be taken into account. In simple terms, they have to be added together to form a total—say ten for ease of example. With five parts aperture plus five parts shutter speed exposure will be perfect, as will seven of one and three of the other, or any similar combination. However, if you had seven parts shutter speed and seven parts aperture, too much light would reach the film and the picture would be over-exposed. If the total was three plus six the picture would be underexposed, or dark. This principle applies to all cameras, irrespective of type or make.

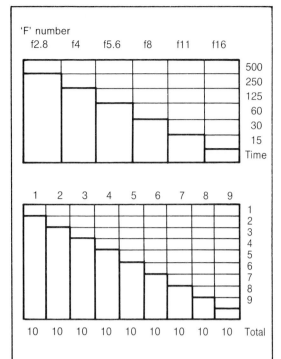

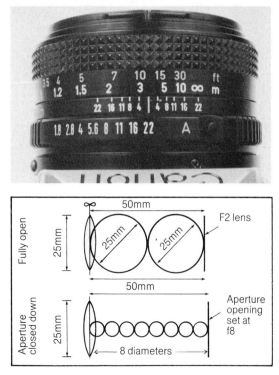

Continued from previous page

Below this is the 35 mm Ricoh ZF, a rangefinder non-interchangeable lens camera. Left is the Hasselblad SLR 500CM, a 6 cm by 6 cm format camera which is manual and requires the use of a separate light meter.

Left To take the theory of exposure and classify it as totalling ten, this can be achieved using two numbers (parts) in a combination of ways. Aperture opening (part 1) + shutter speed (part 2) = the total of the exposure. The aperture and shutter speed are the two parts that are used to make up the exposure, which is determined by the sensitivity of the film to light. The illustration shows a camera fitted with a shutter speed range of 2 seconds through to 1/1000 of a second. The shutter controls the length of time that the light falls on to the film's surface. This is constructed so as to double, allowing twice the time for the light to strike the film's surface, or vice versa. The aperture is also constructed so that it allows twice the amount of light through for each next stop up. Shown is a lens fitted with an aperture range of f1.8 to f22.

The focal length of the lens is divided by its diameter to provide its 'f' number ie. the lens focused at infinity, at the distance of 100 mm is expressed as a 100 mm lens. If the diameter of the lens is 25 mm it divides into 100 mm four times so that the lens is now expressed as being a 100 mm f4 lens.

Opposite page, top left The aperture of the lens set at f3.5.

Top centre The aperture of the lens set at f22.

Top far right The illustration shows the aperture fully open and fully closed. An f3.5 lens, set at its widest aperture, allows through the maximum amount of light, but has a poor depth of field. The lens set at f22 allows through a small amount of light, but provides maximum depth of field.

Opposite page, centre above The effect of perspective using a 35mm lens.

Centre below The effect of foreshortened perspective using a 135mm lens.

THE LENS AND FILM SPEED

The function which the lens of the camera performs is that of focusing the image or 'picture', as it is commonly known, on to the film's surface. Lenses have various focal lengths, the lower the number the wider the angle of view (ie, a 24 mm lens is an ultra wide angle lens, whilst a 1,000 mm lens is an ultra long telephoto lens with a narrow angle of view). The so-called 'standard' lens will depend upon the camera's size (or 'format', to give it its proper name). For the 35 mm format camera the standard lens is of 50 mm focal length and for the larger 6 cm × 6 cm camera format it is 75 mm. These standard focal length lens sizes equate to the zone of picture angle normally seen in sharp focus by the eye. However, the eye actually sees peripherally a greater angle of view, so for this reason a certain focal length of lens is called 'the camera's standard lens'.

The angle of view of the lens affects perspective as well as determining how much of a scene fills the film's picture area (or 'frame', to use the correct term again). Using a 35 mm format camera and fitting a wide angle lens (28 mm) will allow you to fill the frame with a view of a house whilst standing very close to the building. If the lens was changed for a 50 mm standard one the photographer would have to stand further away from the house to fill the frame with the same view. Finally, if a very long telephoto lens (1,000 mm) was used the photographer could well end up half a mile away yet still only fill the frame with a picture of the house. What happens is that the wide angle lens exaggerates the perspective, the telephoto lens foreshortens it, and the standard lens makes things look normal.

The lens in each case will also contain the aperture, which controls the amount of light allowed to pass through the lens. As this is closed down and reduced in its area size it restricts the amount of light passing through (eg, f2, maximum aperture, to f22, minimum aperture size). As it does so, however, it also increases the depth of field of the lens, or in other words the amount of the picture which is in sharp focus. This factor is very important as a picture will be in sharp focus at f22 over a far greater distance than with a low f2 setting, which has practically no depth of field and is useless for model photography. Using f22 does have a disadvantage, though, in that since we are now allowing only a small amount of light to pass through the lens a longer shutter speed will be required (ie, one part aperture plus nine parts shutter speed equalling our exposure of ten).

The necessary exposure will depend upon the film's sensitivity to light, as various types of film are produced. They are rated as ISO, ASA or DIN, followed by a number. These initials stand for various standards recognized throughout the world, but since most countries are now agreeing on one standard this will soon be known as ISO (the International Standards Organization). The number which follows varies from 20 to 32,000 and denotes

The angle of view of the lens is governed by its focal length. On 35 mm format cameras a lens that focuses at 21 mm is classified as a very wide angle lens, a 35 mm lens is a wide and the 50 mm lens is known as the standard lens as its angle of view matches that of the eye. A lens that focuses further away than this is known as a telephoto lens. These range from 55 mm to well over 1,000 mm. All variable focal length lenses are commonly called 'zoom' lenses, because one can apparently move quickly nearer to the subject. Hence to zoom!

Aperture setting

f3.5

f22

he film's sensitivity to light, so an ISO 100 film is half as sensitive to light as ISO 200 and twice as ensitive to light as ISO 50. This provides a choice of 'film speed' to suit the available lighting. On a bright sunny day ISO 50 is a good film to use as here is plenty of available light which also provides acceptable shutter speeds and aperture. At night ime, however, the amount of light is considerably educed, and whilst the film can still be used, the shutter speed required to make the exposure becomes inconveniently long. We can make this shutter speed time shorter by exchanging the slow ISO 50 film with a super-fast ISO 32,000 film, which s 64 times more sensitive to light and will considerably reduce the amount of exposure time equired. But by exchanging our film we pay a penalty, because the film's surface is made up of iny grains of silver light-sensitive crystals, and the smaller they are, the slower they are to react to the ight. By comparing the ISO 50 to ISO 32,000 it can be seen that the grains of the former look like fine sand while the latter look like small pebbles. This change also brings about a loss in picture quality, so hat in the end a compromise has to be reached. An ISO 125 black-and-white film is a good all-round film o use, its speed and resolution both being acceptable due to the grain size. For colour slides ISO 64 is an acceptable film and for colour negatives ISO 100.

Colour film is sensitive to the colour 'temperature' of the light source, whilst black-and-white film is not. f the wrong type of colour film or lighting is used the esulting picture will have an overall colour cast. Daylight film is designed to be exposed in daylight conditions or with electronic flash. Tungsten film is designed to be exposed under colour-balanced artificial lights (not household lamps). If you expose colour films to the wrong lighting conditions without using correction filters the picture will be unacceptable, being either too blue or too yellow, as colour film 'sees' very differently to the way the human eye sees things.

Left Ilford FP4 black and white film, 35mm format, 36 exposures, rated at 125 ASA 22 DIN. All black and white films can be used in mixed lighting situations.

Right The 35 mm SLR camera is very popular due to both its size and versatility. The camera shown has a variable focal length lens fitted, ie 35-70mm. This is a wide angle, standard and short telephoto lens all in one.

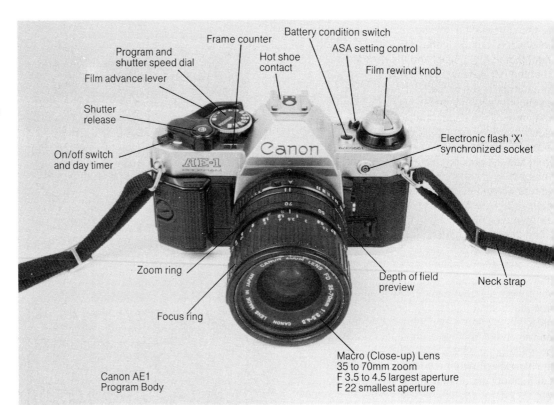

Frame counter

Battery condition switch

ASA setting control

Program and shutter speed dial

Hot shoe contact

Film advance lever

Film rewind knob

Shutter release

On/off switch and day timer

Electronic flash 'X' synchronized socket

Zoom ring

Depth of field preview

Neck strap

Focus ring

Macro (Close-up) Lens
35 to 70mm zoom
F 3.5 to 4.5 largest aperture
F 22 smallest aperture

Canon AE1
Program Body

Right The camera needs the ASA/ISO setting changed to match the film used. The ¼ to 4 section allows re-rating for difficult lighting situations.

Below To enable the lens to focus nearer than normal, extension tubes are used between the camera's body and its lens. By using various combinations of these tubes different close focusing distances are obtained.

LIGHTING AND EXPOSURE

Since the film does see differently to the eye it requires lighting to meet its very special needs irrespective as to the film type (ie, artificial or natural light film). To make sure that the film receives the required amount of light for making the correct exposure, the light has to be carefully measured using a suitable meter. There are two types of light, 'available light' which is continuous, such as daylight, tungsten and fluorescent; or electronic flash. This type of light, since it is of very short duration, requires a special light meter, the continuous available light meter not being suitable. Daylight and electronic flash light are colour balanced, that is to say that the same daylight type of film can be used for both light sources. Daylight film is colour balanced to 5,600k, the standard method of reading colour temperature, whilst tungsten film is colour balanced for 3,200k (photo lamps), much lower in its colour temperature. Effectively daylight film sees tungsten lighting as a warm yellow colour and tungsten film sees daylight as a cold blueish colour each of which will create a colour cast over the entire picture. For this reason daylight and tungsten lighting should never be mixed while using the same film. Since black-and-white film does not see colour in the same way it can be used under various mixed lighting conditions without incurring problems.

All types of film have to be exposed correctly and that is why a light meter is used. The best method of doing this is to measure the reflected light from the surface of the subject, averaging out over the light and dark areas by taking a number of readings, then deciding upon which area to make the exposure for e, the light parts of the subject, the dark parts, or he shadow parts). If the difference between the right part of the subject and the shadow part is too reat the film cannot cope, it will over-expose and urn out on the bright part, be correctly exposed for he middle tones and under-exposed for the shadow rea, producing a soot and white wash result. To vercome this problem, known as 'contrast', either a econd diffused light can be used or the existing ght used by reflecting it back into the shadow, from , piece of white shiny card. This is known as 'fill-in' ght, as it fills in the shadow with additional light and educes the contrast between the bright light and ow light areas.

The maximum difference between the bright and ow light areas which the film can cope with is, for colour transparency film minus 1½ stops, for colour negative film minus 2½ stops and for black and white film, which needs a greater difference to produce an effect, from a minimum of two stops to a maximum of four stops less than the main light reading. The exposure of film to light is very critical; oo much light and it over-exposes, too little light and it under-exposes, too wide a contrast range and t still cannot cope. This is why films are marked up with ISO numbers, so that their effective sensitivity o light is known to the photographer, who can then expose the film accordingly.

USING THE 35MM CAMERA (STUDIO WORK)

The first thing to do after loading a camera with film s to set the camera's light meter, according to the ilm speed used (eg ISO 100). Having done this the camera is 'set' for use. The first two frames (pictures) should be wound on by pressing the shutter and wasted, as the film is already exposed to ght. Once this is done the camera is 'ready' for use. For model photography the aperture of the camera's ens should be set at its smallest aperture—f16, f22 or f32 depending upon the lens and the camera

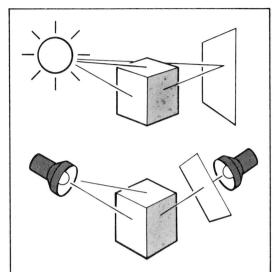

Left By filling in the shadows with reflected or additional diffused light the shadows become less dense, as the film 'sees' in a very different way from the eye.

Below A high contrast photograph with no detail in the shadows.

Bottom A good contrast photograph showing both highlights and details in the shadows as only one light source was used.

Typical information shown in a camera's viewfinder, displaying shutter speed and aperture. The circle in the middle is used to aid focusing.

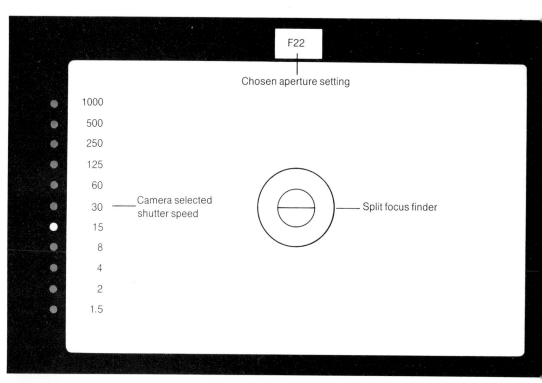

F22

Chosen aperture setting

1000
500
250
125
60
30 —— Camera selected shutter speed
15
8
4
2
1.5

Split focus finder

The Weston hand-held light meter needs to have the ASA/ISO set. The meter has two ranges, from two to ten, then ten to sixteen. The example shows the 10 to 16 range but the meter is set for a reading of 8.75 for ASA/ISO film of 100 and provides a range of exposure settings from f22 at half of one second, to f0.5 at 1/4,000 of a second. The camera's lens limits this range, because if the lens is a f2.8/f22 it would restrict the range to seven of the combinations, not eleven, as shown on the meter and the camera's available shutter speeds restrict this at times still further.

By using a cone over the light meter's photo-electric cell the light arriving on to the scene can be measured.

focused upon the subject. If the subject is too near to focus the camera's lens, extension tubes will be required. These are fitted between the lens and the camera's body so as to enable the lens to focus at a shorter distance than normally used. Once you have focused upon the subject you will notice that the camera is difficult to hold steady and in focus at close range. Also, when the light reading is taken, using a small aperture to provide an acceptable depth of field means that a slow shutter speed will be needed (less than 1/60 of a second), so a tripod will be needed to hold the camera steady and in focus.

The tripod should be of solid construction so that it supports the camera firmly and does not vibrate or shake, as this will also cause unsharp photographs. The tripod is used in several ways: to hold the camera in focus, and to hold the camera steady whilst the photograph is taken. Additionally, once set up in a fixed position, other people can view the scene through the camera, then lenses can be changed so as to study their different effects on the perspective so that good composition within the photograph can be achieved.

Finally the scene is lit. The lighting is set to suit the subject and the shadows filled in with additional lighting. If photographing out of doors, rotate the model to suit the existing lighting and be careful not to cast a shadow over the model by standing in front of the light or putting other items in the way. Take care with the background as well, avoiding out of scale items such as roofs and chimney pots. Mount the camera on a tripod and focus on to the subject. Take a light reading through the camera or use a separate light meter to suit the lighting available, set the shutter speed and, to avoid shaking the camera whilst using the slow shutter speed, use a cable elease. Press the shutter button via this or use the camera's delayed action.

I have found through practice it is well worth making several exposures, by bracketing each. This is a technique by which the adding and reducing time is used (faster and slower shutter speed) on each side of the aperture's unchanged setting, so as to provide a selection of negatives to print from. This is especially important when using colour transparency film, as what you take is the finished photograph.

PHOTOGRAPHY IN PRACTICE

Using a camera is really an applied science. Each part of the camera has a job to do and will do it without question. An automatic camera 'thinks' for the photographer, deciding which settings to use, but it can only act on the information supplied. It cannot interpret the information and can easily be fooled. The same applies with auto-focus cameras, which again can be confused into interpreting the information wrongly. The photographer therefore needs to be aware of these faults and correct them.

The manual camera has one advantage: the photographer has to set it for each photograph, and having been set the camera will then do precisely what is asked of it so if a mistake occurs it is because the photographer has made an error. Ideally the type of camera to purchase is the automatic with a complete manual override, which allows the photographer to let the camera do the thinking for the straightforward photographs, and to use the override to turn it into a manual camera so he can do the thinking and interpreting in difficult lighting and subject situations.

One of the most advanced cameras of this type is the Canon A1 which has five independent functions. In addition the camera also has an 'exposure lock' which allows the photographer to average out difficult lighting scenes, then lock the camera's setting. Finally the camera supplies both aperture and shutter speed information in the viewfinder, which the photographer uses as a guide. This is ideal for back lighting situations or when there is a lot of sky showing in the picture—for example, photographing a church steeple or viaduct from the shadow side is guaranteed to produce a silhouette picture with an automatic camera unless the exposure is altered.

Note Various lenses will have different f number (aperture) settings. For example, page 179 shows a f1.8 to f22 lens. Page 181 shows a f3.5 to f22 lens. The tilt and shift lens shown on page 186 has a f2 to f22 aperture setting. The same applies to a lens's focal length—page 180 shows 35mm, 50mm and 100mm and on page 182 a 35mm to 70mm variable focal length zoom lens is shown.

The lens set at f2.8 has a very shallow depth of field, and is unsuitable for model photography.

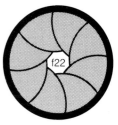

The lens set at f22 provides maximum depth of field. Both the front and the back of the subject are now in focus but because the lighting was poor the dark paintwork and the shadows have clogged into solid black, an easy mistake to make when photographing rolling stock.

Photograph taken with sun behind camera. The camera's light meter coped with the situation with ease.

Photograph taken with sun in front of camera. This fooled the camera's light meter into thinking that a lot of light was available, as it metered the bright sky only and did not allow for the dark shadow areas. To expose this scene properly, the photographer would have to 'set' the camera on manual or lock the exposure setting, taking a meter reading for the shadow areas only.

The tilt and shift lens used for architectural photography. The shift allows verticals to be corected in camera and the tilt permits the plane of focus to be varied.

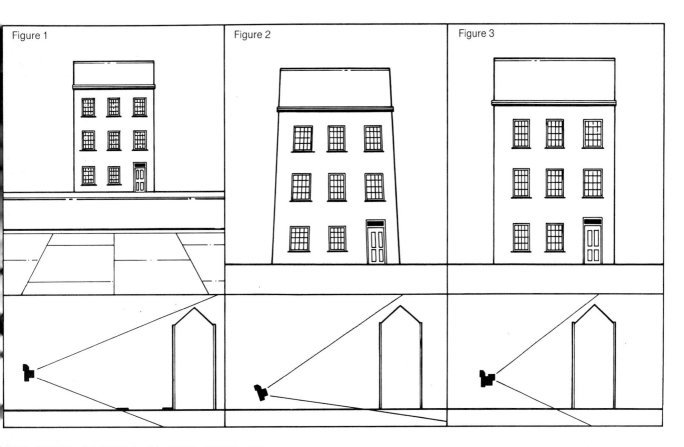

Figure 1   Figure 2   Figure 3

THE 35MM CAMERA IN USE (OUT OF DOORS)

First select a film type suitable for the type of photography to be undertaken then load the camera. Making sure the camera's instructions are followed, set the ASA, DIN or ISO rating of the film, so that the camera knows which speed of film it is using. Point and focus the camera at the subject. Take a light reading and match both aperture and shutter speed to suit the exposure, allowing for light and dark areas. Set the aperture to provide an acceptable depth of field (ie, f8) and set the shutter to a sufficiently high speed to enable the camera to be hand-held (ie, 1/125 second). If there is too much light, stop down the aperture, followed by altering the shutter speed. If there is too little light reduce shutter speed to 1/60 second then adjust the aperture. If the shutter speed needs to be less than 1/60 second mount the camera on a tripod and use a cable release or set the camera on delayed action so that the tripod has time to cease vibrating after pressing the button before taking the picture.

For close-up photography apply the techniques described in the studio photography section and remember that the camera's built in light meter will take care of any difference in exposure caused by the use of the extension tubes and filters as it meters through the lens. Much the same applies when using converters, to change the lens' focal length.

To obtain the most useful results when surveying a building, it should be photographed squarely from all sides (if possible) and you should include roof photographs and obliques to explain how corners relate to each other. I have found through practice that a 35 mm to 70 mm zoom lens is ideal for this. The 35 mm (wide angle) setting allows overall photographs to be taken without too much distortion and the 70 mm setting (short telephoto) is used for photography of roof details, etc.

The camera can photograph the elevations of buildings in such a way that they can be used to make a model, avoiding the majority of the drafting out stage normally used to turn photographs into working drawings. The technique is to set the camera up square on to the elevation of the building to be modelled and keep the back of the camera parallel vertically to the building. Use a wide angle lens and photograph the entire elevation, then in the darkroom enlarge the building to the required scale. If it was impossible to photograph the elevation without tilting the camera upwards, the converging verticals will have to be corrected in the darkroom. The method that the professional photographer uses in this situation is a shift lens, which enables the back of the camera to be held parallel to the building and the lens raised to photograph the building, thus correcting converging verticals in the camera.

BLACK AND WHITE FILM PROCESSING

After the film has been exposed it obviously has to be processed. This is a very straightforward procedure started by winding the film back into the film cassette whilst it is still in the camera. If you carefully listen to the film winding back in the camera the point that it disengages from the take up spool can be heard. At this point stop so that when the

Above

Fig 1 By using a wide angle lens and standing back from the building, keeping the camera vertical, the building will be square in the photograph. Unwanted bits are then trimmed off the print.

Fig 2 If the camera is tilted up at the building the verticals will converge at the top.

Fig 3 By using a shift lens the photographer can move nearer the building and still correct the verticals in the camera.

Right A selection of some of the equipment used to develop a film. Note the developing tank with two spirals, allowing films to be processed together.

Warning Keep all photographic chemicals away from children and foodstuffs.

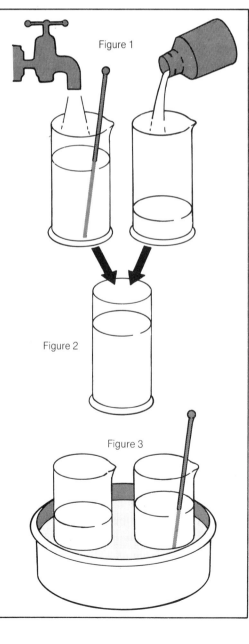

Fig 1 Mix water to the required temperature and measure out both water and chemicals in separate containers.

Fig 2 Then mix together. *Do not* measure by pouring in the water then adding the chemicals, because if too much is added it cannot be taken out.

Fig 3 Keep the chemicals and water to be used at a constant temperature by immersing their containers in a large bowl of correctly heated water.

Figure 1

Figure 2

Figure 3

camera is opened a short length of film will still be protruding from the cassette. Remove the cassette from the camera and cut across the protruding piece of film with a pair of scissors so as to square the end then trim up the sharp corners at 45 degrees. This will enable the film to load in the spiral easily.

In total darkness load the film on to the spiral as per processing tank instructions and when completed cut off the film's cassette spool as this is unwanted. Complete loading the film on to the spiral and place it into the tank, checking to make sure that the sealing washer, if required, is correctly in place. Then screw the lid into position, checking to make sure it is on correctly before turning on the room lights. (Note: A film changing bag will suffice for loading the film into the tank.) The film in its tank is ready for processing.

Processing black-and-white photographic film is very straightforward as it only requires two chemicals known as 'developer' and 'fixer'. These are available in concentrated liquid form, needing to be diluted with water before use.

Mixing up the chemicals requires four containers, two for each chemical so that they do not get contaminated with each other. These are then mixed up as per instructions found on the bottles. If Patterson Acutol developer is used, for example, it is mixed one part chemical to nine parts of water, preheated to twenty degrees centigrade to form a working solution. Much the same applies with the fixer, only this time it is one part chemical to three parts preheated water, also at twenty degrees centigrade. The reason is that developing a film depends on time and temperature; if the mixed chemicals are hot the developing time is reduced and visa versa, so this processing temperature of twenty degrees centigrade is very important.

The procedure for developing the film is to first pour in the working mixture of developer and start the timing (eg, Ilford ISO 125 film requires six minutes using Pattersons Acutol). As soon as the developer is poured in, agitate the tank by inverting it back and forth or using the spiral agitator for thirty seconds. Stop and leave for thirty seconds, then agitate for five seconds, repeating every 25 seconds until the processing time has elapsed. Then pour the used developer away, rinsing the film in the tank with clean fresh water several times or, using a stop bath at the same temperature of twenty centigrade. Empty the tank and pour in the fixer and constantly agitate for the fixing time as found on the instructions (eg, thirty seconds for Ilford high speed fixer). On completion of the fixing time return the fixer for storage as this can be used again. Rinse the film with tap water for fifteen minutes in the processing tank starting at 20°C temperature, cold water being added to this as the fixer must be washed out of the film. When the washing time has finished squeegy the film and hang up in a dust-free place to dry. The processing is now complete. When the film has dried (normal room temperature three hours) cut up and file, as the negatives are ready for printing.

With black-and-white home processing, especially since various types of film and chemicals are available on the market, I have found it very worthwhile to try out different makes, as film can be 'pushed' by regrading its ISO recommended exposure time. This means that an entire length of 100 ISO film can be rated as 400 and developed accordingly, the penalty being that the film's grain size increases, which shows on the print.

PRINTING BLACK-AND-WHITE

After the black-and-white film has been processed it shows a negative image which will require reversing to form a positive. This is easily obtained in the printing stage as the paper goes darker when it is exposed to white light. The negative is used to restrict the amount of white light. The paper masked by the dark areas on the negative remains white whilst in other areas which receive a lot of light it becomes dark (the negative when exposed in the camera works in the same way).

A white border is obtained around a print by using a masking frame. This shields the paper from the light emitted from the enlarger, and since the edge of the paper is covered by the masking frame it remains white. Borderless prints are produced by exposing the entire sheet of photographic paper, without covering the edges.

ENLARGERS

There are many types available on the market, varying from the simple to the very complex self-analyzing type. Each is designed to do the same job, to project the negative on to the photographic paper. The enlarger needs to be of sturdy construction so that it does not vibrate, and also to have a lens fitted that equals the camera's lens in its resolving power, otherwise it will soften the final picture. Unfortunately the camera's lens cannot be used properly in the enlarger as it is designed to focus a curved field of view, while the enlarger's lens is designed for a flat field of view so that the

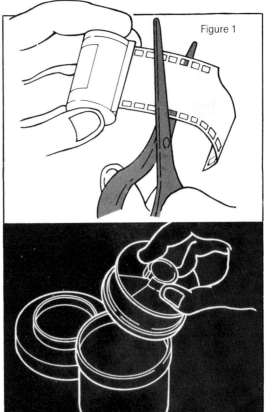

Fig 1 Remove the film from the camera and trim the leader off of the film using scissors, then trim the sharp corners at 45 degrees, missing the perforated holes, so that the film loads into the spiral easily.

Fig 2 Load the film into the spiral and processing tank in total darkness.

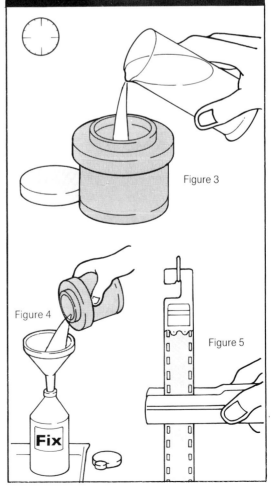

Fig 3 Pour in the developer and start timing, agitating for the first thirty seconds continuously, then leave for 25 seconds. Next agitate every five seconds, leaving for 25 seconds to make up a thirty second cycle as necessary during the development time. Pour away when the time is finished. Rinse in water or use a stop bath of the same temperature then fix continuously agitating throughout the time required.

Fig 4 Returning fixer to the storage bottle on completion.

Fig 5 Wash and squeegy the film and hang up to dry in a dust-free place.

An enlarger set up in a small darkroom, the trays being stored underneath and paper above. Adjustable shelving is used to vary the height of the printing surface, to allow for making very large prints.

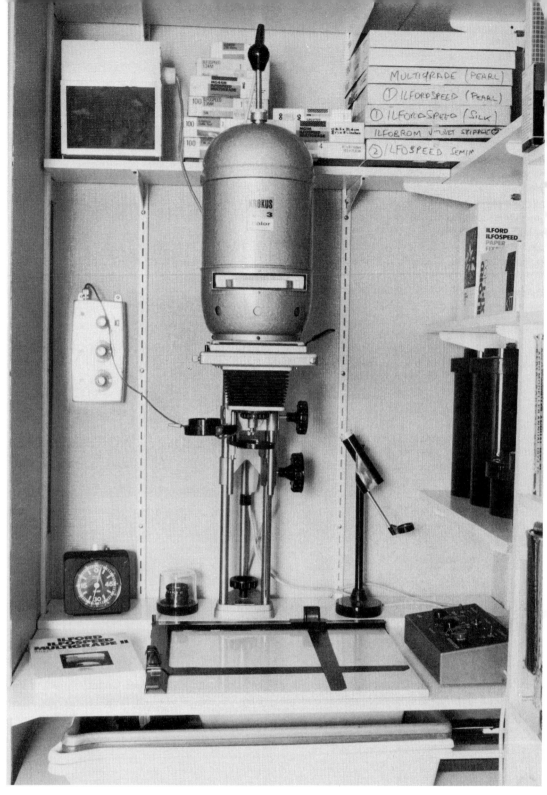

Opposite page Fig 1 Use three trays slightly larger than the paper size.

Fig 2 Prepare chemicals to the manufacturer's specification for each tray.

Fig 3 Place negative emulsion side down in carrier and focus the picture to size.

Fig 4 Adjust aperture to suit.

Fig 5 Adjust masking frame to suit paper size, compose picture and make test wedge.

Fig 6 Place print face down, then turn over.

Fig 7 Keep the developer or fixer moving over the print's surface.

Fig 8 Wash the print in running water, peg up and dry. This can be speeded up by squeegeeing and using a hair dryer.

Fig 9 Inspect the test wedge and select exposure time for the finished print, then repeat the procedure for the final print.

enlarged picture remains square around its edges. If a camera lens is used in an enlarger it will produce either a pincushion shape or a barrel shape edge.

PRINTING

The printing stage of black-and-white prints is also very straightforward and similar to processing the film. The chemicals are slightly different in their composition, although they are still called 'developer' and 'fixer'. This time the developer is designed to develop paper and the fixer is of a non-acid hardening type, mixed up and used in the same way. The main difference is that this time the chemicals are poured into dishes and the procedure of print developing and fixing is carried out under a safe light, of a reddish-orangey-yellow colour of low power, to which the black-and-white photographic paper is not very sensitive. The box of paper can only be safely opened under these lighting conditions.

The negative is placed in the enlarger's carrier emulsion side towards the lens and the enlarger switched on with the room lights switched off, leaving the safe light on. The picture is then sized by moving the enlarger up or down the column and focused. Next the masking frame is set for size to suit the paper, the enlarger's lens aperture is then stopped down three stops and the enlarger switched off. A sample piece of photographic paper is then placed in the masking frame (closing the box after each sheet is removed) emulsion side up and four-fifths covered with a piece of cardboard. The enlarger is then switched on for five seconds, exposing this strip of uncovered paper. The cardboard is then moved across the paper so as to uncover three-fifths of the paper and exposed by switching on again for five seconds. This is repeated across the paper until all the paper has been exposed in a series of strips. The paper is then removed from the masking frame and placed emulsion side down into the developer-filled dish

and agitated by rocking the tray. After five seconds turn the paper over using tongs and continue to develop the paper, agitating the dish all the time for a minute (at twenty degrees centigrade using Ilford Multigrade developer). On completion of the developing time rinse the paper in water or use a stop bath, then place face down into the fixer. Taking care not to touch the fixer with the tongs, use a second pair of tongs to turn the paper over and allow to fix for thirty seconds using higher velocity fixer or ten minutes with slow fixer. After this time has elapsed the room lights can safely be switched on. Now wash the print in running water for three minutes and dry. The test wedge print can now be examined. This will show as a series of progressively darkening strips, the picture starting at 25 seconds (dark)

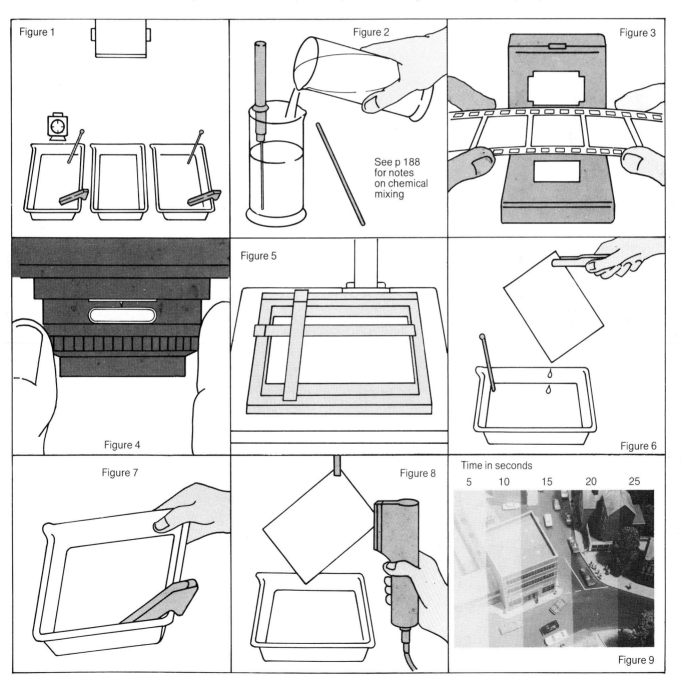

Figure 1

Figure 2

See p 188 for notes on chemical mixing

Figure 3

Figure 4

Figure 5

Figure 6

Figure 7

Figure 8

Time in seconds
5   10   15   20   25

Figure 9

Below By tilting the enlarger sideways, converging elevations can be corrected. To maintain focus, the lens will also have to be re-aligned, by tilting (as shown in the small illustration.) By sizing the enlargement, to model size, the elevation can then be mounted on card in a series of layers as shown on the opposite page from Fig 6 onwards. The photographic paper to use for both these methods is the fibre type, as the modern resin-coated paper tends to have a 'non stick' surface, resulting in the paint used for colouring falling off.

Opposite page
Fig 1 Drawing of the building made on tracing paper.

Fig 2 Under safe light conditions, place the drawing (turn over for opposite hand) on a sheet of photographic paper, then cover with glass to keep the drawing and paper pressed together.

Fig 3 Exposure to white light, the time being established through trial and error.

Fig 4 Develop, rinse or stop, fix and wash the photographic paper in the normal way.

Fig 5 Make several prints.

Fig 6 Mount on to card.

Fig 7 Cut out doors and windows.

Fig 8 Paint to suit and use spraymount on the back.

Fig 9 Fix on to previously mounted photo, trim to required size.

exposure down to five seconds (light). If the overall effect of the test strip is too light open the aperture of the lens, if too dark close the aperture of the lens, and repeat the test wedge.

Select the most suitable exposure (eg, fifteen seconds), then switch off the room lights and place a fresh piece of photographic paper in the masking frame emulsion side up. Expose all the paper for fifteen seconds by switching on the enlarger. Then develop and fix the paper in the pre-mentioned way, wash and dry and the first print is completed.

Normally, since cameras these days produce evenly-exposed negatives shot on the same film under the same conditions, the remaining negatives can be exposed at the same enlarging time for that strip of film, with only the odd print requiring extended or reduced enlarging time.

MAKING USE OF THE ENLARGER
The print's quality depends upon matching the negative to the printing paper. A 'contrasty' negative requires a soft paper (grade 0) and a soft negative a hard paper (grade 5). Ilford produce something called Multigrade which is a single box of paper of eleven different grades, changed by filtration. This resin-coated paper will be found to be very economical, compared with purchasing six boxes of different grades of paper, of which only two will be used most of the time.

The procedure for changing the paper's grade, when using Multigrade, is by exchanging the filter fitted in the enlarger for a different one. The filters are supplied by Ilford to match the various paper grades and range in colour from orange (grade 0) to deep magenta (grade 5). The orange produces a soft grade of paper and the deep magenta a hard grade. The reason for the change of paper grade is that a hard contrasty negative produces an acceptable print on a soft grade of paper, while a soft negative prints to an acceptable standard on hard paper. The average negative prints on a grade 2 or 3. This change of paper grade provides the photographer with control over the tones of the print, permitting the correction of the all-grey or soot and whitewash effect.

Additional control over the print can be made by holding back areas that print too dark (reduced exposure) or by burning in (increased exposure) areas that print incorrectly, using 'dodges'. These control localized areas of printing by preventing light reaching the paper or increasing the light and are made of card. The first is a round disk of card on a piece of wire, the second is a piece of card with a hole cut in it. During the printing exposure they are used between the lens and the paper and are kept moving so as not to form a hard edge on the print.

The enlarger can also be tilted which corrects the

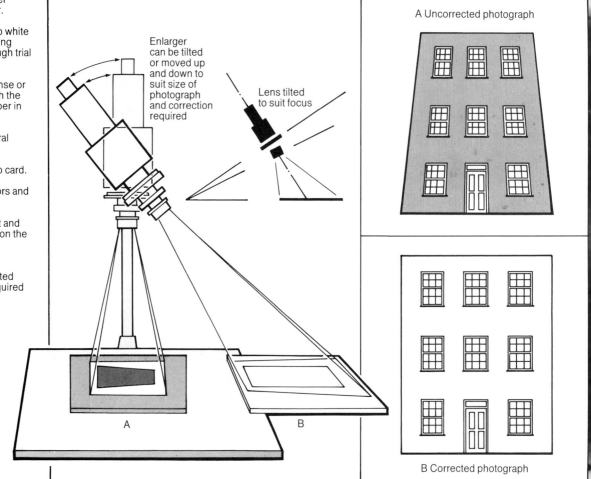

Enlarger can be tilted or moved up and down to suit size of photograph and correction required

Lens tilted to suit focus

A

B

A Uncorrected photograph

B Corrected photograph

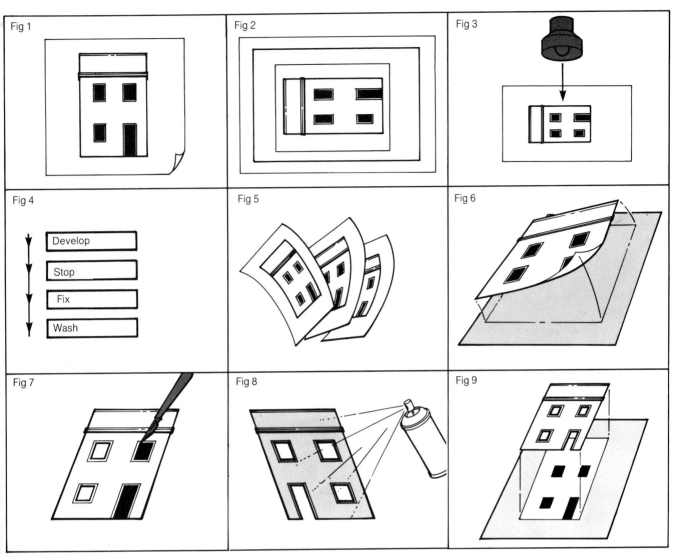

Fig 1 | Fig 2 | Fig 3

Fig 4
- Develop
- Stop
- Fix
- Wash

Fig 5 | Fig 6

Fig 7 | Fig 8 | Fig 9

verticals. The technique used is to draw two parallel lines on the enlarger's masking frame and tilt the enlarger so that the projected image (ie, a building) now becomes parallel with these lines. The lens is also tilted to focus the negative from end to end, followed by making a print on to paper in the usual way, allowing slightly more exposure to the print at the widest end of the picture by 'dodging' with a piece of card.

By sizing the print on non-resin-coated paper to N, HO, or OO standard scales the print can then be cut up and made into an elevation photographically. If several prints are made at the same time they can then be cut up to form overlays, mounted on card and painted. This saves hours of work drawing out the elevations of buildings, etc. Alternatively, the elevation can be drawn out on a sheet of tracing paper and placed under the enlarger, which this time does not have a negative in its carrier. The technique is first to draw the elevations of the building, including the door and window glazing bars, in black ink on a sheet of tracing paper to the required scale. Then, in the darkroom under safe light conditions, place the tracing on top of a sheet of non-resin-coated photographic paper, weighted

down with a sheet of clean clear glass or plastic so as to hold the tracing flat on top of the photographic paper. By switching on the enlarger, the exposure is made, the time being determined by using the test wedge principle so as to produce a mid- to dark grey print and white window glazing bars. By changing the colour background of the paper (eg, from white to red or silver), coloured glazing bars can be obtained. Alternatively again white paper can be dyed with nylon dyes to produce the desired colour.

The tracing paper method can be used with the minimum of equipment, requiring three trays all larger than the paper size to be used, one Patterson red safe light and a desk lamp fitted with a fifteen watt bulb. The procedure is to set up in a dark room (eg, under the stairs) with the premixed developer, water and fixer to temperature in,trays, under safe light conditions, then lay the tracing over the photographic paper on a flat surface and cover with a sheet of glass. Switch on the table lamp for about a second, remove the paper and develop in the usual way. The ideal is to expose the photographic paper through the tracing paper to white light which forms an image on the paper after development.

GLOSSARY

Abutment Structure used for support on each side of an arch or bridge.

Adhesive weight Weight of the locomotive borne by the driving wheels, used as friction grip.

Alternating current (single phase AC) Cycle of household electrical current, pulsing between full power and zero, hence the live side and neutral. Three phase incorporates the other half and doubles the supply.

Ampere or **amp** Unit used to measure electrical strength.

Aqueduct Bridge carrying water.

Armature Series of wire-wound bobbins (each one classified as a pole) fixed to the shaft of an electric motor and, when switched on, forming a rotating electro-magnetic. See Commutator.

Articulation Pivoting driving wheels on separate frames complete with their own steam cylinders or electrical power units to help the locomotive to negotiate tight bends more easily.

Automatic coupler One that locates itself and locks into position. Can be uncoupled with the use of a ramp or electro-mechanical device.

Ballast Chippings spread underneath track, used for bedding and levelling.

Banking See Superelevation.

Baseboard Structure on which the model railway is built.

Bay platform A short platform built on one side of a through platform generally used for terminating local or branch line trains.

Bench-mark Spot height shown on a map and marked at the actual location (usually on a wall etc).

Block train One made up of identical wagons and vans.

Bo-Bo Diesel or electric locomotive with two driving axles (ie four driving wheels) on each of the two bogies.

Body shell Basic structure of a model without the fittings.

Bogie Swivelling assembly carrying wheels mounted below a locomotive or coach.

Bolster Principal weight-carrying cross-member of a bogie on which the pivot is fixed.

Bow Wire strip bent with the aid of string, used to draw curves.

Brake van Sometimes known as the guard's van. Used in trains without continuous brakes to supply braking power at the rear.

Branch line Secondary line departing from a main line.

Buffers (also **end stop**) Used to stop rolling-stock at the end of sidings etc.

Buffers Sprung shock-absorbing fittings, fixed at each end of all rolling stock.

Bunker Coal container built into the rear of a tank locomotive.

Cab Driver and fireman's compartment of a locomotive, usually sheltered with a roof.

Can motor Electric motor enclosed in a tin casing.

Cant See Superelevation.

Catch-points Set of points facing away from the direction of travel used to catch rolling stock running away backwards, as on a gradient.

Catenary Arrangement of suspended wires for overhead current collection.

Centre-swing Amount the centre of the vehicle overhangs the track on the inside of a bend.

Chairs Iron castings bolted or spiked to the sleepers and used to secure the rails.

Chipboard Board made from wood chippings bonded together with resin.

Clearway Clearance gap between running tracks.

Clerestory roof One with a central vertical extension, the sides of which are glazed.

Co-Co Diesel or electric locomotive with three driving axles (ie six driving wheels) on each of the two bogies.

Collector Electrical contact rubbing on the live rail or wire.

Commutator Segmented electrical contact ring fixed on to the shaft of an electric motor, used to pass the electricity from the two brushes into the winding of the armature, the number of segments of the commutator corresponding to the number of poles. As it rotates along with the armature on the shaft of the motor, it switches on or off the windings, controlling the effect of the rotating electro-magnets against the static magnet(s). This produces the driving force of the motor.

Contour Line joining places of equal elevation, used to indicate changing levels on a flat sheet such as a map or plan.

Converter Transformer or other unit for converting AC current to DC or vice versa.

Coupling Device used for connecting items of rolling stock.

Cross-tie Longer than standard sleeper used beneath points etc.

Current Rate of flow of electricity.

Curve, compound One formed from a series of radii.

Curve, reverse Curve followed by one in the opposite direction.

Cut-out circuit breaker Automatic device which operates to open the circuit in the event of an electrical overload.

Cutting Excavation through high ground to maintain railway/road level.

Decal (transfer) Printed logo or lettering, removable from its backing, used instead of hand painting.

Direct current Continuously flowing single direction electrical current.

Distant signal Signal showing approaching trains the condition of stop signals ahead.

Double-heading Use of two locomotives to power one train.

Double-slip point Crossover also incorporating sets of points in both directions.

Down line That travelling away from the company offices (usually London).

Drawbar Device for connecting the locomotive to the tender.

Electric pencil Conductive rod used to make a short electrical contact; its prime use is for changing points.

Embankment Built-up ground to carry a railway/road over low ground.

End stop See buffers.

End-swing Amount the end of the vehicle overhangs the track on the outside of a bend.

Fiddle yard Concealed area of a layout used to manually assemble the trains.

Fishplate Plate used to join lengths of rail together (should not be relied upon for electrical connection).

Flange Part of a wheel's rim which engages the rail's inside edge, used to keep rolling stock on the track. The complete profile is known as the tyre.

Flash Unwanted material on injection moulded components (caused by incorrect fitting of the dies).

Footplate Platform on the locomotive for the driver and fireman.

Frog Break in the rails of points allowing wheels to pass through where they cross.

Gauge Actual width, centre to centre, between rails.

Governor Device used to self regulate a train's speed irrespective of incline or descent.

Gradient Slope or incline usually expressed as a ratio, eg 1:150.

Half-wave rectification Electronic method of controlling the current, providing a very precise control of full power.

Halt Stopping place for local services without normal station facilities.

Headshunt Length of track allowing the locomotive to disengage from the rest of the rolling stock (as at a terminal platform) or track on to which a train can draw before setting back into a goods yard.

Home signal Stop signal at the entrance to the next 'block' of signals controlled by a signal box.

Hopper wagon Vehicle that discharges its load through the floor.

Horn-hook Easy-to-use but out-of-scale coupling.

Hump yard Marshalling yard with an artificial hill down which wagons roll into the selected sidings. Also known as gravity shunting.

Island platform One with tracks on both sides.

Island site Layout with access from all sides.

Jumper cables Wiring fitted with plugs and used to connect portable baseboards.

Leading wheels Wheels fitted in front of the driving wheels on a locomotive.

Level crossing General term for a road, path or railway crossing the track on the level, controlled by gates, lights and bars or signals.

Light engine Locomotive travelling without rolling stock.

'Limit of shunt' Indication board on a main line beyond which any rolling stock may not pass during shunting operations.

Livery Colour scheme used by railway companies.

Loading gauge Hanging framework used to check the height of a load before it leaves a siding.

Loop Up and down lines linked together via a half circle, allowing the turning of rolling stock in a train length without uncoupling.

Main line The route used by the majority of fast rail traffic.

Marshalling yard The area where rolling stock is sorted out into train lengths for different destinations.

Micro-chip Minute electronic integrated circuit designed to do a particular task; used in Zero One control.

Motive power depot Engine shed used for servicing and preparing locomotives for running.

Motor bogie Powered bogie fitted with driving wheels.

Motorman Driver of a diesel or electric engine.

Multiple aspect signals Those using electric lamps to give a series of aspects, red, amber and green.

Multiple track Track with running lines in addition to the up and down line.

Multiple unit Two or more power units or locomotives controlled by one driver.

Narrow gauge Any railway track of less than the standard gauge.

Pannier tank Locomotive carrying water tanks fitted on the sides of the boiler.

Pantograph Current-collecting sprung frame used for collection of electricity from overhead wires.

Pilot engine Locomotive used for marshalling empty rolling stock at a terminal station or an additional engine coupled at the front, providing assistance to help pull a heavy load up a steep incline.

Points Trackwork allowing change from one track to another.

Reception road Track used for the arrival of trains at a goods yard.

Release crossover Set of points towards the buffer end of a headshunt to allow a locomotive to depart leaving other rolling stock at the platform.

Reverse loop Length of track turning back on itself, used to turn a train in the opposite direction. It must be used with a reversing switch and electrically segmented track.

Rolling resistance Drag caused by the friction of the axle bearings, wheels etc, opposing the pulling effort.

Rolling stock General term for all vehicles that travel on the tracks.

Roundhouse Engine shed arranged in a part or full circle with a turntable in the centre.

Saddle tank Engine fitted with a water tank shaped to fit over the boiler.

Scale Relationship of any dimension in direct proportion to that of full size, ie 1 in on a model representing 1 ft on the full size item would be one-twelfth scale.

Scissor-crossing Parallel tracks fitted with points and a diamond crossing allowing trains to change over from any direction.

Semaphore signal Older bar-type indicator, with a painted arm and lamp-lit coloured spectacles.

Shunting neck Similar to headshunt, a single track which then divides up into sidings.

Shuttle Train that runs back and forth normally over a short distance on a regular basis.

Side tanks Water containers fitted on either side of the boiler.

Sidings Lengths of track used for shunting, storage etc away from the main line.

Signal Warning indicator fitted alongside the track, used to control the movement of rolling stock.

Signal box Building from which signals and points are operated, having control over specific area of track.

Single slip Crossover incorporating points in one direction only.

Six-foot way Clearway between tracks.

Sleeper Concrete or wood cross-member used to support the track.

Solebars Main front and back cross-members at each end of the wagon frame.

Starter signal One permitting a train to proceed into the next signalling 'block section' ahead.

Station throat Complex of trackwork outside a large station.

Strapping Metal strip reinforcement on rolling stock bodywork.

Stretcher Locomotive's or bogie frame's cross-member.

Stud contact Metal, round-headed spike fitted on the sleeper between the tracks, used for electrical contact on older types of electric model trains.

Superelevation Laying the outside rail higher than the inside rail on a tight curve, enabling the rolling stock to travel around it at a higher speed.

Tank engine Locomotive which carries its own water and coal supply on one chassis.

Tender Wheeled vehicle carrying coal and water supply, attached directly behind the engine.

Trailer coach Unpowered carriage fitted to a railcar or railbus.

Trammel (beam compass) Used for drawing large-radius curves.

Transfers See Decals.

Transformer Unit for converting mains electricity into safe low voltage suitable for model railway use.

Tread Slightly coned face of a locomotive's wheel which is in contact with the track.

Truss rod Bracing used diagonally in the underframe to make it more rigid.

Turnout See Point.

Turntable Rotating device for turning stock or aligning it with other tracks that radiate from it, eg in a roundhouse.

Underframe Load-carrying structural framework which supports the body of a carriage or wagon.

Underlay Material used beneath the track on a layout to help reduce noise.

Up line That travelling towards the company offices (usually London).

Valve gear Mechanism which opens and closes the steam ports of the cylinders of a steam locomotive.

Voltage Electromotive force measured in volts (equivalent of pressure).

Wheel arrangement (4-6-2, 2-6-0, 0-6-0 etc) Formula representing the number of wheels in front of the driving wheels, the number of driving wheels and the number of wheels behind the driving wheels (on the engine only).

Zero One Hornby system of using two-wire digital control for the entire layout.

ACKNOWLEDGEMENTS

I would first like to thank my wife Jean for all the typing, for the contribution she made towards the book and for putting up with the layouts around the house for some two years.

I would also like to thank the following manufacturers for all their help and support: Wills Finecast, Peco, Ratio, Gauge Master, Form Craft, West Coast Kits, Vulcan, Premier, Seep and Hornby, with special thanks to Graham Farish.

ARTWORK
Andrew Timmins and Christion Still:
Pages 13, 14, top 17, 20, top 21, 24, 26, 27, 30, 32, 33, 37, 64, 69, bottom 70, top 71, 73, 77, 78, 79, 80, 81, top 91, top 93, 97, 105, 108, 110, 112, 122, top 127, bottom 155, 162, 179, 181, 183, top 184, 185, 187, 188, 189, 191, 192, 193.

Paul Wylie:
Pages bottom 62, 76, top 92, top 100, bottom 100, top 131, 133, 143, top 145, bottom 145, 149, bottom 156, bottom 160, top 175.
John Wylie:
Pages 10, 15, 16, 17, 18, 19, bottom 21, 22, top 30, 31, bottom 32, top 34, bottom 34, 35, 38, 42, 43, 44, 49, 50, 51, 52, 53, 54, 55, 56, 57, 58, 60, 85, 86, 87, 88, 89, 90, bottom 92, 93, 97, 99, 105, 106, 114, 121, 123, 135, 136, 144, 146, 147, 148, 150, top 151, bottom 151, 152, 153, 154, top 155, top 156, 157, 159, top 160, 161, 163, 168, bottom 173, 179.
Colour artwork page 67: Andrew Timmins.
Illustration on page 166 and permission to use photograph on page 167, Peco Ltd.

MODELMAKERS
Medway College of Art and Design, Fort Pitt, Rochester, Kent (3 year Higher Dip. Industrial Modelmaking).
Tim Adcock, Damian Barrell, Amanda Bristow, Mark Dawson, Simon Fox, Andrew Freeman, Graham French, Alison Hardy, Paul Higgins, Richard Majillius, Ian Poisden-Watts, Paul Persigetti, Raoul Reesinck, Stella Winter, Stuart Woods.
Additional help: Paul Wylie, Jean Wylie.
Special thanks to Amanda Bristow, Graham French.
All models made under the direction of John Wylie.

PHOTOGRAPHY
Graham Farish, pages 24, 25. Brian Monaghan, page 59. *Your Model Railways,* pages 59, 98, 115, 169. West Coast Kits Ltd, pages 164, 164. Ron Cadman of Vulcan and Premier Kits Ltd, pages 170, 171, 172, 173, 174, 175. All other photographs, John Wylie.

INDEX